Philosophy of Mind

Dimensions of Philosophy Series
Norman Daniels and Keith Lehrer, Editors

Philosophy of Mind, Jaegwon Kim

Philosophy of Social Science, Second Edition, Alexander Rosenberg

Philosophy of Education, Nel Noddings

Philosophy of Biology, Elliott Sober

Metaphysics, Peter van Inwagen

Philosophy of Physics, Lawrence Sklar

Theory of Knowledge, Keith Lehrer

Philosophy of Law: An Introduction to Jurisprudence,
Revised Edition, Jeffrie G. Murphy and Jules L. Coleman

Introduction to Marx and Engels: A Critical Reconstruction,
Richard Schmitt

FORTHCOMING

Political Philosophy, Jean Hampton

Philosophical Ethics, Stephen L. Darwall

Philosophy of Science, Clark Glymour

Philosophy of Language, Stephen Neale

Philosophy of Cognitive Science, edited by Barbara Von Eckardt

Contemporary Continental Philosophy, Bernd Magnus

Normative Ethics, Shelly Kagan

Philosophy of Mind

Jaegwon Kim

BROWN UNIVERSITY

 WestviewPress
A Division of HarperCollins*Publishers*

Dimensions of Philosophy Series

Copyright © 1996 by Westview Press, Inc., A Division of HarperCollins Publishers, Inc.

Published in 1996 in the United States of America by Westview Press, Inc., 5500 Central Avenue, Boulder, Colorado 80301-2877, and in the United Kingdom by Westview Press, 12 Hid's Copse Road, Cumnor Hill, Oxford OX2 9JJ

A CIP catalog record for this book is available from the Library of Congress.
ISBN 0-8133-0775-9; ISBN 0-8133-0776-7 (pbk.)

The paper used in this publication meets the requirements of the American National Standard for Permanence of Paper for Printed Library Materials Z39.48-1984.

10   9   8   7   6   5   4   3   2

Contents

Preface

   This book is an introductory survey of philosophy of mind, with brief incursions into the overlapping and adjoining field of philosophy of psychology. It covers many of the central issues currently debated in the field in a way that is intended to be accessible to those without a formal background in philosophy.

   But the distance between what one hopes and what one actually has to settle for can be great, and I will have to leave it to the reader to judge to what extent I have been successful. In the course of writing this book, I was constantly reminded of what Sir Peter Strawson once said, namely, that there is no such thing as "elementary philosophy." It has remained my intention—and hope—though, to present the issues, claims, and arguments concerning the mind in a way that will make them intelligible, interesting, and challenging to beginning students of philosophy as well as those who are first coming to the philosophy of mind with some general philosophical background. I hope, too, that those with some familiarity with the field will also find something of interest here.

   A book like this must deal with a number of diverse topics that are closely connected and yet relatively independent of one another. This has affected the structure of the book in two ways: First, it seemed to me desirable to make each chapter as self-sufficient as possible so that it could be read as an independent essay on the issues under discussion. To accomplish this, I thought it important to preserve, within each chapter, as much narrative continuity and flow of argument as possible. Second, in the course of pursuing this goal, I have found it desirable, and sometimes even necessary, to tolerate some overlap and repetition of material from chapter to chapter; for example, issues concerning mental causation, mind-body supervenience, content, qualia, and reduction are discussed in various places, and similar or closely related points and arguments make more than one appearance throughout the book.

   Over the past two decades or so, philosophy of mind has been an unusually active and exciting area. The field has grown enormously, and I believe there have been significant advances in our understanding of the issues concerning the mind. A large body of literature has built up during this period, and the rate of research publication shows no signs of abating. In part this boom has been due to the impetus provided by the explosive growth, since around midcentury, of "cognitive science"—a loosely allied group of disciplines, including psychology, linguistics, neuroscience, and artificial intelligence, with aspirations to enhance the scientific understanding of mentality. This has, to some extent (some will say fundamentally), changed the character of philosophy of mind, and there are areas where philosophical work on the nature of mind is continuous with scientific work. These include such topics as mental representation, mental imagery, rationality and decisionmaking, language and language acquisition, the nature of "folk psychology" and its relationship to systematic psychology, and the controversy concerning classical artificial intelligence and connectionism. A separate volume devoted to philosophy of psychology and cognitive science is needed to provide proper coverage of these topics (such a volume, I understand, is forthcoming in the Dimensions of Philosophy series). In this book I have tried to stay with the issues that are standardly and traditionally regarded as falling squarely within philosophy of mind rather than those that emerge primarily from the recent developments in the sciences.

I am indebted to Marian David and Fred Feldman, who have given me helpful comments on earlier versions of various chapters. Lynne Rudder Baker and John Heil, who read the manuscript for Westview, provided me with many useful comments and suggestions that have improved the book. Maura Geisser, my research assistant at Brown, has given me invaluable help with many tedious chores. Spencer Carr, my editor, has treated me with great patience and tact in the face of repeated delays. It goes without saying that I owe intellectual debts to a great many philosophers, too numerous for individual acknowledgments. But it should be apparent from the text and references who many of them are. My thanks go to them all.

Jaegwon Kim

1

Introduction

In coping with the myriad things that come our way at every moment of our waking life, we try to organize them into manageable structures. We do this by sorting them into groups—categorizing them as "rocks," "trees," "insects," "birds," "cows," "telephone poles," "mountains," and countless other kinds, and describing them in terms of their properties and features, as "large" or "small," "tall" or "short," "red" or "yellow," "slow" or "swift," and so on. A distinction that we almost instinctively, though usually unconsciously, apply to just about everything that we come across is whether or not it is a *living* thing (it might be a dead bird, but still we know it is the *kind* of thing that lives, unlike a rock or a pewter vase, which couldn't be "dead"). There are exceptions, of course, but it is unusual for us to know *what something is* without at the same time knowing, or having some ideas about, whether or not it is a living creature. Another example: when we know a person, we almost always know whether the person is male or female.

The same is true of the distinction between things or creatures with a "mind," or "mentality," and those without a mind. This is probably one of the most basic contrasts we use in our thoughts about things in the world. Our attitudes toward things that are conscious and capable of sensations like pain and pleasure, however lowly they may be in the biological hierarchy, are importantly different from our attitudes toward things lacking such capacities, mere chunks of matter or insensate plants, as witness the controversy about vegetarianism and medical experiments performed on live animals. And we are apt to regard ourselves as distinctive and unique in that we are creatures endowed with specially highly developed mental capacities and functions, such as the capacity for abstract thoughts, self-consciousness, artistic sensibilities and creative powers, and complex emotions. Much as we admire the miracle of the flora and fauna, we do not think that every living thing has a mind or that we need a *psychological* theory to understand the life cycles of elms and birches or the behavior and reproductive patterns of amoebas. Except those few of us who have certain mystical inclinations, we don't think that members of the plant world are endowed with mentality, and we would exclude many members of the animal kingdom from the mental realm as well. We would not think that planarians and gnats have a mental life that is fit for serious psychological inquiry. When we come to higher forms of animal life, such as cats, dogs, and chimpanzees, we are willing to grant them a fairly rich mental life. They are surely *conscious* in that they experience *sensations*, like pain, itch, and pleasure and *perceive* their surroundings more or less the way we do. They *remember* things—that is, store and use information about their surroundings—and *learn* from experience, and they even seem capable of *emotions*, such as fear, frustration, and anxiety. We describe their psychological life using the expressions we normally use for fellow human beings: "Phoebe is feeling too cramped inside the pet carrier, and all that traffic noise has made her nervous. The poor thing is dying to be let out."

But are the animals, even the more intelligent ones like horses and dolphins, capable of complex emotions like embarrassment and shame? Are they capable of forming intentions, engaging in deliberation and making decisions, or performing logical inferences? When we go down the ladder of animal life to, say, oysters, crabs, and earthworms, we would think that their mental life is considerably impoverished in comparison with that of, say, a domestic cat. Surely these creatures have sensations, we think; for they have sense organs through which they find out what goes on around them, and they adjust and modify their behavior accordingly. But do they have minds? Are they conscious? Do they have mentality? What do these questions mean anyway?

Minds as Souls: Mental Substances

What is it for something to "have a mind," or "have mentality"? When the ancients reflected on the difference between us and the rest of the natural world, they sometimes described it in terms of having a "soul." For example, Plato said that each of us has a soul that is simple, divine, and immutable, unlike our bodies, which are composite and perishable. In fact, before we were born into this world, our souls existed in a pure, disembodied state, and, according to Plato, what we call "learning" is merely a process of recollecting what we already knew in our prenatal existence as pure souls. Bodies are merely the vehicles of our existence in this earthly world, a transitory stage of our souls' eternal journey. The general idea, then, was that because each of us has a soul, we are the kind of conscious, intelligent, and rational creatures that we are. Strictly speaking, we don't in a literal sense "have" souls since we are in an important sense *identical with* our souls—that is, each of us *is* a soul. My soul is the thing that I am. So each of us "has a mind" because each of us *is* a mind.

Writing about 2,000 years later, Descartes advocated a similar idea. Having established to his satisfaction that he exists, he wonders "what this 'I' is" whose existence he is now certain of. His answer: "I am, then, in the strict sense only a thing that thinks, that is, I am a mind, or intelligence, or intellect, or reason."[1] And he argues that this mind, or soul, is separate from his body:

> On the one hand I have a clear and distinct idea of myself, in so far as I am simply a thinking, nonextended thing; and on the other hand I have a distinct idea of body, in so far as this is simply an extended, non-thinking thing. And accordingly, it is certain that I am really distinct from my body, and can exist without it.[2]

A view like this is called "substance dualism": The idea is that each of us is, at least as we exist on this earth, a composite being made up of two distinct substances, an immaterial mind and a material body.

But the idea of minds as souls or spirits, as *entities* or *objects* of a special kind, has never gained a foothold in a serious scientific study of the mind and has also gradually disappeared from philosophical discussions of mentality. There certainly is no evidence that there is something physical or material that exists in our bodies that fits the traditional description of a soul as "simple," "indivisible," and "immortal"; in fact, on this conception of a soul, nothing physical could be a soul. For only particles like electrons or photons (perhaps only quarks) are "simple" and "indivisible," if anything physical is, and it would surely be absurd to think of these particles as souls.

Might there then be immaterial and purely spiritual objects that could account for our mentality and rationality? Descartes claimed that there are two sorts of substance, mental and material, and that each of us is a "union," as Descartes called it, made up of a material substance (the body) and a mental substance (the mind). What is a "substance"? The core idea of a substance is that of something that can "exist independently" and have properties and enter into relationships with other substances. Ordinary material things, such as rocks, tables, and chairs, are usually thought to qualify as substances; so are living things like trees and animals. But in what sense are they capable of "independent existence"? We get a serviceable idea when we compare tables and chairs with things like surfaces, shadows, and smiles. We can imagine this table existing all by itself; that is, we can conceive of a "possible world" in which this table is the only thing that exists. In contrast, a surface, a two-

dimensional expanse with no thickness, cannot exist without a solid object of which it is a surface; there is no possible world in which a surface
alone exists and nothing else. The humor of the Cheshire cat's grin,
which, we are told, stays in the tree after the cat is gone, is precisely that it
is a metaphysical impossibility. The grin, unlike the branch that the cat
has left, is not a substance and is not capable of independent existence.

According to Descartes, the essence of a material substance is to be *spatially extended*—that is, to occupy a volume of space—whereas the essence
of a mental substance is *thinking*, or to be *conscious*. By "thinking"
Descartes meant a full range of mental states and activities, such as sensing, feeling, perceiving, judging, and doubting as well as thinking narrowly conceived. Further, minds necessarily lack spatial dimensions—
perhaps they are not *in* physical space at all—and matter necessarily lacks
consciousness. But this does not, on Descartes's view, prevent mind and
matter from causally influencing each other: In perception the physical
stimulation of our sensory surfaces causes us to perceive objects and
events around us, and in voluntary action our wants and beliefs cause
our limbs to move in appropriate ways.

But the idea that our mentality consists in the possession by each of us
of some immaterial mental substance is fraught with difficulties. In the
first place, there seems no compelling reason to think that there are
wholly immaterial things in this world. Second, even if there were such
things, it is dubious that they could do the job for which they were intended. For, as many thinkers have pointed out, it simply does not seem
credible that an immaterial substance, with no material characteristics
and totally outside physical space, could causally influence, and be influenced by, the motions of material bodies that are strictly governed by
physical law. Just try to imagine how something that isn't anywhere in
physical space could alter in the slightest degree the trajectory of even a
single material particle in motion. Its inability to explain the possibility of
"mental causation," how mentality can make a causal difference to the
world, doomed Cartesian dualism. But, as we shall see, the problem of
mental causation didn't go away when Cartesian mental substance went
away; it has remained one of the most central and most intractable problems in philosophy of mind.

There has been a near consensus among philosophers that the concept
of mind as a mental substance gives rise to too many difficulties and puzzles without compensating explanatory gains. In addition, the idea of an
immaterial and immortal soul usually carries with it various, often conflicting, religious and theological associations that are best avoided. For
example, the traditional conception of the soul involves a sharp and un-
bridgeable gap between humans and the rest of animal life. Even if our

own mentality could be explained as consisting in the possession of a soul, what might explain the mentality of nonhuman animals?

But if we abandon the idea of a soul, or mental substance, to explain our mentality, in what does our "having a mind" consist?

Mental Properties, Events, and Processes

To reject the substantival view of mentality is not to deny that each of us "has a mind"; it's only that we should not think of "having a mind" as there being some object or substance called a "mind" that we literally "have." Having a mind isn't like having brown eyes or a sore elbow. Think of "dancing a waltz" or "taking a walk": When we say "Sally danced a waltz" or "Sally took a leisurely walk along the river," we don't mean—at least we don't need to mean—that there are *things* in this world called "waltzes" or "walks" such that Sally picked out one of them and danced it or walked it. Where are these dances and walks when no one is dancing or walking them? Having a mind or dancing a waltz isn't like having a Chevrolet or kicking a tire. Dancing a waltz is merely a *manner* of dancing, and taking a walk is a *manner* of moving our limbs in relationship to our surroundings. In using these expressions, we need not accept the existence of entities like waltzes and walks; all we need to admit into our ontology are persons who waltz and persons who walk.

Similarly, when we use such expressions as "having a mind," "losing one's mind," "being out of one's mind," and the like, there is no need to suppose there are things in this world called "minds" that we have, lose, or are out of. Having a mind can be construed simply as a *property, capacity,* or *characteristic* that humans and some higher animals possess in contrast with things like pencils and rocks. To say that something "has a mind" is to classify it as a certain sort of thing capable of certain characteristic sorts of behaviors and functions (sensation, perception, memory, learning, reasoning, consciousness, action, and the like). It is less misleading, therefore, to speak of "mentality" than to speak of "having a mind"; the surface grammar of the latter abets the problematic idea of a substantival mind, mind as an object of a special kind.

Mentality is a broad and complex property. As we just saw, there are various narrower properties and functions through which the mentality of a person manifests itself, such as experiencing sensations, entertaining thoughts, reasoning, making decisions, and feeling emotions. There are also more specific properties falling within these categories, such as experiencing a throbbing pain in the right elbow, believing that snow is white, wanting to visit Tibet, and being angry at one's roommate. When you shut a door on your thumb, you *instantiate* or *exemplify* the property of being in pain; most of us *have*, or *instantiate*, the property of having the belief that snow is white; some of us have the property of wanting to visit Tibet; and so on. This is admittedly a cumbersome way of talking; the point is just that my being in pain or wanting to see Tibet can be understood as my having, or exemplifying, a certain property, namely, the property of being in pain or of wanting to see Tibet. (Throughout this book, the expressions "mental" and "psychological" and their respective cognates will be used interchangeably; similarly for "physical" and "material.")

All this is to make clear the kind of ontological scheme that we presuppose in this book and to explain how we will use certain terms associated with the scheme. We suppose, first of all, that our scheme includes *things* or *objects* (including persons, biological organisms and their organs, computers, etc.) and that they have various *properties* and stand in various *relations* to each other (properties and relations are together called *attributes*). Some of these are physical, like having a certain mass or temperature, being 1 meter long, and being heavier than. Some things—in particular, persons and certain biological organisms—can also instantiate mental properties, like being in pain and liking the taste of avocado. We also speak of mental or physical *events*, *states*, and *processes* and sometimes of *facts*. A process can be thought of as a causally connected series of events and states, and events differ from states only in that they suggest *change* whereas states do not. We can use the terms "phenomena" and "occurrences" to cover both events and states. We will often use one or another of these terms in a broad sense inclusive of the rest (that is, when we say "events," that shouldn't be taken to exclude states, phenomena, and the rest). How events and states are related to objects and their properties is a question of some controversy in metaphysics. We will simply assume here that when a person instantiates a mental property, say, that of being in pain, then there is the event (or state) of that person's being in pain and there is also the fact that the person is in pain. Some events are psychological events, such as pains, beliefs, and onsets of anger, and these are instantiations by persons and other organisms of mental properties. Some events are physical, such as earthquakes, hiccups and sneezes, and the motion of your limbs when you walk to the library, and these are instantiations of physical properties. (Note that for our present purposes the biological and the chemical also count as physical; "physical" is used, roughly, in the sense of "nonmental.") Events, too, have properties and stand in relation to other events. Take a particular occurrence of pain (someone just stepped on your toe); being a pain (that is, falling under the event kind pain) is a property of that event. It stands in the relation of *occurring an instant later than* with respect to your toe's being stepped on and in the relation of *being a cause of* with respect to your crying "Ouch!" Sometimes clarity and precision demand attention to ontological details, but as far as possible we will try to avoid general metaphysical matters that are not directly germane to our immediate concerns about the nature of mind.

Philosophy of Mind

Philosophy of mind, like any other field of inquiry, is defined by a group of problems. As we expect, the problems that constitute this field concern mentality and mental properties. What are some of these problems? And how do they differ from the scientific problems about mentality and mental properties, those that psychologists, cognitive scientists, and neuroscientists investigate in their research?

There is first of all the problem of clarifying the concept of a "creature (structure) with a mind," or "with mentality." What conditions must a thing meet for us to attribute mentality, or a mind, to it? Before we can answer questions like whether inorganic electromechanical devices (e.g., computers and robots) can exhibit genuine mentality, we need a reasonably clear idea about our conception of mentality itself. This general question is difficult, probably impossible, to answer with an explicit definition; it will be briefly discussed in a later section of this chapter, but many of the specific questions we will discuss throughout this book will also be pertinent to the question of what constitutes mentality.

There are also problems concerning specific mental properties or kinds of mental states and events and their relationship to one another. Are pains only sensory events, or do they also have a motivational component (e.g., aversiveness)? Can there be pains of which we are not aware? Do emotions like anger and jealousy necessarily involve felt qualities? Do they also involve a cognitive component, like belief? What is a belief anyway, and how does a belief get to have the content it has (say, that it is raining outside)?

A third group of problems concerns the relation between mental and physical properties. Collectively they are called "the mind-body problem," a central problem of philosophy of mind since Descartes formulated it over 300 years ago. It is a central problem for us in this book as well. This is the problem of clarifying, and making intelligible, the relation between our mentality and the physical nature of our being—or, more generally, the relationship between mental and physical properties. But why should we think there is a problem here? Just what needs to be clarified and explained?

A simple answer is this: because the mental seems so utterly different from the physical and yet the two seem intimately related to each other. When you think of consciousness—of such things as the smell of basil, a pang of remorse, and the painfulness of a burned finger—it is hard to imagine anything that could be more different from mere configurations and motions, however complex, of material particles, atoms and molecules, cells and tissues. How can such conscious events emerge in biological/physical systems? How can biological/physical systems come to have such mental states as thoughts, hopes, and experiences of guilt and embarrassment? It strikes many of us that there is a fundamental, qualitative difference between physical properties and mental properties and that this makes their apparently intimate relationships puzzling and mysterious. But what are these relationships?

For one thing, it seems beyond doubt that mental events occur as a result of physical/neural processes. Stepping barefoot on an upright thumbtack causes a sharp pain in your foot. It is likely that the proximate basis of the pain is some event in your brain; a bundle of neurons deep in your hypothalamus or cortex discharges, and as a result you experience a sensation of pain. Impingement of photons on your retina causes a visual sensation, and as a result you come to have the belief that there is a tree in front of you. How could a series of physical events, little particles jostling against one another, electric current rushing to and fro, and so on, blossom into a conscious experience—the burning hurtfulness of a badly scalded hand, the brilliant red and purple sunset over the dark green ocean, the smell of freshly mown lawn? We are told that when certain special neurons (nociceptive neurons) discharge, we experience pain, and presumably there is another group of neurons that fire when we experience an itch. Why shouldn't pain and itch be switched around? That is, why is it that we feel pain rather than itch when just these neurons fire and experience itch, not pain, when those other neurons fire? Why isn't it the other way around? Why should *any* experience emerge when these neurons fire?

Moreover, we ordinarily take it for granted that our mental events have physical effects. It seems essential to our concept of action that our bodies are moved in appropriate ways by our wants and beliefs. You see a McDonald's sign across the street and you want to get a burger, and the perception and desire apparently cause your limbs to move in such a way that you now find your body at the doors of the McDonald's. Cases like this are among the familiar facts of life, too boring to mention. But how did your beliefs and desires manage to move your body weighing over 150 pounds all the way across the street? You say, That's easy: Beliefs and desires first cause certain neurons in my brain to discharge, and then these neural impulses are transmitted through the network of neural fibers to the peripheral control systems, which cause the appropriate muscles to contract, and so on. All that might be a complicated story, you say, but it's something that neurophysiology, not philosophy, is in charge of explaining. But how do beliefs and desires manage to cause those little neurons to fire to begin with? How can this happen unless beliefs and desires are themselves just physical happenings in the brain? But is it coherent to suppose that these mental states are simply physical processes in the brain? These questions don't seem to be questions that can be solved just by doing more neurophysiological experimentation and theorizing; they seem to require philosophical reflection.

In this book we will be chiefly concerned with the mind-body problem. At bottom, this is the problem of accounting for the place of mind in a world that is essentially physical. There are persuasive (some people will say compelling) reasons to believe that the world we live in is a fundamentally material world, a world made up of material particles and their aggregates, all of which behave strictly in accordance with physical law. How can we accommodate minds and mentality in such a world? That is our main question.

But before we set out to examine specific doctrines concerning the mind-body relationship, let us survey some of the basic concepts and assumptions that will be useful in the discussion to follow.

Supervenience, Dependence, and Minimal Physicalism

Consider the apparatus called the "transporter" in the science-fiction television series *Star Trek*. You walk into a booth. When the transporter is activated, your body is instantly disassembled; exhaustive information concerning your anatomical structure, down to the last molecule, is transmitted, apparently instantaneously, to another location, often at a great distance, where a body that is exactly like yours is reassembled (presumably with locally available material). And someone who looks exactly like you walks out of the receiving booth and starts doing the tasks you have been assigned to do there.

Let us not worry about whether the person who walks out of the destination booth is really you or only someone who replaces you. In fact, we can avoid this issue by slightly changing the story: Exhaustive information about your bodily structure is obtained by a scanner that does no harm to the object scanned, and on the basis of this information an exact physical replica of your body, a molecule-for-molecule identical duplicate, has been created at another location. By assumption, you and your replica have exactly the same physical properties; you and your replica could not be distinguished by any *current* physical characteristics. (We say "current" to rule out the obvious possibility of distinguishing you from your duplicate by tracing the causal chains to the past.)

Given that your replica is a *physical duplicate* of you, will he also be a *psychological duplicate*? That is, will he be identical with you in mental respects as well? Will he be as smart and witty as you, as prone to daydream, share your likes and dislikes in food and music, and behave just as you would when angry? Will he prefer blue to yellow and have a visual experience identical with yours when you and he both look at a Van Gogh landscape of yellow wheat fields drenched in sunlight against a dark blue sky? Will his twinges, itches, and tickles feel to him just the way yours feel to you? Well, you get the idea. An unquestioned assumption of *Star Trek* and similar science fantasies seems to be that the answer is yes to all of these questions. If you are like the many fans of *Star Trek* in going along with this assumption, you would be tacitly endorsing the following "supervenience principle":

> [Mind-body supervenience] The mental supervenes on the physical in that any two things (objects, events, organisms, persons, etc.) exactly alike in all physical properties cannot differ in respect of mental properties. That is, physical indiscernibility entails psychological indiscernibility.

Or as it is sometimes put: No mental difference without a physical difference. Notice that this principle does not say that things that are alike in psychological respects must be alike in physical respects. We seem to be able coherently to imagine intelligent extraterrestrial creatures whose biochemistry is entirely different from ours (say, their physiology is not carbon-based) and yet who share the same psychology with us. If so, the converse of the supervenience thesis is false: Creatures could be physically different and yet psychologically alike. Mind-body supervenience asserts only that creatures could not be psychologically different and yet physically identical.

The supervenience thesis appears to have the following interesting consequence: There can be at most one Cartesian soul! For assume there are two Cartesian souls, mental substances lacking in all physical properties. This means that they are physically indiscernible; that is, there is no physical respect in which they can be said to differ. The supervenience principle, therefore, implies that the two souls must have the same mental properties; they cannot be differentiated in any psychological respects at all. It's difficult to see how one purely mental thing could be differentiated from another purely mental thing except in regard to some psychological feature. So here there must be just one soul, not two. If you think the last step of this argument is not wholly convincing, we can at least prove this: If there were two or more Cartesian souls, their mental lives must be totally identical. It is doubtful that any supporter of the Cartesian doctrine of immaterial mental substances would be willing to accept the consequence that there can be no more than one soul—or at any rate only one qualitatively distinguishable soul. In this sense, the supervenience principle is incompatible with the doctrine of minds as immaterial souls or substances.

These considerations also show that the supervenience principle does not by itself imply that everything with some psychological property must be a physical thing, a thing with some physical property. The idea that nothing that has only mental properties can exist, though not strictly implied by the supervenience principle, is an essential physicalist doctrine closely related to it and is likely to be accepted by anyone who accepts the supervenience thesis. This idea may be set forth as follows:

> [The anti-Cartesian principle] There can be no purely mental beings (for example, Cartesian souls). That is, nothing can have a mental property without having some physical property and hence without being a physical thing.

Many philosophers regard the supervenience principle as affirming a relation of *dependence* or *determination* between the mental and the physical; that is, what mental properties a given thing has depends on, or is determined by, what physical properties it has. To put it another way, our psychological character is wholly determined by our physical/biological nature. The supervenience principle is often read to imply a dependency thesis of this kind; for it says that once the physical nature of a thing is completely fixed, that fixes its mentality in every detail. But strictly speaking, the supervenience principle as stated only makes a claim about how mental properties *covary* with physical properties; it doesn't say that the former are dependent on the latter. But this dependency thesis, as we might call it, is also important, and we can set it down as follows:

> [Mind-body dependence] What mental properties a given thing has depends on, and is determined by, what physical properties it has. That is to say, the psychological character of a thing is wholly determined by its physical character.

We can see that this principle of psychophysical dependence entails the supervenience principle earlier stated.

What does the mind-body dependence thesis say that goes beyond the supervenience thesis? The dependence thesis is important in that it is an explicit affirmation of the *ontological primacy*, or *priority*, of the physical in relation to the mental, thereby opening the possibility of *explaining* the mental in terms of the physical, in the following sense: It says that physical properties of things are basic and what mental features they have is wholly dependent on their physical nature, and this suggests the possibility of explaining why a given thing has the mental features it has, or why it has changed in some mental respect, by pointing to facts about its physical nature. We can also explain why two organisms differ in psychological respects by invoking their relevant physical/biological differences.[3] If you reflect on this for a moment, you will see that we often use these explanatory procedures in everyday life as well as systematic psychological theory. The dependence thesis, then, can be thought of as the philosophical basis of such explanatory practices. Moreover, we can think of the (supposed) fact of psychophysical dependence as an explanation of mind-body supervenience itself—that is, why mental properties of things covary, in the way indicated, with their physical properties.

The mind-body dependence thesis seems to accord well with the way we ordinarily think of the mind-body relation as well as with scientific assumptions and practices. For very few of us would think that there can be mental events and processes that float free, so to speak, of physical processes; most of us believe that what happens in our mental life, including the fact that we have a mental life at all, is dependent on what happens in our body, in particular in our nervous system. Suppose we were called upon to construct a system with mentality. It seems that the only way to proceed is to try to build a physical/biological structure; if we should succeed in constructing an appropriately complex physical system (say, an exact physical replica of an actual human), a mental life would emerge in that system; there is nothing further that needs to be done. It makes little sense to think of constructing something mental *directly*, without going through the design and construction of a physical structure.

We may think of the three principles set forth above—mind-body supervenience, the anti-Cartesian principle, and mind-body dependence—as defining *minimal physicalism* in the following sense: If you accept them, you may properly be called a physicalist, and if you reject them, you are rejecting physicalism. The reason for this is clear; if you accept the principles, you are saying that each and every property of a thing is either a physical property or is determined by its physical properties and that there is nothing in the world that is not a physical thing. To reject one or more of these principles amounts to saying that there are things in the spacetime world other than physical things, like Cartesian souls, or at least that some things in the world have certain properties that are independent of their physical nature. If this were the case, the fixing of the physical character of a thing would not fix its psychological character; the psychological character of a thing would be autonomous from its physical nature.

Thus, the three principles define the basic physicalist position. As we will see, there are stronger forms of physicalism, for example, various forms of reductionist physicalism. But it is plausible to think that anything weaker than what the three principles together affirm amounts to a rejection of physicalism. Contemporary discussions in the philosophy of mind have generally proceeded within a physicalist framework. Something like our three principles is often assumed or taken for granted; the chief aim of constructing theories in the philosophy of mind is often taken to be the formulation of a theory about the nature of mental properties that would explain why these principles hold as well as explaining and making sense of certain further facts about mentality and its relationship to the physical. In subsequent chapters, we will in general follow this procedure, discussing and evaluating some of the major physicalist theories of the mental. But let us first spend a little time looking into what makes a property a mental property—that is, the concept of mentality.

Varieties of Mental Phenomena

It will be useful at this point to look at some major categories of mental events and states. This will give us a rough idea about the kinds of phenomena we are concerned with and also serve as a reminder that the phenomena that come under the rubric "mental" or "psychological" are extremely diverse and variegated. The following list is not intended to be complete or systematic, and some of the categories obviously overlap with one another.

First, we may distinguish those mental phenomena that involve *sensations*: pains; itches; tickles; afterimages; seeing a round, green patch; hearing screeching car tires against pavement; feeling nausea; and so on. These mental states are thought to have "phenomenal" or "qualitative" aspects—the way they *feel* or the way things *look* or *appear*; thus, pains are thought to have a special qualitative feel that is distinctive of pains—they *hurt*. When you look at a green patch, there is a distinctive way the patch looks to you: It *looks green*, and your visual experience involves this green look. And itches are itchy and tickles are ticklish. Each such sensation has its own distinctive feel and is characterized by a sensory quality that we seem to be able to identify in a direct way, at least as to the general type to which it belongs (e.g., pain, itch, etc.). The expressions "raw feel" and "qualia" are also used to refer to these qualitative mental states.

Second, there are mental states that are standardly attributed to a person or organism by the use of that-clauses: For example, Bill Clinton *hopes that* Congress will pass a health care bill this year, Newt Gingrich *believes that* there is no chance that will happen, and Bob Dole *fears that* Clinton may get what he wants. Such states are called "propositional attitudes." The idea is that these states consist in a subject's having an "attitude" (e.g., thinking, hoping, fearing) toward a "proposition" (e.g., that tuna dinner is tastier than beef grill, that Congress will pass the health care bill, etc.). These propositions are said to constitute the "content" of the propositional attitudes, and that-clauses that specify these propositions are called "content sentences." Thus, the content of Clinton's hope is the proposition that Congress will pass the health care bill, which is also the content of Dole's fear, and this content is expressed by the sentence

"Congress will pass the health care reform bill." These states are also called "intentional" (sometimes "intensional") or "contentful" states. Do these mental states have a phenomenal, qualitative aspect? We do not normally associate a specific feel with beliefs, another specific feel with desires, and so on. There does not seem to be any special belieflike feel, a certain sensory quality, associated with your belief that Providence is south of Boston or that 2 is the smallest prime number. Much of our ordinary psychological thinking and theorizing ("folk psychology") involves these propositional attitudes, and it is generally thought that *believing* and *desiring* (or wanting) are the two most basic, and important, propositional attitudes—so much so that the psychology of propositional attitudes is sometimes called "belief-desire psychology."

And then there are various mental states that come under the broad and somewhat vague heading of *feelings* and *emotions*. They include anger, joy, sadness, depression, elation, embarrassment, remorse, regret, and the like. Notice that emotions are often attributed to persons with a that-clause—in other words, some states of emotions are also propositional attitudes: For example, Clinton is *annoyed that* several reporters were overly persistent with their questions about the Whitewater affair, and he is also *embarrassed that* he showed his irritation in public. And as the word "feeling" suggests, there is often a special qualitative component specific to kinds of emotions, such as anger and jealousy, although it is far from certain that all instances of emotion or feeling are accompanied by such a qualitative feel or that there is a single specific sensory feel to each major type of emotion.

There are also what used to be called "volitional" states, like intending, deciding, and willing. These states are propositional attitudes; intentions and decisions have content. For example, I may intend to take the ten o'clock train to New York tomorrow; here the content is expressed by an infinitive construction ("to take . . . "), but it can be spelled out in a full content sentence, as in "I intend that I take the ten o'clock train to New York tomorrow." In any case, these states are closely related to actions. When I intend to raise my arm *now*, I must *now* undertake to raise my arm; when you intend, or decide, to do something, you commit yourself to doing it. You must not only be prepared to take the necessary steps toward doing it but also actually initiate them at an appropriate time. This isn't to say that you can't change your mind or that you will necessarily succeed; it is to say that you need to change your intention to be released from the commitment to action.

Actions typically involve motions of our bodies, but they do not seem to be mere bodily motions. My arm is going up and so is yours. However, you are raising your arm, but I am not (my arm is being pulled up by someone else). The rising of your arm is an action; it is something you do. But the rising of my arm is not an action; it isn't something that I do but something that happens to me. There appears to be something mental about your raising your arm that is absent from the mere rising of your arm; perhaps it is the involvement of your desire, or intention, to raise your arm, but exactly what distinguishes actions from "mere bodily motions" has been a matter of philosophical dispute. Or consider something like buying a loaf of bread. Evidently, someone who can engage in the act of buying a loaf of bread must have certain appropriate beliefs and desires; she must, for example, have a desire to buy bread, or at least a desire to buy something (for you could buy a loaf of bread by mistake, thinking that it is something else that you wanted). And to do something like buying, you must have knowledge, or beliefs, about what constitutes buying rather than, say, borrowing or simply taking, about money and exchange of goods, and so on. That is to say, only creatures with beliefs and desires and an understanding of appropriate social conventions and institutions can engage in activities like buying and selling. The same goes for much of what we do as social beings; actions like promising, greeting, and apologizing presuppose a rich and complex background of beliefs, desires, intentions, and an understanding of social relationships and conventions.

There are other items that are ordinarily included under the rubric of "psychological," such as traits of character and personality (being honest, obsessive, witty, introverted), habits and propensities (being industrious, punctual), intellectual abilities, artistic talents, and the like. But we can consider them to be mental in an indirect or derivative sense: Honesty is a mental characteristic because it is a tendency, or disposition, to form desires of certain sorts (e.g., desire to tell the truth, not to mislead others, etc.) and act in appropriate ways (in particular, saying what one believes).

In the chapters to follow, sensations and intentional states will often be the focus of our discussion. They will provide us with examples of mental states when we discuss the mind-body problem and other issues. We will also be discussing some specific philosophical problems about these two principal types of mental states. However, we will largely bypass such questions as what types of mental states there are, how they are related to one another, and the like.

But in what sense are all these things "mental" or "psychological"? Is there some single property or feature, or a reasonably simple and perspicuous set of properties, in virtue of which they all count as mental?

Is There a "Mark of the Mental"?

Various characteristics have been proposed by philosophers to serve as a "mark of the mental," a criterion that would separate mental properties or phenomena from those that are not mental. Each has a certain plausibility and covers a range of mental phenomena, but as we will see, none seems to be adequate for all the diverse kinds of events and states, functions and capacities that we normally classify as "mental" or "psychological." Although we will not try to formulate our own criterion of the mental, a review of some prominent proposals will give us an understanding of the principal ideas that have traditionally been associated with the concept of mentality and highlight some of the important characteristics of mental phenomena, even if, as noted, no single one of them seems capable of serving as a universal necessary and sufficient condition of mentality.

Epistemological Criteria

You are experiencing a sharp toothache caused by an exposed nerve in a molar. The toothache that you experience, but not the condition of your molar, is a mental occurrence. But what is the basis of this distinction? One influential answer says that the distinction consists in certain fundamental differences in the way you come to have *knowledge* of the two phenomena.

Direct (or immediate) knowledge. Your knowledge that you have a toothache is "direct" or "immediate," not based on evidence or inference. There is no other thing that you know or have observed from which you infer that you are experiencing a toothache; that is, your knowledge is not mediated by other beliefs or knowledge. This is seen in the fact that it makes no sense to ask, "But *how do you know* that you have a toothache?" The only possible answer, if you take the question seriously, is that you *just* know. This shows that here the question of "evidence" is inappropriate: Your knowledge is direct and immediate in that sense. Yet your knowledge of the physical condition of your tooth is based on evidence: In all likelihood, it is based on the testimonial evidence provided by your dentist. And your dentist's knowledge presumably depends on evidence of the X-ray pictures, visual inspection of your teeth, and so on. Evidently, the question, "How do you know that you have an exposed nerve in a molar?" makes good sense and can be given an informative answer.

But isn't our knowledge of certain simple physical facts just as "direct" and "immediate" as knowledge of mental events like toothaches and itches? Suppose you are looking at a large red circle painted on a wall directly in front of you: Doesn't it seem that you would know, directly and without the use of any further evidence, that there is a round red patch in front of you? Don't I know, in the same way, that here is a piece of white paper in front of me or that there is a tree just outside my window?

Privacy, or first-person privilege. One possible response to this challenge is to invoke the privacy of our knowledge of our own mental states, namely, the apparent fact that this direct access to any given mental occurrence is

enjoyed by a single subject, the person to whom the mental event is occurring. In the case of the toothache, it's only you, not your dentist or
anyone else, who are in this kind of specially privileged position, but this
is not the case with the red patch. If you can know "directly" that there is
a round red spot on the wall, so can I and anyone else who is suitably sit-
uated in relation to the wall. There is no single person with a specially
privileged epistemic access to the round red patch. In this sense, knowledge of certain mental events exhibits an *asymmetry* between first person
and third person, but knowledge of physical states shows no such asymmetry. Moreover, this asymmetry seems to hold only for knowledge of
current mental occurrences, not for knowledge of *past* mental occurrences:
You know that you had a toothache yesterday, a week ago, or two years
ago, from evidence of memory (which is fallible), an entry in your diary,
your dental record, and the like. Nor does such an asymmetry hold for
knowledge of one's future mental states.

Infallibility and self-intimacy. Another epistemic feature sometimes associated with mentality is the idea that in some sense one's knowledge of
one's own current mental states is "infallible" or "incorrigible," or that it
is "self-intimating." The main idea is that mental events—at least events
like pains and other sensations—have the following property: You cannot
be mistaken concerning whether or not you are experiencing them. That
is, if you *believe* that you are in pain, then it follows that you *are* in pain,
and if you believe that you are not in pain, then you are not; that is, it is
not possible to have false beliefs about your own pains. In this sense, your
knowledge of your own pain is *infallible*. So-called psychosomatic pains
are pains nonetheless. But when your belief concerns a physical occurrence, there is no guarantee that your belief is true: Your belief that you
have a decayed molar may be true, but its truth is not entailed by the
mere fact that you believe it. Or so goes the claim, at any rate.[4]

"Self-intimacy" is the converse of infallibility: A state or event *m* is said
to be self-intimating to a person just in case, necessarily, if *m* occurs, the
person believes that *m* occurs—in fact, she *knows* that *m* occurs.[5] The
claim, then, is that mental events are self-intimating to the subjects to
whom they occur. If pains are self-intimating in this sense, there could not
be *hidden* pains—pains that the subject is unaware of. Just as the infallibility of beliefs about one's own pains implies that pains with no physiological cause are possible, the self-intimating character of pain would imply
that even if all normal physical and physiological causes of pain were
present, if you are not aware of any pain and do not believe that you are
in pain, then you are not in pain. There are stories about soldiers on the
battlefield and athletes in the heat of competition who report no experience of pain in spite of severe physical injuries; if we assume pains are

self-intimating, we would have to conclude that no pain, as a mental event, is occurring to these subjects. We may give the name "the doctrine of the transparency of mind" to the joint claim of self-intimacy and infallibility of knowledge of one's own mental states. On this doctrine, the mind is a totally transparent medium, but only to a single person.

Whether or not mental events have these characteristics of infallible knowability and self-intimacy, it is clear that most bodily events and states do not have them. But what about those bodily states we are said to detect through "proprioception," such as the positions of our limbs and the spatial orientation of our bodies (e.g., knowing whether your right knee is bent, whether you are lying down or standing, etc.)? Our proprioceptive sense organs and associated neural machinery are in the business of keeping us informed, *directly*, of certain physical conditions of our bodies, and proprioception is, in general, highly reliable. But does this make these bodily states self-intimating and infallibly knowable? This is a question worth pondering, but let us move on.

These epistemological characteristics attributed to the mental are very strong properties indeed. It would be no surprise if physical events and states did not have them; a more interesting question is whether all or even most mental events satisfy them. It is clear that not all mental events or states have these special epistemic properties. In the first place, it is now a commonplace to speak of "unconscious" or "subconscious" beliefs, desires, emotions, and the like—psychological states that the subject is not aware of and would even deny having if he were to consider the matter but that evidently shape and influence his overt behavior. Second, it is not always easy for us to determine whether an emotion that we are experiencing is, say, one of embarrassment, remorse, or regret—or one of envy, jealousy, or anger. And we are often not sure whether we "really" believe or desire something: Do I believe that President Clinton is doing a good job? Do I believe that I am a generous and kind person? Do I want to be a happy-go-lucky type who is open and friendly with everyone, or do I want to be a person who is a bit aloof and prefers to keep strangers at arm's length? I am not quite sure whether or not I believe or want these things. It isn't as though I know I have suspended judgment about them—I don't even know *that*. Epistemic uncertainties can happen with sensations as well. Is this sensation one of pain or one of intense hotness? Special epistemic access is perhaps most plausible for sensations like pains and itches, but here again not all our beliefs about pains appear to have the special authoritative character indicated by the epistemic criteria we have surveyed. Is the pain I am now experiencing more intense than the pain I felt a moment ago in the same elbow? Just where in my elbow is the pain? Clearly, there are many characteristics of pains, even introspectively identifiable ones, about which I could be mistaken.

It is also said that you can misclassify, or misidentify, the type of sensation you are experiencing, say, reporting that you feel an itch in the shoulder when the correct description would have been that you feel a ticklish sensation. However, it is not clear just what such cases show. It might be replied, for example, that the error is a verbal one, not one of belief. Although you are using the sentence "My left shoulder itches" to report your belief, your belief *is* to the effect that your left shoulder tickles, and this belief, one might claim, is true.

Thus, exactly how the special epistemic character of mental events is to be specified is controversial, and there is no agreement among philosophers on this issue. And there are some philosophers, especially those who are physicalistically minded, who would take pains to minimize these prima facie differences between mental and bodily events. But it is apparent that there are important epistemological differences between the mental and the nonmental, however these differences are to be exactly described. Especially important is the first-person epistemic authority noted earlier: We seem to have special access to our own mental states—at least to an important subclass of them, if not all. Our knowledge of our own minds may fall short of infallibility or incorrigibility, and it seems beyond doubt that our minds are not wholly transparent to us. But the differences we have noted, even if they are not quite the way described, do seem to point to a crucial qualitative difference between what is physical and an important subclass of the mental. It may well be that we get our initial purchase on the concept of mentality through the core class of mental states for which special first-person authority holds, deriving the broader class of mental phenomena by extending and generalizing this core in various ways.

Mentality as Nonspatial

As we saw, Descartes characterized the mental as essentially thinking and the material as essentially spatial. A corollary of this, at least for Descartes, is that the mental is essentially nonspatial and the material is essentially lacking in the capacity for thinking. Most physicalists would reject this corollary even if they accept the thesis that the mental is definable as thinking. But there may be a way of developing the idea that the mental is nonspatial that leaves the question of physicalism open.

For example, one might attempt something like this: To say that M is a mental property is to say that the proposition that something, S, has M *does not imply* that S is spatially extended (spatial, for short). This is consistent with saying that anything that has M is in fact a spatial thing; that is, the notion of mentality does not *require* that anything with mentality be a spatially extended material thing, although *as a matter of contingent fact*, all things that have any mental property are spatially extended things, like humans and other biological organisms.

Thus, from the proposition that someone, S, believes that 4 is an even number, it does not follow that S is a spatially extended thing. There may be no immaterial angels in this world, but it seems at least logically consistent to say that there are angels and that angels have beliefs, and perhaps other mental states, like desires and hopes. But it evidently is a logical contradiction to say that something has a physical property, say a red color, a cubic shape, or a rough texture, and at the same time to deny that it has a spatial extension. What about being located at a geometric point? Or *being* a geometric point, for that matter? Aren't these physical properties that do not require their possessors to be spatially extended? But no physical *thing* is a geometric point; geometric points are not physical objects, and nothing has the property of being a point or being located wholly at a point in space.

But what of *abstract objects* such as numbers and propositions? Take the property of being divisible by 4. The number 16 has it, but no number is spatially extended; numbers, if they exist, aren't in physical space at all. To take account of numbers, propositions, and other abstracta, we may modify the criterion as follows: A property M is a mental property just in case the proposition that x has M, where x is not an abstract object, does not logically entail that x is spatially extended.

Perhaps there are other complications that call for further adjustments. But how useful is this general approach toward a mark of the mental? It would seem that one who takes this approach seriously must also take the idea of mental substance seriously. For she must allow the existence of possible worlds in which mental properties are instantiated by nonphysical beings, beings without spatial extension. Since it makes no sense to think of abstract entities, like numbers, as subjects of mental properties, the only other possibility is Cartesian mental substances. Thus, anyone who accepts the criterion of the mental as the nonspatial must accept the idea of mental substance as a coherent one, an idea that makes sense. This means that if you have qualms about the coherence of the Cartesian conception of minds as pure mental substances, you should be very cautious about the nonspatiality criterion of mentality.

Intentionality as a Criterion of the Mental

Schliemann looked for the site of Troy. He was fortunate; he found it. Ponce de León looked for the fountain of youth, but he never found it. He couldn't have, for it wasn't there. It remains true, though, that he searched for the fountain of youth. The nonexistence of Bigfoot or the Loch Ness monster has not prevented people from looking for them. Not only can you *look for* something that in fact does not exist, but you can apparently also *believe in*, *think of*, *write about*, and even *love* a nonexistent object. Even if God should not exist, he could be, and in fact has been, the object of these mental acts or attitudes on the part of many people. Contrast them with physical acts and relations, such as cutting, kicking, and being to the left of. You cannot cut, kick, or be to the left of something that does not exist. That you kick something x logically entails the existence of x. That you believe in x does not logically entail the existence of x.

The Austrian philosopher Franz Brentano called this feature of mentality "the intentional inexistence" of psychological phenomena, claiming that it is this characteristic that separates the mental from the physical. In a well-known passage, he wrote:

> Every mental phenomenon is characterized by what the Scholastics of the Middle Ages called the intentional (or mental) inexistence of an object, and what we might call, though not wholly unambiguously, reference to a content, direction toward an object (which is not to be understood here as meaning a thing), or immanent objectivity. Every mental phenomenon includes something as object within itself, although they do not all do so in the same way. In presentation something is presented, in judgement something is affirmed or denied, in love loved, in hate hated, in desire desired and so on.6

This feature of the mental, namely, that mental states have, or are directed upon, an object, or content, which may not exist, has been called "intentionality."

The concept of intentionality may be subdivided into *referential intentionality* and *content intentionality*. Referential intentionality concerns the "aboutness" or reference of our thoughts, beliefs, intentions, and the like. When Ludwig Wittgenstein asked, "What makes my image of him into an image of *him*?"7 he was asking for an explanation of what makes it the case that a given mental state (my "image of him") is *about*, or *refers to*, a particular object—him—rather than someone else. (That person may have an identical twin, and your image may fit his twin just as well as him, perhaps even better, but your image is of him, not of his twin.) Our words, too, refer to, or are directed upon, objects; "Mount Everest" refers to Mount Everest, and "horse" refers to horse.

Content intentionality concerns the fact that, as we saw, an important class of mental states, such as beliefs, hopes, and intentions, have contents or meanings, often expressed by full sentences. It is in virtue of having contents that our mental states represent things and states of affairs outside us—external to those states at any rate. My perceiving that there are flowers in the field *represents* the fact, or state of affairs, of there being flowers in the field, and your remembering that there was a thunderstorm last night *represents* the state of affairs of there having been a thunderstorm last night. The capacity of our mental states to represent things external to them—that is, that they have *representational content*—is clearly a very important fact about them.

But can intentionality be taken as the mark of the mental? There are at least two difficulties. The first is that some mental phenomena—in particular, sensations like pains and tickles, do not seem to exhibit either kind of intentionality. The sensation of pain does not seem to be "about," or refer to, anything, nor does it have a content in the way beliefs and intentions do. Doesn't the pain in my knee "mean" that I hurt the ligament in the knee again? But the sense of "meaning" involved here seems something like causal indication; the pain means a damaged ligament in the same sense in which your nice new suntan "means" that you spent the weekend on the beach. In any case, there seem to be mental states that are not unproblematically characterized by either type of intentionality. Second, it may be argued that mental states are not the only things that show intentionality. In particular, words and sentences can refer to things and have content and meaning. The word "London" refers to London, and the sentence "London is large" refers to, or represents, the fact, or state of affairs, that London is large. A string of 0s and 1s in a computer data structure can mean your name and address, and such strings are ultimately electronic states of a physical system. If these physical items and states are capable of reference and content, how can intentionality be considered an exclusive property of mentality?

Two lines of reply are open to this challenge. First, as some have argued,[8] one might distinguish between *genuine*, or *intrinsic*, intentionality, which our minds and mental states have, and *make-believe*, or *derived*, intentionality that we attribute to objects and states that do not have intentionality in their own right. Thus, when I say of my computer printer that it "likes" to work with my Windows programs but "hates" the DOS programs, I am not really saying that my printer has likes and dislikes in a literal sense. It's at best an "as-if" or metaphorical use of language and doesn't imply the presence of genuine mentality in the machine. And it is not implausible to argue that the word "London" refers to London only because language users use the word to refer to London. If we used it to refer to Paris, it would mean Paris, not London. Or if the inscription "London" weren't a word in a language, it would not have any referential function at all but would be meaningless scribbles on paper. Similarly, the sentence "London is large" represents the state of affairs it represents only because speakers of English use this sentence to represent that state of affairs—for example, in affirming this sentence, they express the judgment that London is large. The point, then, is that the intentionality of language depends on, and is derived from, the intentionality of language users and their mental processes. It is the latter that have intrinsic intentionality, intentionality that isn't derived from, or borrowed from, anything else. Or so one could argue.

A second and perhaps more direct reply may go as follows: To the extent that some physical systems can be said to refer to things, represent states of affairs, and have meanings, they should be considered as exhibiting mentality and be dealt with on that basis. No doubt, as the first reply indicates, analogical or metaphorical uses of intentional idioms abound, but this fact should not blind us to the possibility that physical systems and their states may possess genuine intentionality and hence mentality. After all, some would argue, we, too, are complex physical systems, and the physical/biological states of our brains are capable of referring to things and states of affairs external to them and store their representations in memory. Of course it may turn out not to be possible for purely physical states to have such capabilities, but that would only show that they are not capable of mentality. It remains true, the reply goes, that intentionality is at least a sufficient condition for mentality.

An Unresolved Puzzle

In surveying these candidates for "the mark of the mental," we realize that our notion of the mental is far from monolithic and that it is in fact a cluster of many ideas. Some of the ideas are fairly closely related to one another, but others appear independent of each other (why should there be a connection between special epistemic access and nonspatiality?). The diversity and possible lack of unity in our conception of the mental implies that the class of things and their states that we classify as mental, too, may be a varied and heterogeneous lot. It is standardly thought that there are two broad basic categories of mental phenomena: sensory or qualitative states (qualia), like pains and sensings of colors and textures, and intentional states, like beliefs, desires, and intentions. The former seem paradigm cases of states that satisfy the epistemic criteria of the mental, such as direct access and privacy, and the latter are the prime examples of mental states that satisfy the intentionality criterion. A question to which we do not as yet have an answer is this: In virtue of *what common property* are both sensory states and intentional states "mental"? What do our pains and beliefs have in common in virtue of which they fall under the single category of "mental phenomena"? They of course satisfy the disjunctive property "qualitative or intentional," but that's like trying to find a commonality between red and round by saying that both red things and round things satisfy "red or round." To the extent that we lack a satisfying answer to this question, we fail to have a unitary conception of what mentality consists in.

Further Readings

There are several fine introductory books on philosophy of mind, each with its own distinctive focus and approach. They include: William Bechtel, *Philosophy of Mind: An Overview for Cognitive Science* (Hillsdale, NJ: Lawrence Erlbaum, 1988); Paul M. Churchland, *Matter and Consciousness* (Cambridge: MIT Press, 1988); Barbara Hannan, *Subjectivity and Reduction* (Boulder: Westview Press, 1994); George Graham, *Philosophy of Mind: An Introduction* (Oxford: Blackwell, 1993); John Heil,

The Nature of True Minds (Cambridge: Cambridge University Press, 1992). Readers interested in issues that specifically concern cognitive science may consult Barbara von Eckardt, *What Is Cognitive Science?* (Cambridge: MIT Press, 1993).

Readers will also find the following two reference works useful: *A Companion to Philosophy of Mind*, ed. Samuel Guttenplan (Oxford: Blackwell, 1994); *A Companion to Metaphysics*, ed. Jaegwon Kim and Ernest Sosa (Oxford: Blackwell, 1995).

The following are good general anthologies of writings on philosophy of mind: *Readings in Philosophy of Psychology*, vol. 1, ed. Ned Block (Cambridge: Harvard University Press, 1980); *Mind and Cognition*, ed. William G. Lycan (Oxford: Blackwell, 1990); *The Nature of Mind*, ed. David M. Rosenthal (New York: Oxford University Press, 1991).

Notes

1. René Descartes, *Meditations* I. The translation is by John Cottingham, Robert Stoothoff, and Dugald Murdoch in *The Philosophical Writings of Descartes* (Cambridge: Cambridge University Press, 1985).

2. Descartes, *Meditations* VI.

3. Whether or not such explanatory strategies can be carried through for the entire mental realm, in particular for consciousness, is a controversial issue; see Chapters 7 and 9.

4. "Incorrigibility" is sometimes used in a different sense from "infallibility": To say that a person's belief is incorrigible is to say, roughly, that no independent evidence may overturn—that is, "correct"—that belief. That is, the person's epistemic authority in regard to that belief cannot be challenged by anyone else. This sense of incorrigibility allows the possibility that an incorrigible belief may in fact be false.

5. This is so because the belief is guaranteed true and there seems to be no question about the person's being entitled to such a belief.

6. Franz Brentano, *Psychology from an Empirical Standpoint*, trans. Antos C. Rancurello, D. B. Terrell, and Linda L. McAlister (New York: Humanities Press, 1973), p. 88. Originally published in 1874 in Leipzig as *Psychologie vom empirischen Standpunkt*.

7. Ludwig Wittgenstein, *Philosophical Investigations*, trans. G.E.M. Anscombe (Oxford: Blackwell, 1953), p. 177.

8. See, for example, John Searle, *Intentionality* (Cambridge: Cambridge University Press, 1983) and *The Rediscovery of the Mind* (Cambridge: MIT Press, 1992).

2

Mind as Behavior:
Behaviorism

Behaviorism arose as a doctrine on the nature and methodology of psychology, early in the twentieth century, in reaction to what some psychologists took to be the subjective and unscientific character of introspectionist psychology. In his classic *The Principles of Psychology*, published in 1890, William James, who had a major role in establishing psychology as an independent field of science, defined the scope of psychology in these words: "Psychology is the Science of Mental Life, both of its phenomena and of their conditions. The phenomena are such things as we call feelings, desires, cognitions, reasonings, decisions, and the like."[1] For James, then, psychology was the scientific study of mental phenomena, and he took the study of consciousness as an important core of psychology. Compare this with the declaration in 1913 by J. B. Watson, who is generally considered the founder of the behaviorist movement: "Psychology . . . is a purely objective experimental branch of natural science. Its theoretical goal is the prediction and control of behavior."[2] This view of psychology as the study of publicly observable human and animal behavior, not of inner mental life, dominated scientific psychology and associated fields until the late 1960s and made the term "behavioral science" a preferred name for psychology in universities and research centers around the world, but especially in North America.

The rise of behaviorism and the influential position it attained was no fluke. Even James saw the importance of behavior to mentality; in *The Principles of Psychology* he wrote: "*The pursuance of future ends and the choice of means for their attainment are thus the mark and criterion of the presence of mentality* in a phenomenon. We all use this test to discriminate between an intelligent and a mechanical performance."[3] It will be agreed on all sides that behavior has a lot to do with mentality. But what precisely is the relationship between them? Does behavior merely serve, as James seems to be suggesting, as an indication, or a sign, that a mind is present? And if behavior is a sign of mentality, what makes it so? If something serves as a sign of something else, there must be a reason. Or is the relationship between behavior and mentality a more intimate one? Philosophical behaviorism takes behavior as *constitutive* of mentality: According to this position, having a mind just *is* a matter of exhibiting, or having the propensity to exhibit, certain appropriate patterns of observable behavior. Although behaviorism, in both its scientific and philosophical forms, has lost the sweeping influence it once enjoyed, it is a doctrine that we need to understand, since not only does it form the historical backdrop for much of the current thinking about the mind but its influence lingers and can be discerned in some important current philosophical positions. In addition, a proper appreciation of its motivation and arguments will help us gain a better understanding of the relationship between behavior and mentality.

Reactions Against the Cartesian Conception

On the traditional conception of the mental deriving from Descartes, the mental is essentially private and subjective: For any mental phenomenon, be it a sensation of pain or an intentional state such as believing or doubting, only a single subject, the one to whom it occurs, has direct cognitive access to it. Others must depend on the subject's verbal reports or other observable behavioral clues to *infer* that she is experiencing a pain or thinking a certain thought. We see a person holding up a bleeding thumb, groaning, and infer that she must be experiencing a very bad pain in her thumb. You see your roommate leaving the apartment with her raincoat on and carrying an umbrella, and you infer that she thinks it's going to rain today. On the one hand, then, our knowledge of our own mental states, on the traditional conception, is direct and certain; on the other hand, our knowledge of other persons' mental states is indirect and must be based on inference from observable physical and behavioral evidence. Many philosophers, and also psychologists, have thought that this view of mentality entails unacceptable consequences.

The difficulty with this conception of how we come to know other minds is *not* that such knowledge, based as it is only on "outer" signs, is liable to error and cannot attain the kind of certainty with which we supposedly know our own minds. The problem, as some saw it, is rather that it makes knowledge of other minds not possible at all! Take a standard case of inductive inference—that is, inference based on premises that are less than logically conclusive—such as this: You find your roommate listening to the weather report on the radio, which is predicting heavy rain, and say to yourself, "She is going to be looking for her old umbrella!" This inference, too, is liable to error; perhaps she misunderstood the weather report or wasn't really paying attention, or she has already packed the umbrella in her backpack, or she doesn't mind getting wet. Now compare this with our inference to a person's pain on the basis of her "pain behavior." You notice the following apparent difference: With the former you can check by further observation whether or not your inference was correct (you can wait and see if she looks for her umbrella), but with the latter further observation will only yield more observations of her behavior, never an observation of her pain. Only she can experience her pains; all you can do is to see what she does and says. And what she *says* is only behavior of another kind. So what reason is there for thinking that she has an inner mental life at all?

We can illustrate this point further with a striking analogy used by Wittgenstein, "the beetle in the box." Suppose that each of us has a little box with something in it and that we can look only into our own box, never the inside of another person's box. You have a beetle in your box, and your friends say that they, too, have beetles in their boxes.[4] But what can you know from their utterance, "I have a beetle in my box"? How do you know what they mean by the word "beetle"?

It is clear that you can't know what others mean by "beetle": For all you know, some may have a butterfly or a little rock or perhaps nothing. Nor can they know what you mean when they hear you say, "I have a beetle in my box." As Wittgenstein says, the thing in the box "cancels out, whatever it is"; it's difficult to see how it can have a role in communication between persons.

In the same way, it is mysterious how, on the Cartesian conception of the mental, we could ever learn the meaning of the word "pain" and be able to use utterances like "I have a sharp pain in my elbow" for interpersonal communication, to impart information to another person. The apparently evident fact that such utterances can be used to transmit information from person to person and that expressions like "pain" and "the thought that it's going to rain" have intersubjective meanings, meanings that can be communicated from person to person, seems to give the lie to the Cartesian model of mind as an inner private theater at which only a single subject can take a peek.

Behaviorism, in one form or another, is a reaction to these seeming implications of the Cartesian conception. It attempts to construe the meanings of our mental expressions not as designating some private inner events and states accessible to a single person but as referring to publicly accessible and intersubjectively verifiable conditions and facts about people. According to the behavioristic approach, in short, the meanings of mental expressions, such as "pain" and "thought," are to be explained by reference to facts about publicly observable behavior, not inner episodes in private minds. But what is behavior?

What Is Behavior?

We may take "behavior" to mean whatever people or organisms or even mechanical systems *do* that is *publicly observable*. "Doing" is to be distinguished from "having something done." If you grasp my arm and pull it up, the rising of my arm is not something I do; it is not my behavior (although your pulling up my arm is behavior). It isn't something that a psychologist would be interested in investigating. But if I raise my arm—that is, if I cause it to rise—then it's something I do, and it counts as my behavior. It is not assumed here that the doing must in some sense be "intentional" or done for a purpose; it is only required that it is caused by some occurrence internal to the behaving system. If a robot moves toward a table and picks up a book, its motions are part of its behavior, whether or not the robot "knows" what it's doing. If a bullet punctures its skin, that is not part of its behavior, not something it does.[5]

What are some examples of things that humans and other behaving organisms "do"? The following four types can be distinguished:

(i)   Physiological reactions and responses: For example, perspiration, salivation, increase in the pulse rate, increase in blood pressure, twitching of muscles

(ii) Bodily motions: For example, my arm's rising, my moving toward the fridge in the kitchen, throwing a baseball, a cat scratching at the door, a rat turning left in a T maze

(iii) Actions involving bodily motions: For example, typing an invitation, greeting a friend, checking a book out of the library, going shopping, writing a check, telephoning your mother

(iv) Actions not involving overt bodily motions: For example, reasoning, guessing, calculating, judging, deciding

Behaviors falling under (iv), sometimes called "mental acts," are "inner events," and behaviorists will not consider them "behavior" in their intended sense (this of course does not necessarily rule out behavioral analyses of these activities). Those falling under (iii), although they involve physical motions, also have clear and substantial inner psychological components. Consider the act of writing a check: Only someone with certain cognitive capacities, beliefs, desires, and an understanding of relevant social institutions can write a check. You must have a desire to make a payment and the belief that writing a check is a means toward that end. You must also have some understanding of exchange of money for goods and services and the institution of banking. A person whose overt behavior is observationally indistinguishable from yours when you are writing a check is not necessarily writing a check (try to think how that can happen). Something like this is true of the other actions listed under (iii), and this means that none of them can count as behavior for behaviorists.

Since public observability is of central concern to behaviorists, they will exclude items under (iii) and (iv) as behavior, counting only those under (i) and (ii), what Gilbert Ryle called "motions and noises," as meeting their requirements. In much behaviorist literature, there is an implicit assumption that only those physiological responses and bodily motions that are in a broad sense "overt" and "external" (or "molar," as some behaviorists used to put it) are to count as behavior. This would rule out events and processes occurring in the internal organs as behavior; thus, internal physiological states, including states of the brain, would not, on this view, count as behavior, although they are of course among the physical states and conditions of psychological subjects that are intersubjectively accessible. The main point to remember, though, is that however the domain of behavior is circumscribed, behavior is taken to be bodily events and conditions that are publicly observable and that do not give rise to the kind of first-person epistemic asymmetry noted earlier for "inner" mental phenomena.

Logical Behaviorism: Hempel's Argument

Writing in 1935, Carl Hempel said: "We see clearly that the meaning of a psychological statement consists solely in the function of abbreviating the description of certain modes of physical response characteristic of the bodies of men and animals."[6] A claim of this form, usually called "logical behaviorism" or "analytical behaviorism," is about the translatability of psychological sentences, which can be put as follows:

[Logical behaviorism I] Any meaningful psychological statement, that is, a statement describing a mental phenomenon, can be *translated*, without loss of content, into a statement solely about behavioral and physical phenomena.

The claim can be formulated somewhat more broadly as a thesis about the behavioral definability of all meaningful psychological expressions:

[Logical behaviorism II] Every meaningful psychological expression can be *defined* solely in terms of behavioral and physical expressions, that is, those referring to behavioral and physical phenomena.

Here "definition" is to be understood in the following fairly strict sense: if an expression E is defined as E^*, then E and E^* must be either synonymous or necessarily equivalent (i.e., there is no conceivable situation to which one of the expressions applies but the other does not). Assuming translation to involve synonymy or at least necessary equivalence, we see that logical behaviorism II entails logical behaviorism I.

Why should anyone believe in logical behaviorism? The following argument extracted from Hempel represents one important line of thinking that leads to this position:

(1) The content, or meaning, of any meaningful statement is exhausted by the conditions that must be verified to obtain if we are to consider that statement true (we may call them the "verification conditions" of the statement).

(2) If a statement is to have an intersubjective content, that is, meaning that can be shared by different persons, its verification conditions must be publicly observable.

(3) Only behavioral and physical phenomena are publicly observable.

(4) Therefore, the content of any meaningful psychological statement must be specifiable by statements of publicly observable verification conditions, that is, statements describing appropriate behavioral and physical conditions that must hold if and only if the psychological statement is to count as true.

Premise (1) is often called "the verifiability criterion of meaning," a central doctrine of the philosophical movement in the early twentieth century known as "logical positivism." The idea that meanings are verification conditions is no longer accepted by many philosophers, and anyone who rejects it can reject this argument. However, we can see, and appreciate, the motivation for going for something like the intersubjective verifiability requirement in the following way. We want our psychological statements to have public, sharable meaning and serve as vehicles of interpersonal communication. Suppose someone asserts a sentence S. For me to understand what S means, I must know what state of affairs S represents (e.g., whether S represents snow's being white or the sky's being blue). But for me to know what state of affairs this is, it must be one that is accessible to me; it must be the kind of thing that I could in principle determine to obtain or not to obtain. This means that the meaning of S, namely, the state of affairs S represents, must be specifiable by conditions that are intersubjectively accessible. Therefore, if psychological statements and expressions are to be part of public language suitable for intersubjective communication, their meanings must be governed by publicly accessible criteria, and only behavioral and physical conditions can qualify as such criteria. And if anyone insists that there are inner subjective criteria for psychological expressions as well, we should reply, argues the behaviorist, that even if such existed, they (like Wittgenstein's beetles) could not be part of the meanings that can be understood and shared by different persons. One way of summarizing all this is to say: Insofar as psychological expressions have interpersonal meanings, they must be definable in terms of behavioral/physical expressions.

A Behavioral Translation of "Paul Has a Toothache"

As an example of behavioral/physical translation of psychological statements, let us see how "Paul has a toothache" can be given such a translation. Hempel offers the following five conditions:[7]

(a) Paul weeps and makes gestures of such and such kinds.
(b) At the question "What is the matter?" Paul utters the words "I have a toothache."
(c) Closer examination reveals a decayed tooth with exposed pulp.
(d) Paul's blood pressure, digestive processes, the speed of his reactions, show such and such changes.
(e) Such and such processes occur in Paul's central nervous system.

Hempel suggests that we regard this list as open-ended; there may be many other such "test sentences" that would help to confirm the statement that Paul is having a toothache. But how plausible is the claim that these behavioral/physical sentences together constitute a translation of "Paul has a toothache"?

It seems clear that as long as translation is to preserve "meaning" in the ordinary sense, we must disqualify (d) and (e): It is not a requirement on the mastery of the meaning of "toothache" that one know anything about blood pressure, reaction times, and conditions of the brain (the latter would be disqualified by some behaviorists as well). Even (c) is questionable: Why can't someone have the mental experience of toothache (that is, "toothachy pain") without having a decayed tooth or in fact any tooth at all (think about "phantom pains")? (If "toothache" means "pain caused by a physical condition of a tooth," then "toothache" is no longer a purely psychological expression.) This leaves us with (a) and (b).

Consider (b): It associates *verbal behavior* with toothache. Unquestionably, verbal reports have a crucial role in our finding out what our fellow humans are thinking and feeling, and we might think that verbal reports, and verbal behavior in general, are observable behavior that we can depend on to yield knowledge of other minds. But there is a problem: Verbal behavior is not pure physical behavior, behavior narrowly so called. In fact, it can be seen that verbal behavior, such as responding to a question with an utterance like "I have a toothache," presupposes much that is psychological; it is a behavior of kind (iv) distinguished earlier. For

Paul's response to be relevant here, he must *understand* the question "What is the matter?" and *affirm* the sentence "I have a toothache" to *mean* that he has a toothache. That is, Paul must be a competent speaker of English. Understanding a language and being a competent user of that language for interpersonal communication is a sophisticated, highly complex psychological ability, not something we can subsume under "motions and noises." Moreover, given that Paul is having a toothache, he will respond in the way specified in (b) *only if Paul wants to tell the truth*. But "want" is a psychological expression, and building this clause into (b) would again destroy its behavioral/physical character. We must conclude that (b) could hardly count as an unalloyed behavioral/physical condition; it makes huge assumptions about the psychology of Paul. We will return below to condition (a) in Hempel's translation.

Difficulties with Behavioral Translation

Consider beliefs: How might one define "*S* believes that there are no native leopards in North America" in terms of *S*'s behavior? Pains are associated with a rough but distinctive range of behavior patterns that are appropriate to pain, such as winces, groans, screams, the distinctive ways in which we favor the affected bodily parts, and so on, which we can collectively call "pain behavior" (recall Hempel's condition [a] above). However, it is much more difficult to associate higher cognitive states with specific patterns of behavior. Is there even a loosely definable range of bodily behavior that is characteristically exhibited by people when they believe, say, that an independent judiciary system is essential to a democratic government, or that there is no largest prime number? Surely the very idea of looking for bodily behaviors correlated with these beliefs is entirely misguided.

This is why it is tempting to resort to the idea of *verbal behavior*—the disposition to produce appropriate verbal responses when prompted in certain ways. A person who believes that there are infinitely many prime numbers has a certain behavioral disposition—for example, she would tend to utter the sentence "There are infinitely many primes" or its synonymous variants under certain conditions. This leads to the following schematic definition:

S believes that $p =_{\text{def.}}$ If *S* is asked, "Is it the case that p?" *S* will answer, "Yes, it is the case that p"

The right-hand side of this formula (the "definiens") states a *dispositional property* (*disposition*, for short) of *S*: *S* has a disposition to produce behavior of an appropriate kind under certain specified conditions. It is in this sense that such properties as solubility in water or being magnetic are called dispositions: Water-soluble things dissolve when immersed in water, and magnetic things will attract iron filings that are placed nearby. To be soluble at time *t*, it need not be dissolving at *t* or ever. To have a belief that *p* at time *t*, you only need to be disposed, at *t*, to respond appropriately if prompted certain ways; you need not be actually emitting that response at *t*.

There is no question that something like this definition plays a role in finding out what our fellow humans feel and believe. The importance of verbal behavior in the ascription of beliefs can be seen when we reflect on the fact that we are willing to ascribe to nonverbal animals only crude and simple beliefs. We routinely attribute to a dog beliefs like "The food bowl is empty" and "There is a cat sitting on the fence," but not beliefs like "Either the food bowl is empty or there is no cat sitting on the fence" and "The day after tomorrow, that cat will be sitting on the fence again." It is difficult to think of nonverbal behavior on the basis of which we could attribute logically complex beliefs, for instance, those expressed by "Everyone can be fooled some of the time, but no one can be fooled all of the time" and "If tomorrow is Sunday, Fred will stay home and weed his garden or tend to his ponies, unless he decides to go windsurfing or motorcycling." It is arguable that in order to have beliefs or entertain thoughts like these, you must be a speaker of a language with resources to formulate sentences with complex logical structures.

But how well does the proposed definition of belief work as a behavioristic definition? There are some serious difficulties with it. First, as we saw with Hempel's example, the definition presupposes that the person in question *understands* the question "Is it the case that *p*?" (In fact, the definition as formulated presupposes that the subject understands English, but this feature of the definition can be removed by modifying the antecedent thus: "*S* is asked a question in a language *S* understands that is synonymous with the English sentence 'Is it the case that *p*?'") But understanding is a psychological concept, and if this is so, the proposed definition cannot be considered behavioristically acceptable (unless we had a prior behavioristic definition of "understanding a language"). The same point applies to the consequent of the definition: In uttering the words "Yes, it is the case that *p*," *S* must *understand what these words mean and intend them to be understood by his or her hearer with the intended meaning*. It is clear that saying something, or uttering words with the intention of meaning something, is an action that carries substantial psychological presuppositions about the subject, and if it is to count as "behavior," it must be classified under type (iii) or (iv).

A second difficulty (this, too, was briefly noted with Hempel's example): When *S* is asked the question "Is it the case that *p*?" *S* will respond in the desired way only if *S* wants to tell the truth. Thus, the condition "if *S* wants to tell the truth" must be added to the antecedent of the definition, but this again threatens its behavioral character. The belief that p leads to an utterance of a sentence expressing p only if we combine the belief with a certain desire, the desire to tell the truth. This point can be generalized: Behavior or action issues only from complexes of mental states, not from single, isolated mental states. As we just saw, beliefs alone will not produce any behavior unless they are combined with appropriate desires. Nor will desires: If you want to eat a ham sandwich, this will lead to your ham-sandwich-eating behavior only if you believe what you are handed is a ham sandwich; if you thought it was a beef-tongue sandwich, you might pass it up. If this is so, this would make it impossible to define belief without building desire into the definition, and if you try to eliminate desire from the definition by defining it behaviorally, you will find that that's not possible unless you build belief into *its* definition.[8]

This point can be further generalized. Consider the following schema relating desire, belief, and action:

[The desire-belief-action principle (DBA)] If a person desires that p and believes that by doing A she can secure p, she will do A.

There are various ways of sharpening this principle; perhaps it's more accurate to say "she will try to do A" rather than "she will do A," and so on. Some such principle as DBA underlies our "practical reasoning," the means-ends reasoning that issues in action. It's by appeal to such a principle that we "rationalize" actions—that is, give reasons that can explain why people do what they do. DBA is also useful as a predictive tool: When we know that a person has a certain desire and that she takes a certain action as a good, or perhaps the best or only, way of securing what she desires, we could reasonably predict that she will do, or attempt to do, the required action. Something like DBA is often thought to be fundamental to the very concept of "rational action."

Consider now a special instance of the principle:

(1) If Sally desires that fresh air be let in and believes that by opening the window she can have that happen, she will open the window.

Is (1) true? If she did open the window, we could explain her behavior by appealing to her desire and belief as specified in (1). But it is clear that she may have the desire and belief but not open the window—not if, for example, she thought that opening the window would also let in the horrible street noise. So perhaps we could say:

(2) If Sally desires fresh air to be let in and believes that by opening the window she can have that happen but if she also believes that by opening the window she would let in the horrible street noise, she would not open the window.

Could we depend on (2) to be true? Well, given that the three antecedents of (2) are true, she would open the window if she also thought that her ill mother very badly wants and needs some fresh air. It is clear that this process can go on indefinitely. This suggests something interesting and very important about the relationship between mental states and behavior, which could be formulated as follows:

> [Defeasibility of mental-behavioral entailments] If there is a plausible entailment of behavior B by mental states $M_1, \ldots, M_n$, there is always a further mental state M_{n+1} such that $M_1, \ldots, M_n, M_{n+1}$ together plausibly entail not-B.

If we assume not-B (i.e., the failure to produce behavior B) to be behavior as well, the principle can be iteratively applied, without end, as we saw with Sally and the window opening: There exists some mental state M_{n+2} such that $M_1, \ldots, M_n, M_{n+1}, M_{n+2}$ together plausibly entail B. And so on.[9]

This shows that the relationship between mental states and behavior is quite complex: The moral is that mind-to-behavior connections are always *defeasible*—and defeasible by the occurrence of a *further mental state*, not merely by physical barriers and hindrances (as when Sally can't open the window because her arms are paralyzed or the window is nailed shut). This makes the success of producing for each mental expression a purely behavioral/physical definition highly unlikely. But we should not lose sight of the fact that the defeasibility thesis does state an extremely important connection between mental phenomena and behavior. Strictly speaking, this thesis doesn't say that there are no mental/behavioral entailments. What it does is to give us a way of understanding DBA and other such principles connecting mind with behavior: It says that any such entailments have mental defeaters, not just physical defeaters.

What Kinds of Behavior Are Entailed by Mental States?

Suppose you want to greet someone. What behavior is entailed by this want? We might say greeting behavior. But what is that? When you see someone across the street and want to greet her, you will, say, wave your hand. The entailment is defeasible since you wouldn't greet her, even though you want to, if you also thought that by doing so you might cause her embarrassment. Be that as it may, saying that wanting to greet someone issues in greeting doesn't say much about the behavior entailed by the wanting. The reason is that greeting is an action that includes a robustly psychological component (behavior of type [iii] distinguished earlier): Greeting Sally involves noticing or recognizing her, believing (at least hoping) that she will notice your physical gesture and recognize it as expressing your intention to greet, your desire to show welcome or respect, and so on. Greeting will not count as behavior of kind (i) or (ii)—that is, physiological response or bodily motion.

So does wanting to greet entail any bodily motions? If so, what bodily motions? There are innumerable ways of greeting if the "ways" are counted as ways in which you could produce bodily motions: You can greet by waving your right hand, waving your left hand, waving both, saying "Hi!" or "How are you?" or "Hey, how're you doing, Sally?", saying these things in French or Chinese (you and Sally are in a Chinese class), rushing up to Sally and shaking her hand, giving her a hug, and countless other ways. In fact, any physical gesture will do as long as it is socially recognized as a way of greeting.[10]

Moreover, a gesture that is recognized as a friendly and respectful greeting in one culture may be one of insult and disdain in another, something often noted in travel guides. Indeed, within our own culture, the very same physical gesture could count as greeting someone, cheering your basketball team, bidding at an auction, signaling for a left turn, and any number of other things. The factors that determine exactly what it is that you are doing when you produce a physical gesture include the customs, habits, and conventions that are in force, as well as the particular features of a given situation—a complex network of entrenched rules, mutual expectations based on these rules, the agent's beliefs and intentions, and many other social and psychological factors.

Considerations like these make it highly unlikely that anyone could ever produce correct behavioral definitions of mental terms, those linking each mental expression with an equivalent behavioral expression referring solely to pure physical behavior ("motions and noises"). In fact, they show how futile it would be to look for interesting generalizations, much less definitions, connecting mental states, like wanting to greet someone, with physical behavior. To have even a glimmer of success, you would need, it seems, to work at the level of intentional action, not of physical behavior—at the level of greeting, buying and selling, and the like.

Do Pains Entail Pain Behavior?

As was noted, however, some mental phenomena seem more closely tied to physical behavior—occurrences like pains and itches that have "natural expressions" in behavior. When you experience pain, you wince and groan and try to get away from the source of the pain; when you itch, you scratch. This perhaps is what gives some substance to the talk of "pain behavior"; it would obviously be much easier to recognize pain behavior than, say, greeting behavior, in an alien culture. We sometimes try to hide our pains and suppress winces and groans and succeed in doing so; nonetheless, pains do seem, under normal conditions, to issue in a roughly identifiable range of physical behavior. Does this mean that pains do entail, albeit "defeasibly," certain specific types of physical behavior?

Let's first get clear about what "entailment" is to mean for the present purposes. When we say that pain "entails" winces and groans, we are saying that "Anyone in pain winces and groans" is *analytically, or conceptually, true*—that is, like "Bachelors are unmarried" and "Vixens are females," it is true *solely by virtue of the meanings of the terms involved (or the concepts expressed by these terms).* If "toothache" is definable, as Hempel claims, in terms of "weeping" and "making gesture *G*" (where we leave it to Hempel to specify *G*), toothache will entail weeping and making gesture *G* in our sense. And if pain entails winces and groans, no organism, no person anywhere could count as "being in pain" unless it could evince wincing and groaning behavior. That is, there is no "possible world" in which something is in pain but does not wince and groan.

Some philosophers have argued that there is no pain-behavior entailment because pain behavior can be completely and thoroughly suppressed by some people, "super-Stoics" and "super-Spartans" who for various reasons have trained themselves not to manifest their pains in overt behavior.[11] This objection can be met, at least partially, by pointing out that these super-Spartans, although they do not actually exhibit pain behavior, can still be said to have a *propensity*, or *potential*, to exhibit pain behavior—that is, they *would* exhibit overt pain behavior *if certain conditions were to obtain*. It is only that some of these conditions do not obtain for them, and so the behavior disposition associated with pain remains unrealized. Thus, there is this difference between a super-Spartan who is in pain and another super-Spartan who is not in pain: It is true of the former, but not the latter, that if certain conditions were true of her (e.g., she has given up her super-Spartan code of conduct), she would wince and groan. It seems, therefore, that the objection based on the conceivability of super-Spartans can be substantially mitigated by formulating the entailment claim in terms of behavior dispositions or propensities ("possible behavior") rather than actual behavior.

So the modified entailment thesis says this: It is an analytic, conceptual truth that anyone in pain has a propensity to wince or groan. Is this true? Consider animals: Dogs and cats can surely feel pain. Do they wince or groan? Perhaps. How about squirrels or bats? How about snakes and octopuses? Evidently, in order to groan or wince or to emit a specified type of behavior (e.g., screaming and writhing in pain), an organism needs a certain sort of body and bodily organs with certain capacities and powers. Only organisms with vocal cords can groan. Thus, the entailment thesis under consideration has the consequence that organisms without vocal cords (e.g., snakes and octopuses) cannot be in pain, which is absurd. The point can be generalized: Whatever behavior type is picked, we can coherently imagine a pain-capable organism that is physically un-suited to produce behavior of that type.

If this is the case, there is no specific behavior type that is entailed by pain. More generally, the same line of consideration would show that no specific behavior type is entailed by any mental state. And yet the follow-ing weaker thesis may be true: For any pain-capable species[12] there is a certain behavior type B such that, for that species, being in pain entails a disposition to emit behavior of type B. According to this thesis, then, each species may have its own special way of behaviorally expressing pain, al-though there are no universal and species-independent pain-to-behavior entailments. If this is correct, the concept of pain involves the concept of behavior only in this sense: Any organism in pain must be disposed to be-have in some specific way or other. But there is no behavior pattern that can count as "pain behavior" across all pain-capable organisms. Again, this makes the prospect of defining pain in terms of behavior exceedingly remote.

Ontological Behaviorism

Logical behaviorism is a claim about the meanings of psycho-logical *expressions*; as you recall, the claim is that the meaning of every psychological term is definable by the use of behavioral or physical terms. But we can also consider a behaviorist thesis about psychological *states* or *phenomena* as such, independently of the language in which they are described. Thus, a behaviorist might claim:

There are no psychological facts over and above behavioral facts, and there are no psychological states or events over and above actual and possible behavior.

Compare the following two claims about pain:

(1) Pain = winces and groans.

(2) Pain = the cause of winces and groans.

Claim (1) expresses what we may call ontological behaviorism about pain; if it is true, there indeed would be nothing more to pain than pain behavior, that is, winces and groans. But (2) is not a form of ontological behaviorism, since the *cause* of winces and groans need not be just more behavior. Clearly, (2) may be affirmed by someone who thinks that it is the *internal states* of organisms (perhaps physiological states, including those of the central nervous system) that cause them to display appropri-ate pain behavior. Moreover, a Cartesian dualist can accept (2): He would say that a subjective private mental event, an inner pain experience, is the cause of pain behavior. Moreover, one might even claim that (2) is analytically or conceptually true: The concept of pain is that of an internal state apt to cause characteristic pain behaviors like winces and groans.[13] Thus (2) can be taken as a form of logical behaviorism about the expression "pain," since it allows us to eliminate "pain" wherever it occurs with an expression free of mentalistic terms. We may then say this: Logical behaviorism does not entail ontological behaviorism.

Does ontological behaviorism entail logical behaviorism? Again, the answer has to be in the negative. From the fact that Xs are Ys, nothing interesting follows about the meanings of the expressions "X" and "Y"—in particular, nothing follows about their interdefinability. Consider some examples: We know that bolts of lightning are electric discharges in the atmosphere and that the gene is a DNA molecule. But the expressions "lightning" and "electric discharge in the atmosphere" are not semantically related, much less synonymous; nor are the expressions "gene" and "DNA molecule."

In a similar vein, one could say, as some philosophers have said, there are in this world no inner private episodes like pains, itches, and twinges but only observable behaviors or dispositions to exhibit such behaviors. One may say this because one holds a certain form of logical behaviorism or a certain view about mentalistic expressions like "pain" and "itch" (although, as we have just seen, not all forms of logical behaviorism entail ontological behaviorism). But one may be an ontological behaviorist on a methodological ground, affirming that there is *no need to posit* private inner events like pains and itches since, on account of their essentially subjective character, they can play no role in intersubjective communication and cannot be scientifically studied. A person holding such a position may well concede that the purported meaning of "pain" is some inner subjective state but will insist that there is no reason to think that the word refers to anything that actually exists (compare with "phlogiston," "witch"). We will discuss this latter position, "methodological behaviorism," in a later section of this chapter.

The True Relationship Between Pain and Pain Behavior?

Our earlier discussion has revealed serious difficulties with any entailment claims about the relationship between pain and pain behavior, or more generally between mental states and types of behavior. The considerations seemed to show that though our pains may cause our pain behaviors, this causal relation is a contingent, not a necessary, fact. But leaving the matter there is somehow unsatisfying: Surely pain behaviors—groans, winces, screams, writhings, attempts to get away, and all the rest—have something important to do with our notion of pain. How else could we learn, and teach, the concept of pain or the meaning of the word "pain"? Wouldn't we rightly deny the concept of pain to a person who doesn't at all appreciate the connection between pains and these behaviors characteristic of pain? What we need is a positive account of the relationship between pain and pain behavior that explains their apparently intimate connection without making it into one of analytic entailment.

The following is one possible account. Let's begin with an analogy: How do we fix the meaning of "1 meter long"—that is, the concept of a meter?[14] Consider the Standard Meter: a bar of platinum-iridium alloy kept in a vault near Paris.[15] Is the following statement necessarily true?

The Standard Meter is 1 meter long.

Does being the Standard Meter (or having the same length as the Standard Meter) entail being 1 meter long? The Standard Meter is a particular physical object, manufactured at a particular date and now located somewhere in France, and surely this metallic object might not have been the Standard Meter and might not have been 1 meter long (it could have been fashioned into a bowl, or it could have been made into a longer rod of 2 meters). In other words, it is a contingent fact that this particular platinum-iridium rod was selected as the Standard Meter, and it is a contingent fact that it is 1 meter long. No physical object has the length it has necessarily; anything could be longer or shorter—or so it seems. We must conclude, then, that the statement that something has the same length as the Standard Meter does not entail that it is 1 meter long; and it is not analytically, or conceptually, true that if the length of an object coincides with that of the Standard Meter it is 1 meter long.

But what, then, is the relationship between the Standard Meter and the concept of the meter? After all, one speaks of the Standard Meter as a "definition" or "criterion" or "standard" of the meter; there must be some intimate connection between the two. The answer is that we specify the property of being 1 meter long (the meaning, if you wish, of the expression "1 meter long") by the use of a contingent relationship in which the property stands. One meter is the length of this thing (namely, the Standard Meter) here and now. It is only contingently 1 meter long, but that's no barrier to our using it to specify what counts as 1 meter. This is no more mysterious than the ostensive specification of, say, the color red—by pointing to a ripe tomato. After all, it is a contingent fact that ripe tomatoes are red.

Let us see how a similar account might go for pain: We specify what pain is (or fix the meaning of "pain") by reference to a contingent fact about pain, namely, that pain causes winces and groans (in humans). This is a contingent fact about this world. In worlds in which different laws hold or worlds in which the central nervous system of humans and those of other organisms are hooked up differently to peripheral sensory surfaces and motor output systems, the patterns of causal relations involving pain may be very different. But as things are in this world, pain is the cause of winces and groans and other behaviors (which we count in this world as "pain behavior"). In worlds in which pains don't cause winces and groans, different behaviors may count as pain behavior, in which case pain specifications in those worlds could advert to the behaviors caused by pains there. This is similar to the color case: If cucumbers but not ripe tomatoes were red, we would be specifying what "red" means by pointing to cucumbers, not tomatoes.

The foregoing is only a sketch of an account but not an implausible one. It keeps the relationship between pain and pain behavior a contingent one but gives an important role to pain behavior in specifying what pain is. And it seems to show a good fit with the way we learn, and teach, the use of "pain" and other mental expressions denoting sensations. The approach brings mental expressions under the same rubric with many other expressions, as we have seen, such as those denoting colors and basic physical magnitudes. It may well be that most terms for basic properties can be subsumed under the same general account.

Methodological Behaviorism

So far we have been discussing behaviorism as a philosophical doctrine concerning the meanings of mental terms and the nature of mental states. But as we noted at the outset, "behaviorism" is also a name of an important and influential psychological movement initiated early in this century that came to dominate scientific psychology and the social sciences in North America and many other parts of the world. It held its position as the reigning methodology of the "behavioral sciences" until the latter half of the century, when "cognitivism" and "mentalism" began a strong and steady comeback.

Behaviorism as a precept on how psychology should be conducted as a science is called "methodological behaviorism." What are its major tenets? We have room here for only a brief and sketchy discussion of the claims of methodological behaviorism. We can begin with the following doctrine:

(I) The only admissible data for the science of psychology are behavioral data—that is, data concerning the observable behavior of organisms.

What do we mean by "data"? Data serve two related purposes in science: First, they constitute the domain of phenomena for which theories are constructed to provide explanations and predictions; second, they serve as the evidential basis that can support or undermine theories. What (I) says, therefore, is that psychological theories should attempt to explain and predict only data concerning observable behavior and that only such data should be used as evidence against which psychological theories are to be evaluated. These two points can be seen to collapse into one when we realize that explanatory and predictive successes and failures constitute, by and large, the only measure by which we evaluate how well theories are supported by evidence.

The main reason some psychologists and philosophers have insisted on the observability of psychological data is to ensure the *objective testability* of psychological theories. It is thought that introspective data, data obtained by a subject by inwardly inspecting her own inner mental theater, are in principle private and subjective and hence cannot serve as the basis for intersubjective validation of psychological theories. In short, the idea is that intersubjective access to data is essential for ensuring the possibility of intersubjective agreement in science, and the only psychological data that meet this requirement are behavioral (more broadly, physical) data.

What about the subject's verbal reports of her inner experience? A subject in an experiment involving mental imagery might report: "I am now rotating the figure counterclockwise." What's wrong with taking the following as an item of our data: Subject *S* is rotating her mental image counterclockwise? Someone who holds (I) will say something like this: Strictly speaking, what we can properly consider an item of data here is *S*'s utterance of the words "I am now rotating the figure counterclockwise." Counting *S*'s actual mental operation of rotating her mental image as a datum involves the assumption that she is a competent speaker of English, that intersubjective meaning can be attached to reports of inner experience, and that she is reporting her experience correctly. These are all psychological assumptions going beyond reports of the subject's observable behavior. Therefore, unless these assumptions themselves can be behaviorally translated out, the psychologist is entitled only to the subject's utterance of the words, not the presumed content of those words, as part of her basic data.

One point to note about (I), which makes it a form of methodological behaviorism, is this: It regards consciousness as falling outside the province of psychological explanation. Inner conscious states are not among the phenomena it is the business of psychological theory to explain or predict. In any case, many psychologists will find (I) acceptable, although they are likely to disagree about just what is to count as *observable* behavior (some may but others won't consider verbal reports as observable behavior). A real disagreement will arise, though, concerning the following stronger version of methodological behaviorism:

(II) Psychological theories must not invoke internal states of psychological subjects; that is, psychological explanations must not appeal to internal states of organisms, nor should references to such states occur in deriving predictions about behavior.

On this principle, organisms are to be construed as veritable black boxes whose internal structure is forever closed to the psychological investigator. Psychological generalizations, therefore, must correlate behavioral responses as output with observable stimulus conditions as input; stimulus-response (S-R) correlations are the only permissible generalizations. But isn't it obvious that when the same stimulus is applied to them, two organisms often respond with different behavior output? How can we explain this behavioral difference unless we invoke differences in their internal states?

The usual answer is to say that such behavioral differences can be explained by reference to the differences in the *history* of reinforcement for the two organisms; that is to say, the two organisms emit different behavior in response to the same stimulus because their *past histories* involving external stimuli, elicited behaviors, and rewards received for them are different. But if such an explanation works, isn't that because the differences in the history of the two organisms led to differences in their present internal states? Isn't it plausible to suppose that these differences *here and now* are directly implicated in the production of different behaviors *now*? To suppose otherwise would be to embrace "mnemic causation," a causal influence that leaps over a temporal gap with no intermediate links bridging cause with effect. Anyhow, why is it impermissible to invoke present internal differences as well as differences in past histories to explain differences in behavior output?

Notice how sweeping the constraint expressed by (II) really is: It outlaws references not only to private mental states of the organism but also to its internal physical/biological states. Methodological concerns with the objectivity of psychology as a science provide some intelligible motivation for banishing the former, but it does not justify banning the latter from psychological explanations. Even if it is true, as some claim,[16] that invoking internal neurobiological states doesn't help psychological theorizing, that hardly constitutes a sufficient ground for prohibiting it as a matter of methodological principle.

In view of this, we may consider yet a further version of behaviorism as a psychological methodology:

(III) Psychological theories must make no reference to inner mental states in formulating psychological explanations.

This principle allows the introduction of internal biological states, including states of the central nervous system, into psychological theories and explanations, prohibiting only inner mental states. But what is to count as such a state? Does this principle permit the use of such concepts as "drive," "information," "memory," "attention," "mental representation," and the like in psychological theories? To answer this question we would have to analyze these concepts in some detail, a task that goes beyond the scope of our discussion. We should keep in mind, though, that the chief rationale for (III)—in fact, the driving motivation for the entire behaviorist methodology—is the insistence on the objective testability of theories and public access to sharable data, and this means that what (III) is intended to prohibit is the introduction of inner subjective states for which objective access is thought to be problematic, not the use of theoretical constructs posited by psychological theories for explanatory and predictive purposes, as long as these meet the requirement of intersubjectivity. Unlike overt behavior, these constructs are not as a rule "directly observable," and they are not definable or otherwise reducible in terms of observable behavior. However, they differ from the paradigmatic inner mental states in that they apparently do not show the first-person–third-person asymmetry of epistemic access. Scientific theories often introduce theoretical concepts for entities (electrons, magnetic fields) and properties (spin, polarization) that go far beyond the limits of human observability. Psychological theory should be entitled to such theoretical constructs like any other science.

But in excluding private conscious states from psychological theory, (III) excludes them from playing any causal/explanatory role in relation to behavior. If we think that some of our behavior is caused by inner mental states disallowed by (III), our psychological theory would obviously be incomplete: There will be behavior for which no theory meeting (III) can provide explanations.

Are there other methodological constraints for psychological theory? How can we be sure that the states and entities posited by a psychological theory (e.g., "intelligence," "representation," "drive reduction") are "real"? If in explaining the same data, one psychological theory posits one set of unobservable states and another theory posits an entirely different set, which theory, if any, should be believed? That is, which theory represents the *actual states* of the psychological subjects? Does it make sense to raise such questions? If it does, should there be the further requirement that the entities and states posited by a psychological theory must have a "biological reality"—that is, they must somehow be "realized" or "implemented" in the biological/physical structures and processes of the organism? These are important questions about the science of psychology; we will be dealing with some of them later in our discussion of various mind-body theories and the issue of reductionism.

Further Readings

The influential classic work representing behaviorism as a philosophical doctrine is Gilbert Ryle, *The Concept of Mind* (New York: Barnes and Noble, 1949). See also Carl Hempel, "The Logical Analysis of Psychology," in *Readings in Philosophy of Psychology*, vol. 1, ed. Ned Block (Cambridge: Harvard University Press, 1980). For an accessible Wittgensteinian perspective on mentality and behavior, see Norman Malcolm's contributions in *Consciousness and Causality* by D. M. Armstrong and Norman Malcolm (Oxford: Blackwell, 1984). For scientific behaviorism, see B. F. Skinner, *Science and Human Behavior* (New York: Macmillan, 1953).

For a historically important critique of Skinnerian behaviorism, see Noam Chomsky's review of Skinner's *Verbal Behavior* in *Language* 35 (1959):26–58. For criticism of philosophical behaviorism, see Roderick M. Chisholm, *Perceiving* (Ithaca: Cornell University Press, 1957), pp. 173–185; Hilary Putnam, "Brains and Behavior," in Block, *Readings in Philosophy of Psychology*, vol. 1.

Notes

1. William James, *The Principles of Psychology* (1890; reprint, Cambridge: Harvard University Press, 1981), p. 15.

2. J. B. Watson, "Psychology as the Behaviorist Views It," *Psychological Review* 20 (1913):158–177.

3. James, *The Principles of Psychology* (Harvard edition), p. 21. Italics in the original.

4. Ludwig Wittgenstein, *Philosophical Investigations*, trans. G.E.M. Anscombe (Oxford: Blackwell, 1953), sec. 293. To make this story work, we must assume that there are no beetles around us, outside the little boxes.

5. For the notion of behavior as internally caused bodily motion, see Fred Dretske, *Explaining Behavior* (Cambridge: MIT Press, 1988), chs. 1 and 2.

6. Carl Hempel, "The Logical Analysis of Psychology," reprinted in *Readings in Philosophy of Psychology*, vol. 1, ed. Ned Block (Cambridge: Harvard University Press, 1980), p. 19.

7. Ibid., p. 17.

8. For an early statement of this point concerning psychological concepts, see Roderick M. Chisholm, *Perceiving* (Ithaca: Cornell University Press, 1957).

9. See Donald Davidson, "Mental Events," reprinted in his *Essays on Actions and Events* (Oxford: Oxford University Press, 1980); it was originally published in 1970.

10. The phenomena discussed in this paragraph and the next are noted by Berent Enc, "Redundancy, Degeneracy, and Deviance in Action," *Philosophical Studies* 48 (1985):353–374.

11. Hilary Putnam, "Brains and Behavior," reprinted in Block, *Readings in Philosophy of Psychology*, vol. 1.

12. Species may be too wide here, given the fact that expressions of pain are, at least to some extent, culture-specific and even differ from person to person within the same culture.

13. See Chapters 4 and 5 for discussion of the functionalist conception of pain as that of a "causal intermediary" between certain stimulus conditions (e.g., tissue damage) and characteristic pain behaviors.

14. This account is due to Saul Kripke, *Naming and Necessity* (Cambridge: Harvard University Press, 1980).

15. The meter is no longer defined this way; the current definition, adopted in 1984 by the General Conference on Weights and Measures in Paris, is reportedly based on the distance traveled by light through a vacuum in a certain (very small) fraction of a second.

16. See, for example, B. F. Skinner, *Science and Human Behavior* (New York: Macmillan, 1953).

3

Mind as the Brain: The
Mind-Brain Identity Theory

Some ancient Greeks thought that the heart was the organ responsible for thoughts and feelings—an idea that has survived, we are told, in the traditional symbolism of the heart to signify love and romance. But they got it wrong: We think, with good reason, that the brain is where the action is, as far as our mental life is concerned. If you ask most people where they think their minds are, they will point to their heads. But does this mean that they only think that the mind *is where the brain is* or that they think that the mind *is* the brain? We consider here a theory that asserts that the mind is identical with the brain, that to have mentality is to have a functioning brain of appropriate structure and complexity.

Mind-Brain Correlations

But why are we inclined to think that the brain is "the seat of our mental life," as Descartes would have put it? The answer seems obvious: There is a *pervasive and comprehensive system of correlations between mental events and brain processes.* This isn't something we know a priori; Descartes, as mathematically talented as he was, couldn't figure it out by a priori reasoning. We know it from empirical evidence: For example, injuries to the brain can have a dramatic impact on our mental life, affecting our ability to reason, recall, and perceive and sometimes can permanently alter our personality traits. Chemical changes in the brain (e.g., a high level of alcohol in the blood) can make a huge difference to our moods, emotions, and judgments. A brain concussion can knock us out, and our conscious life goes blank. Severe brain injuries can lead to brain death, a state in which the loss of consciousness and mental functions is irreversible. We now have overwhelming evidence from neurophysiological research for the centrality of the brain and its activities as determinants of our mental life.

A badly scraped elbow will cause you a searing pain, and a mild food poisoning is often accompanied by stomachaches and queasy sensations. Irradiation of your retinas will cause visual sensations, which in turn may cause beliefs about things in your surroundings. Stimulations of your sensory surfaces lead to mental events of various kinds. However, they are just remote causes, which bring about mental events only because they cause appropriate states of the brain. This is why anesthesia works: If the nerve signals coming from sensory peripheries are blocked or the normal functions of the brain are interfered with so that appropriate central neural processes are prevented from occurring, there will be no experience of pain. It's plausible to think that everything that occurs in mental life has a state of the brain (or the central nervous system) as its *proximate* physical basis. There is compelling evidence for thinking that the very existence of mentality depends on the existence of appropriate neural structures: If all the molecules that make up a person's brain were taken away, her whole mental life would be lost, just as surely as taking away all the molecules making up her body would result in her ceasing to exist. At least that is the way things seem. We may summarize all this in the following thesis:

> [The mind-brain correlation thesis] For each type M of mental event that occurs to an organism o, there exists a brain state of kind B (M's "neural correlate" or "substrate") such that M occurs to o at time t if and only if B occurs to o at t.

According to this thesis, then, each type of mental event that can occur to an organism has a neural correlate that is both necessary and sufficient for its occurrence. So for each organism there is a set of mind-brain correlations covering every kind of mental state it is capable of having.

Two points may be noted about these brain-mind correlations:

1. They are taken to be "lawlike": The fact that pain is experienced when certain of your neural fibers (C-fibers and A-delta-fibers) are activated is a matter of *lawful regularity*, not accidental co-occurrence.
2. Even the smallest change in your mental life cannot occur unless there is some specific (perhaps still unknown) change in your brain state; where there is a difference between two conscious mental states, there must be a difference between the two corresponding neural states.

Another way of putting these points is to say that mentality *supervenes* on brain states and that this supervenience holds as a matter of law. Remember that this supervenience, if it indeed holds, is something we know from observation and experience, not a priori. Moreover, specific correlations—that is, correlations between specific mental states (say, pain) and specific brain states (say, the activation of certain neural fibers)—are again matters of empirical research and discovery, and we may assume that many of the details about these correlations are still largely unknown. However, it is knowledge of these specific correlations, rough and incomplete though it may be, that ultimately underlies our confidence in the mind-body correlation thesis and mind-body supervenience. If the ancients had been correct (and they *might* have been correct) about the heart as the engine of mentality, we would have mind-heart supervenience rather than mind-brain supervenience.

Explaining Mind-Body Correlations: Mind-Body Theories

When a systematic correlation between two properties or event types has been observed, we often want an explanation of the correlation: Why do the properties F and G correlate? Why is it that an event of type F occurs just when an event of type G occurs? What underlies and explains this systematic relationship? Let us first look at some examples outside the mind-brain case:

(a) Whenever the atmospheric temperature falls below 20°F and stays there for a few days, the local lakes and ponds freeze over. Why? Well, the low temperature *causes* the water in the ponds to freeze. The two events are *causally related,* and that is why the observed correlation occurs.

(b) You enter a clock shop and find an astounding scene: Dozens and dozens of clocks of all shapes and sizes are busily ticking away, and they all show exactly the same time, 2:15. A while later, you see all of them showing exactly 2:30, and so on. What explains this marvelous correlation among these clocks? One possible answer is that the shopkeeper synchronized all the clocks before the shop opened in the morning and that the clocks have been working properly. Here a *common past cause,* the shopkeeper's action in the morning, explains the correlations that are now observed. We do not suppose that there are direct relationships among the clocks that are responsible for the correlations.

(c) We can imagine a somewhat different explanation of why the clocks are keeping the same time: These clocks actually are not very accurate, and some of them gain or lose time markedly every five minutes. There is a little man whose sole job is to run around the shop, unseen by the customers, synchronizing the clocks every two or three minutes. That is why every time you looked, the clocks showed the same time. This again is a *common-cause* explanation of a correlation, but it's different from the story in (b) in the following respect: This explanation involves a continued intervention of a causal agent, whereas in (b) a single cause in the past was sufficient. In neither case, however, is there a direct cause-effect relationship among the clocks.

(d) Why do temperature and pressure covary for gases confined in a rigid container? The temperature and pressure of a gas are both dependent on the motions of molecules that make up the gas: The temperature is the average kinetic energy of the molecules and the pressure is the total momentum imparted to the walls of the container (per unit area) by the molecules colliding with them. Thus, the rise in temperature and the rise in pressure can be viewed as *two aspects* of one and the same underlying microprocess.

(e) Why does lightning occur just when there is an electric discharge between clouds or between clouds and the ground? Because lightning simply *is* an electric discharge involving clouds and the earth. There is here only one phenomenon, not two, and what we thought were distinct phenomena turn out to be one and the same. Here the relationship is one of *identity*.

(f) Why do the phases of the moon (full, half, quarter, etc.) covary with the ocean tides (spring tides, neap tides, etc.)? Because the relative positions of the earth, the moon, and the sun determine both the phases of the moon and the combined strength of gravitational forces of attraction exerted on the ocean water by the moon and the sun. So the changes in gravitational force are the proximate cause of the changes in the tides, and the relative positions of the three bodies can be thought of as their remote cause. The phases of the moon are merely collateral effects of the positions of the three bodies involved and serve only as an indication of what the positions are (full moon when the earth is between the sun and the moon on a straight line, and so on), having no causal role whatever on tidal actions.

What about the explanation of mind-brain correlations? Which of the models we have surveyed best fits the mind-body case? As you would expect, all of these models have been tried. First, we have various causal approaches to the mind-body relation:

Causal interactionism. Descartes thought that causal interaction between the mind and the body occurred in the pineal gland. He speculated that "animal spirits," fluids made up of extremely fine particles flowing around the pineal gland, caused it to move in various ways, and these motions of the gland in turn caused conscious states of the mind. Conversely, the mind could cause the gland to move in various ways, affecting the flow of the surrounding animal spirits. This in turn influenced the flow of these fluids to different parts of the body, ultimately issuing in various physiological changes and bodily movements.[1]

"Preestablished harmony" between mind and body. Leibniz thought that no coherent sense could be made of Descartes's idea that the mind, which isn't even in physical space, could causally interact with a material body like the pineal gland, managing to move this lump of matter hither and thither. On his view, the mind and the body are in a "preestablished harmony," rather like the clocks that were synchronized by the shopkeeper in the morning, with God having started off our minds and bodies in a harmonious relationship.

Occasionalism. According to occasionalists like Malebranche, whenever a mental event appears to cause a physical event or a physical event appears to cause a mental event, this is only an illusion. There is no direct causal relation between "finite minds," namely, human minds, and bodies; when a mental event, say, your will to raise your arm occurs, that only serves as an *occasion* for God to intervene and cause your arm to rise. Divine intervention is also responsible for the apparent causation of mental events by physical events: When your finger is burned, God quickly steps in to cause you pain. The role of God, then, is rather like that of the little man in the clock shop whose job is to keep the clocks synchronized at all times by continuous interventions.

The double-aspect theory. Spinoza claimed that mind and body were simply two correlated aspects of a single underlying substance that is in itself neither mental nor material. This theory, like the doctrine of preestablished harmony and occasionalism, denies a direct causal relation between the mental and the physical; however, unlike them, it does not invoke God's causal action to explain the mental-physical correlations. The observed correlations are there because they are two distinguishable aspects of one underlying reality.

Epiphenomenalism. According to T. H. Huxley,[2] every mental event is caused by a physical event in the brain, but mental events have no causal power of their own, being the absolute terminal links of causal chains. So all mental events are effects of the physiological processes going on in our nervous system, but they are powerless to cause anything else, even other mental events. Thus, you "will" your arm to rise, and it does rise. But to think that your will is the cause of the rising of the arm is to commit the same error as thinking that the changes in the phases of the moon are the cause of the changes in tidal motions. The real cause of the arm's rising was a certain brain event that also caused your desire to raise the arm, just as in the case of the moon and the tides the relative positions of the earth, the moon, and the sun were the true cause of both the tidal motions and the phases of the moon. We will have a chance to examine issues concerning mental causation in detail later (Chapter 6).

The mind-body (or psychophysical, psychoneural) identity theory. This position, formulated and explicitly advanced as a solution to the mind-body problem in the late 1950s, advocates the *identification* of mental states and events with the physical processes in the brain. Just as there are no bolts of lightning as phenomena over and above atmospheric electric discharges, there are no mental events over and above the neural (ultimately, physicochemical) processes in the brain. "Lightning" and "electric discharge" of course are not synonyms, and the Greeks probably knew something about lightning but nothing about electric discharges; nonetheless, lightning just is electric discharges, and the two expressions "lightning" and "atmospheric electric discharge" refer to the same phenomenon. In the same way, "pain" and "C-fiber activation" do not have the same meaning, and our ancestors knew a lot about pains but nothing about C-fiber activations. Still, "pain" and "C-fiber activation" may pick out the same phenomenon, and, according to the identity theory, pains just turn out to be the activations of C-fibers.

Emergentism. There is another interesting response to the question "Why are mental events and states correlated with physical states in the way they are?" It is this: The question is unanswerable—the correlations are "brute facts" that we must accept; they are not subject to further explanation. This is the position of emergentism. It holds that when biological processes attain a certain level of complexity, a wholly new type of phenomenon, namely, consciousness, emerges, and these "emergent" phenomena are not explainable in terms of the underlying physical/biological phenomena from which they emerge. There is no explanation of why, say, pains rather than itches emerge from C-fiber activations or why pains emerge from C-fiber activations rather than A-fiber activations. Indeed, there is no explanation of why anything conscious should emerge from this or any other biological process. That there are just these emergent relationships and not others must be accepted, in the words of Samuel Alexander, a leading theoretician of the emergence school, "with natural piety."[3] Thus, emergentism presents another possible response to the mind-body problem: Mental phenomena are brute emergent phenomena, and we should expect no further explanation of why they emerge. That they do must be accepted as a fundamental fact about the natural world.

Arguments for Psychoneural Identification

J.J.C. Smart, whose essay "Sensations and Brain Processes"[4] played a major role in establishing the psychophysical identity theory as the most influential mind-body theory during the 1960s, emphasized the importance of *simplicity* as the ground for accepting the theory. He wrote:

> Why do I wish [to identify sensations with brain processes]? Mainly because of Occam's razor. . . . There does seem to be, so far as science is concerned, nothing in the world but increasingly complex arrangements of physical constituents. All except for one place: in consciousness. That is, for a full description of what is going on in a man you would have to mention not only the physical processes in his tissues, glands, nervous system, and so forth, but also his states of consciousness: his visual, auditory, and tactual sensations, his aches and pains. That these should be correlated with brain processes does not help, for to say that they are correlated is to say that they are something "over and above." . . . So sensations, states of consciousness, do seem to be the one sort of thing left outside the physicalist picture, and for various reasons I just cannot believe that this can be so. That everything be explicable in terms of physics . . . except the occurrence of sensations seems to me frankly unbelievable.[5]

But just how do considerations of simplicity and parsimony support psychoneural identification? Various lines of argument may be considered.

1. Obviously, identification in general reduces the number of entities and thereby enhances ontological simplicity. When you say x is the same thing as y or, as Smart says, that x is not something "over and above" y, you are saying that there is just one thing here, not two. So if pains are identified with their neural correlates, there are no pains *in addition to* C-fiber activations. This is one sense in which the identity theory simplifies our ontology—the total scheme of things we accept as real.

2. It may also be argued that psychoneural identification can be conducive to conceptual or linguistic simplicity as well. If all mental states are systematically identified with their neural correlates, there is a sense in which mentalistic language, language in which we speak of pains and thoughts, is *in principle* replaceable by a physical language in which we speak of brain processes. The mentalistic language may in practice be indispensable; however, descriptions formulated in the mentalistic vocabulary do not report facts or states of affairs distinct from those reported by a comprehensive physical language, a language in which we report phys-

ical phenomena, and in that sense they are theoretically dispensable. There are no excess facts beyond physical facts to be reported in mentalistic language.

3. Suppose we stop short of identifying pains with C-fiber activations. We then have the problem of explaining why this correlation obtains. The emergentists say that psychophysical correlations are not further explainable and that they must simply be accepted as fundamental facts about the world. They would be "nomological danglers," to use an expression of Herbert Feigl.[6] The emergentist approach, therefore, asks us to accept these dangling laws as brute, unexplainable laws—that is, we are asked to count them among our fundamental laws, laws that are basic in the sense that no further explanation is possible for them. But this proposal is highly implausible, for we expect fundamental laws of nature to be reasonably simple, but these psychophysical correlations involve, on the physical side, tens of thousands of cells, millions and billions of molecules and basic particles. We expect laws governing such complex structures to be derivable from simpler laws about smaller groups of basic entities. But is there any hope for deriving a psychophysical law from more fundamental laws? Perhaps there is; but however the derivation is made, at least one of the premises must refer to a mental state, correlating it with a physical state. How else could we get a psychophysical correlation as our conclusion? This means that we have only postponed the task of explaining how psychophysical correlations are possible; for we must now explain the psychophysical correlation assumed in the premises. This evidently leads to an infinite regress. By identifying the correlated mental and physical states, we prevent this explanatory regress from getting started. Thus, by interpreting psychoneural correlations as identities, the identity theory gets rid of them as laws, thereby simplifying the total set of laws we need to countenance.

Armstrong's Argument

Some identity theorists, including David Armstrong,[7] have advanced the following line of argument in support of psychoneural identification. As a useful analogy, let us first consider how we came to identify the gene as a DNA molecule. The discovery of this identity was of course not an a priori matter; it required a massive amount of empirical and theoretical research. But before we could look for the gene, we must have had a *concept* of the gene—we must have known what was meant by the expression "the gene." What is the concept of the gene? Roughly, the concept of the gene is the concept of an internal factor in the organism that is causally responsible for the transmission of heritable characteristics. The gene was, therefore, defined in terms of its causal function or role. What the molecular biologists discovered, through empirical research, was precisely this: The DNA molecule fills this causal role—that is, it is the DNA molecule that is the causal agent of the transmission of inherited characteristics of organisms. The identity of the gene with the DNA molecules follows as a simple conclusion.

According to Armstrong, the same pattern of reasoning yields the identification of, say, pain with C-fiber activation. The concept of pain, on his view, is the concept of an internal state that is normally caused by tissue damage and that typically causes such behaviors as winces and groans. This is an a priori fact about our concepts: If you have a correct understanding of the concept of pain, you will see that this conceptual identity holds. Now, research in neurophysiology has discovered (let us suppose) that C-fiber activation is precisely the internal state that is normally caused by tissue damage and that in turn typically causes winces and groans. We are thus able to conclude that pain *is* the activation of C-fibers.

How plausible is Armstrong's argument? Two points are worth thinking about. First, is our concept of pain really the concept of a state that is normally caused by tissue damage and that normally issues in winces and groans? Is "pain" definable in this way? We discussed issues relevant to this question earlier in connection with behaviorism (Chapter 2). Second, is the deliverance of empirical neurophysiological research as simple and clear-cut as it is represented in this argument? Do all pain-capable organisms have C-fibers? Isn't it possible—in fact, isn't it probable—that some such organisms have a very different neural organization from humans and that in them pain is realized in a quite different neural process? Isn't it at least coherently conceivable that there might be "organisms" with a psychology relevantly like humans whose biology, unlike human biology, is not protein-based, perhaps not even organic? This is the famous "multiple realization" argument; we will return to it later—briefly at the end of this chapter and more fully in our discussion of functionalism in Chapter 4.

An Argument from Mental Causation

By mental causation we mean any causal relation involving a mental event. A pin is stuck in your hand, and the sharp pain causes your hand to withdraw in a jerky motion. Here is a mental event causing a physical event. Such causal relations are part of our everyday experience.

But pains don't occur without a physical basis; let us assume that pains are lawfully correlated with C-fiber excitation. So the sharp pain that caused the jerky withdrawal of your hand has an occurrence of C-fiber excitation as its neural correlate. Is there any reason for not regarding the latter event, a brain event, as a cause of your hand's jerky motion?

Consider this event's credentials as a cause of the motion of your hand: If the pain–hand-withdrawal causal relation is covered by a law, then given the invariable correlation between pains and C-fiber activations, there must also be a law relating C-fiber activations with hand withdrawals. And it is plausible to assume that if we were to trace back the causal chain involving the hand withdrawal, we would be tracing a series of physiological events back to the C-fiber activation. The pain must somehow make use of this causal chain to be causally efficacious in the production of the movement of the hand; it is difficult to think that it can act directly on the muscles—that is, by telekinesis—and cause them to contract or can work through an independent causal path! All these considerations seem to favor the C-fiber activation as the "real cause" of the hand motion; the pain's role as cause is in danger of being preempted. The simplest way to rescue the pain's causal role seems to be to identify the pain with the C-fiber activation: If they are one and the same event, there is here one single cause of the hand withdrawal. It makes no difference to its causal status whether it is referred to as "pain" or "C-fiber activation."

If in spite of these considerations you still want to insist on the pain as a separate cause of the hand movement, think of a new predicament in which you will find yourself. For the hand movement would now appear to have two distinct causes—the pain and the C-fiber activation—each presumably sufficient to bring it about. Doesn't that make this (and every other case of mental-to-physical causation) a case of causal overdetermination? Given that the hand withdrawal has a sufficient physical cause, what *further* causal contribution can the pain make? There seems no leftover causal work that the pain needs to be called on to perform. Again, the identification of the pain with its underlying neural event appears to dissolve all these puzzles. There is, of course, the epiphenomenalist solution: Both the hand withdrawal and the pain are caused by the C-fiber excitation, and the pain itself has no further causal role in this situation. But unlike the identity solution, the epiphenomenalist move renders the pain causally inert and ends up simply denying our initial assumption that a sharp pain caused the hand's jerky withdrawal.

We discuss mental causation in detail later (Chapter 6), but even this brief discussion here seems sufficient to show that psychoneural identification is particularly helpful in understanding the possibility of mental causation. It makes mental causation entirely unmysterious: Mental causation turns out to be a species of physical causation.

What Does "Identity" Mean?

The identity theory states that mental events are identical with brain processes. Sometimes, such expressions as "state," "phenomenon," and "occurrence" are used interchangeably with "event" and "process." As a specific example of psychoneural identity, let us again consider the statement "Pains are C-fiber excitations." This is sometimes glossed as follows: "For a person (organism) to be in pain is for him to be in the C-fiber excitation state." For a proper understanding and evaluation of the identity theory, we need to be clearer about the logic and ontology of such statements. Let us first consider the notion of "identity."

By expressions such as "the same" or "identical," we sometimes mean *equality* in some magnitude, or being *instances or tokens falling under the same kind* or *type*, rather than *strict identity* or *identity proper*. When we say that the two base angles of an isosceles triangle are the same or identical, we only mean that their magnitude is the same, not that they are one and the same angle. (If the latter were the case, there would be only one angle here, not two!) And when we say, "I just bought the same book you bought yesterday," what we have in mind are two copies, or tokens, of the *same title*, not a single copy (whereas, when you say, "I have five books in my backpack," you likely have in mind five individual books, some of which may be copies of the same title). When X is identical with Y in the strict sense, we have one thing, not two. Socrates is identical with Xanthippe's husband. What we have two of here are names, "Socrates" and "Xanthippe's husband." These names happen to pick out, or refer to, one and the same person.

Some identities are known a priori; for example, "$5 + 7 = 12$" and "$2 =$ the smallest prime number." But the fact that water is H_2O or that the morning star is the evening star, is something we have discovered from observation and experience, not something that could have been ascertained a priori or by merely investigating the meanings or concepts associated with the expressions "water," "H_2O," "morning star," and "evening star." So these identities are empirical, not a priori, truths.

The identity theorist will say that mind-body identities are empirical in the same way. The concept of pain and the concept of C-fiber excitations are distinct and independent concepts, and this explains how it is possible for someone to know a lot about pains but nothing about C-fibers or their excitations. So this psychoneural identity is not certifiable conceptually, solely from the meanings of "pain" and "C-fiber activation." It is an empirical truth (assuming that it is a truth) that depends on sophisticated and laborious neurophysiological research. For this reason, mind-brain identities, it is claimed, are like "theoretical identities" in the sciences, like the following:

- Water is H_2O.
- Heat is molecular motion.
- The cause of AIDS is infection by HIV.
- Light is electromagnetic radiation.

In each such case, a phenomenon or object is identified with something described in the theoretical vocabulary of science. Identities like these are an important part of our scientific knowledge of the world; in a sense, each tells what something "really is"—its true *nature* as revealed by scientific investigation. Similarly, research in neurophysiology has revealed to us what pain really is—it is the excitation of C-fibers.

"Strict identity" is governed by the following law:

[The indiscernibility of identicals] If X is identical with Y, X and Y share all their properties in common—that is, for any property P, either both X and Y have P or both lack it.

This is sometimes called Leibniz's law, although this term is also used to refer to the following, somewhat controversial, principle, which is the converse of the above:

[The identity of indiscernibles] If X and Y share all their properties in common, X is identical with Y.

The first law, the indiscernibility of identicals, is uncontroversial and manifestly true: If X *is* indeed identical with Y, there is here only one thing and not two. So how could any property be instantiated by X and not Y? Saying that it could is to say that the property is both instantiated and not instantiated by a single object, which is a manifest contradiction. In any case, this law tells us that all we need in order to falsify a claim of identity "$X = Y$" is a single property P, however trivial and humble it may be, such that X has it and Y does not or Y has it but X does not. We can call such a property a "differentiating property" for X and Y. As we shall soon see, that is the strategy employed by the foes of the identity theory: They have proposed various properties as differentiating properties for the mental and the physical.

Token Physicalism and Type Physicalism

The identity theory standardly talks of "events," saying, as we have seen, that mental events are physical events in the brain. But what is an event? There are two alternative views about events, however, and the choice between them does make an important difference to the ways in which the identity theory can be understood. One view takes events as basic concrete particulars of this world, along with material objects;[8] and like material things, they have properties and fall under kinds. Thus, an event may be an explosion or the collapse of a bridge; it can be swift, violent, and unexpected. On this view, a particular occurrence of pain is an event that falls under the event kind pain; alternatively, we may say that that occurrence has the property of being a pain event. It can fall under other event kinds and have other properties: It is a dull, pounding pain; is caused by a decayed tooth; wakes you up in the middle of the night; and lasts for over three hours. And if the identity theory is correct, it is also a brain event, an event falling under the brain event kind C-fiber excitation.

On this view of events as basic particulars, therefore, the assertion that a given pain event *e* is a C-fiber excitation is to say that *e* falls under two event kinds, pain and C-fiber excitations—that is, *e* is both a pain and a C-fiber excitation. To put it another way, this event, *e*, has both the property of being a pain and the property of being a C-fiber excitation.

Consider now the standard formulation of the identity theory:

(I) Every mental event is a physical event.

On the present construal of events, this comes to:

(Ia) [Token physicalism] Every event that falls under a mental-event kind also falls under a physical-event kind (or every event that has a mental property has also some physical property).

We may consider talk of "event kinds" as equivalent to talk of "properties" of events, since every property of events can be thought of as defining a kind of event, namely, the kind comprising events with that property. This claim (Ia) is also called "token-identity theory," since it identifies each mental "event token" with a physical "event token." An event token, or token event, is a dated individual occurrence, like the occurrence of pain to a particular person at a particular time. Event tokens are contrasted with event types, or event kinds, say pains and itches. Token physicalists will stress that their thesis, (Ia), does not entail a claim about the identity of mental types with physical types, a thesis called "type physicalism" or "type-identity theory":

(Ib) [Type physicalism] Mental-event types are physical-event types; alternatively, mental properties are physical properties.

What is the relationship between token and type physicalism? That the former does not entail the latter can be shown by the use of an analogy; consider:

(1) Every object that has a color has a shape.

(2) Colors are identical with shapes.

Statement (1) is obviously true; equally obviously, (2) is false. Colors and shapes don't even systematically correlate with each other; a red object can be a sphere or a cube or any other shape. In the same way, even if every event that has a mental property has a physical property, that doesn't even entail that mental properties are systematically correlated with physical properties, much less that they are identical with physical properties.

As you will recall, we have been using the statement "Pains are C-fiber excitations" as an example of psychoneural identity. This statement identifies pain as a kind with C-fiber excitation as a kind; it is a type-identity statement and as such falls under type physicalism. As this example indicates, the psychoneural identity theory is standardly interpreted as type physicalism, not token physicalism.

There is another approach to events that makes type physicalism a natural way (in fact, the only way) of formulating the identity theory. On this view, an event is the exemplification (or instantiation) of a property by an object at a time. So my now being in pain (my instantiating the property of being in pain) is an event; your now being in pain and my being in pain yesterday are also events, but these events are all distinct. For events e and e' to be "the same event," on this account, they must be the instantiations of the same property by one and the same object at the same time; that is:

The event of x's instantiating property P at time t = the event of y's instantiating property Q at time t' if and only if $x = y$, property P = property Q, and $t = t'$.

Unlike the earlier view that takes events as basic and unanalyzed, the present view construes events as structured particulars consisting of properties, objects, and times. A mental event, then, is the instantiation of a mental property (by an object at a time), and, similarly, a physical event is the instantiation of a physical property. Unless mental substances or souls are countenanced, the objects that do the instantiating in mental events as well as physical events must be material things, like biological organisms and, possibly, certain complex electromechanical systems. This general account of events is called the "property exemplification theory."[9]

Take a particular mental event, say, George's being in pain at a time. If this event is identical with a physical event, George's being in a C-fiber excitation state, then the mental property of being in pain must be identical with the physical property of being in a C-fiber excitation state. So on the property exemplification account of events, the identity between a token mental event and a token physical event entails an identity between a mental property and a physical property. In general, then, there is no interesting distinction between token physicalism and type physicalism on the property exemplification approach to the nature of events.

As already noted, the classic formulation of the identity theory due to Smart and Feigl is type physicalism—at least, this is the way it is usually understood. That is the main reason why we have presented the identity theory as a form of type physicalism here. Another reason is that token physicalism is a weak doctrine that doesn't say much; essentially, it only says that mental and physical properties are instantiated by the same entities. Any event or occurrence with a mental property has some physical property or other. But the theory says nothing about the relationship between mental properties and physical properties, the relation between pains, itches, thoughts, consciousness, and the rest, on the one hand, and types of neural events on the other. Token physicalism can be true even if there is nothing remotely resembling a systematic relationship between the mental and the physical (remember the example of colors and shapes). In a world in which token physicalism is true, there can be all sorts of mental properties and characteristics, the hurting sensation of pains, the bluish gray of an afterimage, the bright red phenomenal color of a visual datum, and countless other sensory qualities, but there need be no dependencies, or even correlations, between mental and physical properties. As far as token physicalism goes, there could be another world just like it in every physical detail except that mentality and consciousness are totally absent. *Token physicalism, therefore, can be true even if mind-body supervenience fails*: What mental features a given event has is entirely unconstrained by what biological/physical properties it has, as far as token physicalism goes, and there could be a molecule-for-molecule physical duplicate of you who is wholly lacking in consciousness, that is, a zombie. This means that the theory says nothing about how mental properties of an event might be physically based or explained. Token physicalism, then, is not much of a physicalism. In fact, if we accept mind-body supervenience as defining minimal physicalism, token physicalism falls outside the scope of physicalism altogether.

A systematic property-to-property relationship between mentality and our bodily nature is of fundamental importance to a robust physicalist position. This issue about properties arises also in debates concerning the possibility of "reducing" mentality to more basic physical/biological properties and processes. Token physicalism is a form of nonreductivism: It says nothing about property-to-property relationships between the mental and the physical, and such relationships are usually thought to be necessary for the reduction of the mental to the physical. It is not that token physicalism denies mind-body reduction; rather, it makes no commitment either way. However, most philosophers who accept token physicalism do so because they believe that mind-body reductionism is false and that for them token physicalism is physicalism enough. We shall discuss questions concerning reduction and reductionism in greater detail later (in Chapter 9).

Type physicalism, in contrast, is thought to be a form of "reductive physicalism," since the thesis that mental properties are physical properties is simply the claim that there are no mental properties over and above physical properties. This arguably entails that there are no Cartesian mental substances; for if mental properties are just physical properties, either immaterial mental substances have physical properties, which is prima facie absurd, or they can have no properties of much interest, which only shows that they have no work to do, making them dispensable. It also entails that there are. no mental facts over and above physical facts. This means that though we may continue to find mentalistic expressions useful and practically indispensable, their expulsion will not affect the total descriptive power of our language; physical language will in principle be adequate for the description of all facts. Type physicalism is a strong and robust materialist doctrine. Perhaps it is too strong to be true. We shall see.

Objections to the Identity Theory

We will consider here several of the principal objections against the identity theory. (Some important objections to the general thesis of physicalism, discussed at various points throughout this book, are also relevant to the identity theory.)

Objection 1: An Epistemological Objection

There is a group of objections based on the claim that the mental and the physical differ in their epistemological properties. One such objection may run as follows: Medieval peasants knew lots about pains but nothing about C-fibers and in fact little about the brain. So how can pains be identical with C-fiber excitations?[10]

This objection assumes that the two statements "S knows something about X" and "$X = Y$" logically entail "S knows something about Y." But is this true? Perhaps there is a sense of "knows something about" in which the entailment holds. Little Billy knows something about lightning; and since lightning is an electric discharge, it follows, according to this pattern of reasoning, that Billy knows something about electric discharges. But then in this sense "S knows something about Y" does not imply that S has the concept of Y or can use the expression "Y" to make judgments, ask questions, and so on. The person S may not know, and have no idea, that $X = Y$; S may even lack the cognitive capacity to entertain the thought that $X = Y$, for this requires the possession of the concept of Y. Therefore, in this sense of "knowing something about," there is nothing incoherent about saying that the medieval peasants did know something about C-fiber excitations.

It is perhaps more plausible to argue that the entailment doesn't hold. To be sure, the two statements "S knows something about X" and "S knows that $X = Y$" plausibly entail "S knows something about Y." But it is false that the medieval peasants knew that pains are C-fiber excitations, and it is perfectly coherent to assert that even though pain = C-fiber excitation, they knew nothing about C-fiber excitations but knew lots about pains. Another way of putting this is to say that "being known by person *S* to be such and such" and other similar expressions like "being believed by *S* to be such and such" do not express properties—or at least properties that can serve as differentiating properties. If the present objection were sound, the same argument would show that water isn't H_2O, that light isn't electromagnetic radiation, and so on.

Objection 2: The Location Problem

Some philosophers have argued that mental states can't be brain states because the latter, but not the former, have *locations in space*. We know where the *brain correlates* of thoughts and sensations occur: Although we may not now know their precise locations, we do know that they occur in the central nervous system, and as our knowledge of brain physiology grows, we will have better knowledge of their precise locations.

But just where does your sudden thought that you might miss your flight occur? It's difficult to say, unless you beg the question and say that it must occur where its brain correlate occurs. Unless we have already assumed that thoughts are neural states, why should we locate them where their neural correlates occur? The phases of the moon correlate with tidal motions, but we surely don't locate tidal motions on the moon! We just don't have a procedure for locating thoughts, desires, emotions, and the like.

But isn't it easy enough to locate a pain, say, in my right thumb? There seem to be various senses in which we can speak of a pain's location. First, a pain can be located at the site of the tissue damage or other physiological cause in the body, and that is the sense in which I locate a pain in my bleeding thumb. Second, many pains have "felt" locations; it can be part of the felt quality of a pain that it is in my right thumb; it is a "right-thumby" sort of pain, which even a person without a right thumb could experience. Such locations can be called "phenomenal locations." Amputees report pains ("phantom pains") in nonexistent parts of their bodies, pains that can be subjectively as real and intense as pains with normal causes. Phenomenal locations of pains usually coincide with the locations of the tissue damage causing them; this fact obviously is important for the biological utility of pains (just imagine what it would be like if we had unpredictable, random correlations between these two kinds of location). But it is clear that neither the location of the tissue damage nor the phenomenal location provides the experience of pain itself with a location in public physical space.

Perhaps the best strategy is to locate a pain where the correlated brain state, C-fiber excitation, is located. But why would we want to do this unless we want to identify the pain with the brain state? Suppose we grant that our ordinary concept of pain does not include a rule about how an experience of pain is to be given a location in physical space. If we are now to adopt a rule, a supplementary convention, to locate pains and other mental states where their correlated brain states occur, would we do some important damage to our original concept of pain? In reflecting on this and related questions, we should keep in mind the following point: Different concepts may pick out, or answer to, the same properties or phenomena in the world. In philosophical jargon, different intensions can determine the same extension. From this it follows that a concept can change in certain ways without a change in its extension, a change in the things and phenomena that fall under it. So suppose we add the rule about locating pains to our present concept of pain, yielding the concept of pain*. Question: Are all pains pains*? If the answer is yes, then from the fact that pains* are C-fiber excitations, it will follow that pains, too, are C-fiber excitations, and everything will be fine for the identity theory. We shall leave it to the reader to reflect on the question whether pains are pains*.

Another way of dealing with the location problem is explicitly to adopt the property exemplification account of events. The location of an event, on this account, is the same as the location of the object involved in it. Thus, my breathing is located where I am located (that is, where my body is located), and the house fire on Elm Street is located where the burning house is located. Consider a pain: On the property exemplification account, a given pain event is, say, Sally's instantiating the property of being in pain (or experiencing pain) at noon today. And this pain is located where Sally is located. But that is exactly the location of Sally's C-fiber excitation state. The fact that Sally's pain and her C-fiber excitation occur at the same location follows trivially from the assumption that the two events occur to the same person (or are instantiations of properties by the same person).

Objection 3: Phenomenal Properties of Mental Events

Consider a pain (again!): Suppose that it is a pounding, sharp pain and shoots up from my foot to the groin. Pounding, sharp, and shooting up from the foot are properties of this pain. If this pain is indeed a brain state, some brain state must have these properties as well, but it obviously makes no sense to speak of a brain state that is "pounding," "sharp," "shooting up from the foot to the groin," and so on. What could count as "a sharp brain state"? Or take an orangish yellow visual image. If the visual image is a brain state, then, by the indiscernibility of identicals, some brain state must be orangish yellow, which seems absurd or at best simply false. So what does the identity theorist do with these "psychic features," or phenomenal properties, of mental events?

The way you would handle this objection can depend crucially on whether you are a token physicalist or a type physicalist. If your physicalism goes just as far as token physicalism and not beyond, you need not worry about this objection; it simply doesn't apply to you. For you make no claim about mental properties, including phenomenal properties, only about individual events that have these mental properties. As far as token physicalism goes, mental properties can be irreducibly distinct from physical properties; it is only that certain events have both mental properties and physical properties. So here is an event that is both a sharp, pounding pain and a C-fiber excitation; that is, it has the phenomenal property of being a sharp, pounding pain and the physiological property of being a C-fiber excitation. To say something like, "This event, which is a C-fiber excitation, is also sharp, pounding, and unbearable," is perhaps a bit unusual, the token physicalist may argue, but not meaningless or incoherent; in fact, token physicalism provides a scheme in which such an utterance can be seen to make a perfectly intelligible and true statement.

But the type physicalist cannot simply accept "sharp," "pounding," and "orangish yellow" as denoting phenomenal properties and leave it at that, since her theory is supposed to cover all mental properties. So how can she deal with these psychic features of mental events? Her reply might take the following tack: We should not think of "sharp," "pounding," and "orangish yellow" as denoting distinct phenomenal properties that characterize mental events. Rather, we should think of "sharp pain," "sharp, pounding pain," "orangish yellow image," and the like as denoting mental properties or event-kinds and identify these properties—being a sharp pain; being a sharp, pounding pain; being an orangish yellow image with frayed borders; and the like—with their correlated brain-state kinds. To put it another way: What is being identified with a brain state is the experiencing of an orangish yellow visual image, not an orangish yellow experiencing of a visual image. And this seems intuitively right.

This point can be stated more perspicuously within the property-exemplification account of events: When we speak of your sharp, pounding pain, we are not describing the event, your being in pain at *t*, as sharp, pounding, and so on. Rather, we are speaking of *your being in sharp, pounding pain.* That is, expressions like "sharp" and "pounding" in the present context are not to be taken to refer to properties that qualify individual occurrences of pain; rather, they qualify, or modify, the property of being in pain in various ways, yielding more finely specified properties, such as being in sharp pain, being in pounding pain, being in sharp and pounding pain, and so on. And these properties, according to type physicalism, are brain-state kinds, presumably subkinds falling under the broader brain-state kind with which being in pain is identical. The case of the orangish yellow afterimage is handled in the same way: It isn't that your having an afterimage has the further property of being orangish yellow; as we said, it's rather that the event is one of your having an orangish yellow afterimage. The mental property being instantiated is that of having (or experiencing) an orangish yellow afterimage, and this is just a physical/neural property.

Objection 4: Phenomenal Properties Again

According to the identity theory, specific psychoneural identities (e.g., "Pains are C-fiber excitations") are empirical truths discovered through scientific observation and theoretical research. If "$D_1 = D_2$" is an empirical truth, the two names or descriptions, D_1 and D_2, must have *independent criteria of application*. Otherwise, the identity would be a priori knowable as true: consider "Bachelor = unmarried adult male," "The husband of Xanthippe = Xanthippe's male spouse," and the like. When some occurrence is picked out by a subject as a pain rather than an itch or tingle, the subject must do so by recognizing, or noticing, a certain distinctive felt character, a phenomenal quality, of the occurrence—its experienced painfulness or hurtfulness. If pains were picked out by neurophysiological criteria (say, if we used C-fiber excitation as the criterion of pain), the identity of pain with a neural state could not be empirical; it would simply follow from the very criterion governing the concept of pain. This means, the objection goes, that to make sense of the *empirical* character of psychoneural identities, we must acknowledge the existence of phenomenal properties.[11]

Sometimes the objection goes further, arguing that these phenomenal properties by which the subject is supposed to recognize her pains as pains must be *irreducibly psychic*. And this claim seems plausible: Intuitively, the hurtfulness by which we identify our own pains is nothing like a physical property. As with Objection 3, the token physicalist has nothing to fear here: She can cheerfully accept these phenomenal properties as irreducible mental properties. The type physicalist, of course, must provide a substantive answer: She must show that subjects do not identify mental states by noticing their irreducibly psychic features. Here, the kind of ontological move that we used in behalf of the type physicalist, in her reply to Objection 3, doesn't work. Even if we switch from the orangish yellow experience of an image to the experience of an orangish yellow image, the question still remains how the subject recognizes that she is having an experience of this particular phenomenal character. Does she do it by noticing some irreducibly psychic feature of her experience?

Could the type physicalist reply that a person does identify her experience by noticing its qualitative phenomenal features but that they are not irreducible, since phenomenal properties as mental properties are identical, on her view, with physical/biological properties? But this reply isn't likely to satisfy many people; it will invite the following response: "But surely when we notice our pains as pains, we don't do that by noticing biological or neural features of our brain states!" We immediately distinguish pains from itches and tickles; if we identified our experiences by their neurophysiological features, we should be able to tell which neurophysiological features represent pain, which represent itches, and so on. But is this credible?

Some philosophers have tried to respond to this question by analyzing away phenomenal properties—more precisely, by analyzing statements that apparently refer to such properties in terms of statements that do not. The two best-known attempts are Armstrong's causal conception of mental states, which we have already looked at, and what Smart calls "topic-neutral translation."[12]

Smart argues as follows: When we say, "Ernest is experiencing an orangish yellow afterimage," the content of our report may be conveyed by the following "topic-neutral" translation—topic-neutral because it says nothing about whether what is being reported is mental or physical:

Something is going on in Ernest that is like what goes on when he is looking at an orangish yellow color patch illuminated in good light

(where we suppose "looking" is explained physically in terms of his being awake, his eyes' being open and focused on the color patch, etc.). How does Smart's approach differ from Armstrong's? Compare what they will say about "Ernest is experiencing a sharp pain in his left thumb":

[Smart] Something is going on in Ernest that is like what goes on when a pin is stuck in his left thumb and he is holding up his thumb and groaning.

[Armstrong] Ernest is in an internal state apt to be caused by a pin stuck in his left thumb and apt to cause him to hold up his left thumb and groan.

Notice that Armstrong's translation is also topic-neutral; it simply speaks of an "internal state" without saying anything about what kind of state it is (although of course Armstrong thinks it turns out to be a brain state).

There are interesting differences and similarities between the two proposed translations. But will either satisfy someone concerned with the problem of explaining how someone manages to identify what kind of experience she is having? There is perhaps something to be said for these translations if we approach the matter strictly from the third-person point of view. But when you are reporting your own experience by saying, "I have a sharp pain in my left thumb," are you saying something like what Smart and Armstrong say that you are? Do you have to know the normal causes and effects of pains or anything about a pin stuck in the thumb when you correctly report that you are experiencing a pain in your thumb?

Objection 5: "Pain" as a "Rigid Designator"

Type physicalists used to say that mind-brain identities, for example, "pain = C-fiber activation," are *contingent*, not necessary. That is, although pain is in fact C-fiber excitation, it could have been otherwise; there are possible worlds in which pain is not C-fiber excitation but some other brain state—perhaps not a brain state at all. The idea of contingent identity can be explained by an example such as this: "Bill Clinton is the forty-second president of the United States." The identity is true, but it might have been false: We can easily imagine possible worlds in which the identity does not hold—for example, one in which Clinton lost the election to George Bush in 1992, one in which he gave up the campaign for the democratic nomination after his loss in the New Hampshire presidential primary election, one in which he didn't get a Rhodes Scholarship and joined the marines, and countless other ways in which things might have gone differently in such a way that someone other than Clinton became president in 1992.

But this is only possible because the expression "the forty-second president of the United States" can refer to different persons in different possible worlds; things might have gone in such a way that the expression designated someone other than Clinton. Expressions like "the forty-second president of the United States," "the winner of the 1994 Kentucky Derby," and "the tallest man in China," which can name different things in different possible worlds, are what Saul Kripke calls "nonrigid designators."[13] In contrast, proper names like "Bill Clinton" and "George Bush" are, according to Kripke, "rigid"—they designate the same object or person in all possible worlds in which it exists. It is true that the forty-second president of the United States might not have been the forty-second president of the United States (for example, if Clinton had lost to Bush), but it is not true that Bill Clinton might not have been Bill Clinton. (Of course, Bill Clinton might not have been called "Bill Clinton," but that's another matter.) This seems to show that a contingent identity, "$X = Y$," is possible only if either of the two expressions "X" or "Y" is a nonrigid designator, an expression that can refer to different things in different worlds.

It follows, then, that "pain = C-fiber excitation" can be a contingent identity only if either "pain" or "C-fiber excitation" is nonrigid. But is that possible? Could "C-fiber excitation" be nonrigid? It would seem not:

How could an event that in fact is the excitation of C-fibers not have been one? A world in which no C-fiber excitation ever occurs is a world in which this event, which is a C-fiber excitation, does not occur. Could "pain" then be nonrigid? The approaches by Smart and Armstrong we reviewed in our discussion of Objection 4 are attempts to give nonrigid readings of "pain": On Armstrong's account, for example, "pain" designates, in a given world, whatever state it is in that world that fulfills a certain causal role, namely that of being typically caused by tissue damage and typically causing winces and groans. On this understanding of "pain," then, it is true that a state that is in fact a pain might not have been a pain (just as the forty-second president might not have been the forty-second president). That would be the case if in this world C-fiber activation fills pain's causal role but in another possible world a different neural state fills the role. Since causal role depends on laws and laws can vary from world to world, "pain" cannot be rigid if it designates a causal role.

But how plausible is this account of pain? If you are inclined to take the painfulness of pain as its essential defining property, you will find the Armstrong-style account implausible: You will say that "pain" rigidly designates an event or state with this quality of painfulness and that the expression designates an event of that sort across all possible worlds no matter what causal role it happens to fulfill in a given world, or whether or not it has any causal role at all in relation to physical events or behavior. So the strength of the present objection depends on the viability of the Armstrong-Smart-style approach to mental expressions discussed in connection with the preceding objection.

Can the type physicalist say that mind-brain identities are necessary, not contingent, although, like other theoretical identities, they are empirically based? She would then have to say that the correlation between pains and C-fiber excitations is necessary and that it holds in every possible world. But isn't it conceivable—at least consistent to suppose—that pains can occur without C-fiber excitations or that C-fiber excitations can occur without being accompanied by pains? This is exactly what Descartes thought he could coherently imagine: He claimed it is conceivable that he was a pure mental being not attached to any material body. The correlation may be lawlike—that is, nomologically necessary—but doesn't seem to be necessary without qualification.

Objection 6: The Multiple Realization Argument

Type physicalism says that pain is C-fiber excitation. But that implies that unless an organism has C-fibers or a brain of an appropriate biological structure, it cannot have pain. But aren't there pain-capable organisms, like reptiles and mollusks, with brains very different from the human

brain? Perhaps in these species the neurons that work as nociceptive neurons—pain-sensitive neurons—aren't like human C-fibers at all. Can the
type physicalist reply that it should be possible to come up with a more
abstract and general physiological description of a brain state common to
all organisms, across all species, that are in pain state? This is highly unlikely, but how about inorganic systems? Could there not be intelligent
extraterrestrial creatures with a complex and rich mental life, one that is
very much like ours, but whose biology is not carbon-based? And isn't it
conceivable—in fact, at least nomologically if not practically possible—to
build intelligent electromechanical systems (that is, robots) to which we
would be willing to attribute various mental states?[14] Moreover, the
neural substrates of certain mental functions can differ from person to
person and may change over time even in a single individual through
maturation, learning, and injuries to the brain. We should keep in mind
that if pain is identical with physical state *C*, then pain is identical with
state *C* not only in actual organisms and systems but in all possible organisms and systems.

These considerations are usually taken to show that any given mental
state is "multiply realizable"[15] in a large variety of physical/biological
structures, with the consequence that it is not possible to identify a mental state with a physical state. If pain is identical with a physical state, it
must be identical with some *particular* physical state; but there are indefinitely many physical states that can "realize" (or "instantiate," "implement," etc.) pain in all sorts of pain-capable organisms and systems. So
pain, as a type of mental state, cannot be a neural-state type or any other
physical-state type.

This, in brief, is the influential "multiple realization" argument against
type physicalism Hilary Putnam advanced in the late 1960s (we will recur
to multiple realization in the next chapter). It had a critical impact on the
way philosophy of mind has developed since then: It effectively retired
type physicalism as the reigning doctrine on the mind-body problem,
throwing the very term "reductionism" into disrepute and ushering in
the era of "nonreductive physicalism." Further, it inspired a new conception of mentality, "functionalism," which has been highly influential since
the 1970s and which is arguably still the most widely accepted view on
the nature of mind. In the following two chapters we turn to this important approach to mentality.

Further Readings

The classic sources of the identity theory are J.J.C. Smart,
"Sensations and Brain Processes," in *The Nature of Mind*, ed. David M.
Rosenthal (New York: Oxford University Press, 1991); and Herbert Feigl,
"The 'Mental' and the 'Physical,'" in *Minnesota Studies in the Philosophy of*

Science, vol. 2, ed. Herbert Feigl, Michael Scriven, and Grover Maxwell (Minneapolis: University of Minnesota Press, 1958). David Armstrong's *A Materialist Theory of Mind* (New York: Humanities Press, 1968) presents a sustained development of the theory. For criticisms of the theory, see Jerome Shaffer, "Mental Events and the Brain," in Rosenthal, *The Nature of Mind*; and Saul Kripke, *Naming and Necessity* (Cambridge: Harvard University Press, 1980), lecture 3.

For a defense of token physicalism and considerations against type physicalism, see Donald Davidson, "Mental Events," reprinted in his *Essays on Actions and Events* (Oxford: Oxford University Press, 1980). Christopher S. Hill defends type physicalism in *Sensations: A Defense of Type Materialism* (Cambridge: Cambridge University Press, 1991).

For the multiple realization argument against the identity theory, see Hilary Putnam, "Psychological Predicates," later retitled as "The Nature of Mental States" and reprinted in his *Mind, Language, and Reality: Philosophical Papers*, vol. 2 (Cambridge: Cambridge University Press, 1975); Jerry A. Fodor, "Special Sciences, or the Disunity of Science as a Working Hypothesis," *Synthese* 28 (1974):97–115; Ned Block and Jerry A. Fodor, "What Psychological States Are Not," *Philosophical Review* 81 (1972):159–181, both reprinted in *Readings in Philosophy of Psychology*, vol. 1, ed. Ned Block (Cambridge: Harvard University Press, 1980).

For a comprehensive discussion of the identity theory, see Cynthia Macdonald, *Mind-Body Identity Theories* (London: Routledge, 1989).

Notes

1. See René Descartes, *The Passions of the Soul* I, in *The Philosophical Writings of Descartes*, vol. 2, ed. John Cottingham, Robert Stoothoff, and Dugald Murdoch (Cambridge: Cambridge University Press, 1985).

2. See Thomas H. Huxley, *Methods and Results: Essays* (New York: D. Appleton, 1901), ch. 5.

3. Samuel Alexander, *Space, Time, and Deity*, 2 vols. (London: Macmillan, 1920).

4. J.J.C. Smart, "Sensations and Brain Processes," *Philosophical Review* 68 (1959):141–156; reprinted in *The Nature of Mind*, ed. David M. Rosenthal (New York: Oxford University Press, 1991). However, U. T. Place's "Is Consciousness a Brain Process?" published in 1956 (*British Journal of Psychology* 47, pt. 1:44–50), predates Smart's article as perhaps the first modern statement of the identity theory.

5. Smart, "Sensations and Brain Processes," pp. 169–170 in Rosenthal, *The Nature of Mind*.

6. Herbert Feigl, "The 'Mental' and the 'Physical,'" in *Minnesota Studies in the Philosophy of Science*, vol. 2, ed. Herbert Feigl, Michael Scriven, and Grover Maxwell (Minneapolis: University of Minnesota Press, 1958).

7. See David Armstrong, *A Materialist Theory of Mind* (New York: Humanities Press, 1968).

8. This view is usually associated with Donald Davidson; see Davidson, "The Individuation of Events," reprinted in his *Essays on Actions and Events* (New York: Oxford University Press, 1980).

9. See Jaegwon Kim, "Events as Property Exemplifications," reprinted in Kim, *Supervenience and Mind* (Cambridge: Cambridge University Press, 1993).

10. For other epistemological objections, see discussions of the qualia problem in Chapters 5, 7, and 9.

11. This objection is worked out in detail in Jerome Shaffer, "Mental Events and the Brain," *Journal of Philosophy* 60 (1963):160–166; reprinted in Rosenthal, *The Nature of Mind.*

12. See Smart, "Sensations and Brain Processes."

13. See Saul Kripke, *Naming and Necessity* (Cambridge: Harvard University Press, 1980), especially lecture 3, in which his arguments against the identity theory are presented.

14. These considerations were first advanced by Hilary Putnam in his paper "Psychological Predicates," originally published in 1967 and since reprinted in his *Mind, Language, and Reality: Philosophical Papers*, vol. 2 (Cambridge: Cambridge University Press, 1975), and elsewhere, with the new title "The Nature of Mental States."

15. The term "variably realizable" is sometimes used, especially by British writers.

4

Mind as a Computer:
Machine Functionalism

In 1967 Hilary Putnam published a paper with the title "Psychological Predicates."[1] This paper of modest length changed the debate in philosophy of mind in a fundamental way by doing three amazing things: First, it quickly brought about the demise of type physicalism, in particular the mind-brain identity theory, as the reigning theory of mind; second, it gave birth to functionalism, which has since been a highly influential—arguably the preeminent—position on the nature of mind; and third, it helped to install antireductionism as the received view on the nature of mental properties and other "higher-level" properties of the special sciences. Mind-brain type physicalism, which had been promoted as the only view of mentality properly informed by the best contemporary science, turned out to be unexpectedly short-lived, and during the 1970s most philosophers abandoned reductive physicalism not only as a view about psychology but as a doctrine about all special sciences.[2]

All this arose out of a single idea: *the multiple realizability of mental properties.* We have already discussed it as an argument against the mind-brain identity theory and, more generally, as a difficulty for type physicalism (Chapter 3). What sets the multiple realization argument apart from sundry other objections to the mind-brain identity theory is the fact that it has served as a basis for a new conception of the mental that has played a central role in shaping the current thinking on the status of psychology and, more generally, the cognitive sciences.

Multiple Realizability and the Functional
Conception of the Mental

Perhaps not many of us now believe in angels, purely spiritual and immortal beings supposedly with a full mental life. Angels, as traditionally conceived, are wholly immaterial beings with knowledge and beliefs, able to experience emotions and desires and capable of performing actions. It's only that there is no evidence that there are beings fitting that description. But the idea of such a being may be a perfectly coherent one, like the idea of a unicorn or Bigfoot, although there are no unicorns and probably no Bigfoot. So like unicorns but unlike married bachelors or four-sided triangles, there seems nothing conceptually impossible about angels. If the idea of an angel with beliefs, desires, and emotions is a consistent idea, that would show that there is nothing in the idea of mentality itself that precludes purely nonphysical, wholly immaterial realizations of psychological states.3

It seems then that we cannot set aside the possibility of immaterial realizations of mentality as a matter of a priori conceptual fact. Ruling out such a possibility requires commitment to a substantive metaphysical thesis, perhaps something like this:

[The physical realization principle] If something x has some mental property M (or is in mental state M) at time t, then x is a material thing and x has M at t in virtue of the fact that x has at t some physical property P that realizes M in x at t.4

It is useful to think of this principle as a way of characterizing physicalism:5 It says that anything that exhibits mentality must be a physical system—for example, a biological organism. Although the idea of mentality permits nonphysical entities to have mentality, the world is so constituted, according to this principle, that only physical systems turn out to realize mental properties—perhaps because they are the only things that exist in spacetime. Moreover, the principle requires that every mental property be physically based. Another way of putting the point would be this: Minds, if they exist, must be embodied.

Notice that this principle provides for the possibility of multiple realization of mental properties. Mental property M—say, being in pain—may be such that in humans C-fiber activation realizes it but in other species (think of octopuses and reptiles) the physiological mechanism that realizes pain may well be vastly different. And perhaps there are biological systems—at least no laws of nature rule out such a possibility—that are not carbon- or protein-based, and there can be electromechanical systems, like robots in science fiction, that are capable of having beliefs, desires, and even sensations. All this seems to point to an interesting feature of mental concepts: They include no constraint on the actual physical/biological mechanisms or structures that, in a given system, realize or implement them. In this sense, psychological concepts are like concepts of artifacts: For example, the concept of an "engine" is silent on the actual physical mechanism that realizes it—whether it uses gasoline or electricity or steam and, if it is a gasoline engine, whether it is a piston or rotary engine, how many cylinders it has, whether it uses a carburetor or fuel injection, and so on. As long as a physical device is capable of performing a certain specified job, namely, that of transforming various forms of energy into mechanical force or motion, it counts as an engine. The concept of an engine is specified by a job description, not a description of mechanisms that can execute the job.

What, then, is the job description of pain? The ability to experience pain in the "right" circumstances—for example, when an organism suffers tissue damage—is probably very important to its chances for adaptation and survival. There are unfortunate people who congenitally lack the capacity to sense pain, and few of them survive into adulthood.[6] In the process of coping with the hazards presented by their environment, animal species must have had to develop pain mechanisms, what we may call "tissue-damage detectors," and it is only plausible that different species, confronted by different environmental conditions and evolving independently of one another, have developed different mechanisms for this purpose. It is natural to expect to find diverse evolutionary solutions to the problem of developing a tissue-damage detector. As a start, then, we can think of pain to be specified by the job description "tissue-damage detector."

Thinking of the workings of mind in analogy with the operations of a computing machine is a commonplace, both in the popular press and in serious philosophy and cognitive science, and we will soon begin looking into the mind-computer analogy in detail. A computational view of mentality, too, shows that we must expect mental states to be variably realized. We know that any computational process can be implemented in a huge variety of physically diverse computing machines. Not only are there innumerable kinds of electronic digital computers (in addition to the semiconductor-based machines we are now familiar with, think of the vacuum-tube computers of olden days), but also computers can be built with wheels and gears (as in Charles Babbage's original "analytical engine") or even with hydraulically operated systems of pipes and valves, although these would be unacceptably slow (not to say economically prohibitive) by our current standards. And all of these physically diverse computers can be performing "the same computation," say, solving a differential equation. If minds are like computers and mental processes are, at bottom, computational processes, we should expect no prior constraint on just how minds and mental processes are physically implemented. Just as vastly different physical devices can execute the same computational program, so vastly different biological or physical structures should be able to subserve the same psychological processes. At least that is the starting idea of the functionalist conception of the mind.

What these considerations point to, according to some philosophers, is the *abstractness* or *formality* of psychological properties in relation to physical or biological properties: Psychological kinds abstract from physical and biological details of organisms so that states that are vastly different from a physicochemical point of view can fall under the same psychological kind, and organisms and systems that are widely diverse biologically and physically can instantiate the same psychological regularities. To put it another way, psychological kinds seem to concern *formal* patterns or structures of events and processes rather than their material constitutions or mechanisms.[7] Conversely, the same physical structure, depending on the way it is causally embedded in a larger system, can subserve different psychological capacities and functions (just as the same computer chip can be used for different computational functions in various subsystems of a computer). After all, most neurons, it has been said, are pretty much alike and largely interchangeable.[8]

What is it, then, that binds together all the physically diverse instances of a given mental kind? What do all pains—pains in humans, pains in canines, pains in octopuses, and pains in Martians—have in common in virtue of which they all fall under a single psychological kind, pain?[9] That is, what is *the principle of individuation* for mental kinds?

Let's first see how the type physicalist and the behaviorist answer this question. The brain-state type physicalist will say this: What all pains have in common that makes them cases of pain is a certain neurobiological property, namely, being an instance of C-fiber excitation (or some such state). That is, for the type physicalist, a mental kind is a physical kind (a neurobiological kind, for the mind-brain identity theorist). You could guess how the behaviorist will answer the question: What all pains have in common is a certain behavioral property—or, to put it another way, two organisms are both in pain at a time just in case at that time they exhibit, or are disposed to exhibit, the behavior patterns definitive of pain (e.g., escape behavior, withdrawal behavior, etc.). For the behaviorist, then, a mental kind is a behavioral kind.

If you take the multiple realizability of mental states seriously, you will reject both these answers and opt for a "functionalist" conception. According to functionalism, a mental kind is a *functional kind*, or a *causal-functional kind*, since the "function" involved is to fill a certain causal role.[10] Let us go back to pain as a tissue-damage detector.[11] The concept of a tissue-damage detector is a *functional concept*, a concept specified by a job description, as we said: Any device is a tissue-damage detector for an organism just in case it can reliably detect occurrences of tissue damage in that organism. We can see that functional concepts are ubiquitous: What makes something a table, a carburetor, or a thermometer is its ability to perform a certain function, not any specific physicochemical structure or mechanism. These concepts are specified by the functions that are to be performed, not structural blueprints. Many concepts, in ordinary discourse and in the sciences, are functional concepts in this sense; even many biological concepts (e.g., the gene, heart) appear to have an essentially functional component.

To return to the example of pain: An organism has the capacity to be in pain just in case it is equipped with a mechanism that detects damage to its tissues, regardless of exactly how this mechanism is physically configured. To work as a tissue-damage detector, the mechanism must causally respond to tissue damages: Ideally, every instance of tissue damage, and nothing else, must activate this mechanism—turn it on—and this must further activate other mechanisms with which it is hooked up, finally resulting in, among other things, behavior that will in normal circumstances spatially separate the damaged part, or the whole organism, from the external cause of the damage (that is, it must trigger escape behavior). Thus, the concept of pain is defined in terms of its function, and the function involved is to serve as a *causal intermediary* between typical pain inputs (tissue damage, trauma, etc.) and typical pain outputs (winces, groans, escape behavior, etc.). The functionalist will say that this is generally true of all mental kinds: Mental kinds are causal-functional kinds, and what all instances of a given mental kind have in common is the fact that they serve a certain causal role distinctive of that kind. As Armstrong has put it, the concept of a mental state is that of an internal state apt to be caused by certain sensory inputs and apt for causing certain behavioral outputs.

Functionalism and Behaviorism

Both functionalism and behaviorism speak of sensory input and behavioral output—or "stimulus" and "response"—as central to the concept of mentality. In this respect, functionalism is part of a broadly behavioral approach to mentality and can be considered a generalized and more sophisticated version of behaviorism. But there are also significant differences between functionalism and behaviorism, of which the following two are the most important.

First, the functionalist, on the one hand, takes mental states to be real *internal* states of an organism with causal powers; for an organism to be in pain is for it to be in an internal state (e.g., a neurobiological state for humans) that is typically caused by tissue damage and that in turn typically causes winces, groans, and escape behavior. The behaviorist, on the other hand, eschews talk of internal states in connection with mental states, identifying them with actual or possible behavior. Thus, to be in pain, for the behaviorist, is to wince and groan or be disposed to wince and groan but not, as the functionalist would have it, to be in some *internal state that causes* winces and groans.

Although both the behaviorist and the functionalist may refer to "behavioral dispositions" in speaking of mental states, what they mean by "disposition" can be quite different: The functionalist takes a "realist" approach to dispositions whereas the behaviorist embraces an "instrumentalist" line. To see how realism and instrumentalism differ on this issue, let us consider how water solubility (that is, the disposition to dissolve in water) would be analyzed on each approach:

[Instrumentalist analysis] x is soluble in water = $_{def.}$ if x is immersed in water, x dissolves

[Realist analysis] x is soluble in water = $_{def.}$ x is in a certain internal state S such that S causes x to dissolve when it is immersed in water

According to instrumentalism, therefore, the water solubility of a sugar cube is just the fact that a certain conditional (if-then) statement holds for it; thus, on this view, water solubility turns out to be a "conditional" or "hypothetical" property of the sugar cube—that is, the property of *dissolving if immersed in water*. Realism, in contrast, takes solubility to be a categorical (though microstructurally unspecified) internal state of the cube of sugar that is causally responsible for its dissolving when placed in water (further investigation might reveal the state to be that of having a certain crystalline molecular structure). Neither analysis requires the sugar cube to be immersed in water or actually to be dissolving in order to be water soluble. However, we may note the following difference: If x dissolves in water and y doesn't, the realist will give a causal explanation of the difference in terms of a difference in their microstructure. For the instrumentalist, the difference may just be a brute fact: It's just that the conditional "if placed in water, then it will dissolve" holds true for x but not for y, a difference that may not be grounded in any further difference between x and y.

In speaking of mental states as behavioral dispositions, then, the functionalist takes them as actual inner states of persons and other organisms that in normal circumstances cause behavior of some specific type under certain specified input conditions. In contrast, the behaviorist takes them merely as input-output, or stimulus-response, correlations. Many behaviorists (especially methodological behaviorists) think that speaking of mental states as "inner causes" of behavior is scientifically unmotivated and philosophically unwarranted.[12]

The second major difference between functionalism and behaviorism, one that gives the former a substantially greater power, is in the way "input" and "output" are construed for mental states. For the behaviorist, input and output consist entirely of observable physical stimulus conditions and observable behavioral responses. However, the functionalist will include reference to *other mental states* in the characterization of a given mental state. It is a crucial part of the functionalist conception of a mental state that its typical causes and effects may include other mental states. Thus, for a light pinprick to cause pain, you must be normally alert and not deeply engrossed in an unrelated activity. Along with the pinprick, these mental states play a part in causing pain. Moreover, pain would normally cause you a sense of distress and a desire to be rid of it, and these are mental states in their own right.

The two points that have just been reviewed are related: If you think of mental states as actual inner states of psychological subjects, you would regard them as having real causal powers, powers to cause and be caused by other states and events, and there is no obvious reason to exclude mental states from figuring as causes or effects of other mental states. In conceiving mentality this way, the functionalist is espousing *mental realism*—a position that considers mental states as having a genuine ontological status, counting them among the phenomena of the world with a place in its causal structure. Mental states are real for the behaviorist, too, but only as behaviors or behavioral dispositions; for him there is nothing mental over and above behavior. For the functionalist, mental states are inner causes of behavior, and as such they are in addition to behavior.

Including other mental events among the causes and effects of a given mental state is part of the functionalist's general conception of mental states as forming a complex causal network anchored to the external world at various points. At these points of contact a psychological subject interacts with the outside world, receiving inputs and emitting outputs. And the identity of a given mental kind, whether it is a sensation like pain or a belief that it's going to rain or a desire for a ham sandwich, depends solely on the place it occupies in the causal network. That is, what makes a mental event the kind of mental event it is is the way it is causally linked to other mental-event kinds and input/output conditions. Since each of these other mental-event kinds in turn has its identity determined by *its* causal relations to other mental events and inputs/outputs, the identity of each mental kind depends ultimately on the whole system—its internal structure and the way it is causally linked to the external world via its inputs and outputs. In this sense, functionalism gives us a *holistic* conception of mentality.

This holistic approach enables functionalism to sidestep one of the principal objections to behaviorism. This is the difficulty we saw earlier that a desire issues in overt behavior only when combined with an appropriate belief and that, similarly, a belief leads to appropriate behavior only when a matching desire is present. For example, a person with a desire to eat an apple will eat an apple that is presented to her only if she believes it to be an apple (she would not eat it if she thought it was a fake wooden apple); a person who believes that it is going to rain will take an umbrella only if she has a desire not to get wet. As we saw, this apparently makes it impossible to define desire without reference to belief or define belief without reference to desire. The functionalist would say that this only points to the holistic character of mental states: It is an essential feature of a desire that it is the kind of internal state that in concert with an appropriate belief causes a certain behavior output, and similarly for belief and other mental states.

But doesn't this make our definitions circular? If the concept of desire cannot be defined without reference to belief, and the concept of belief in turn cannot be explained without reference to desire, how can either be understood at all? We will see below how the holistic approach of functionalism deals with this question.

Turing Machines

Functionalism was originally formulated by Putnam in terms of "Turing machines," computing machines as abstractly characterized by the British mathematician-logician Alan M. Turing.[13] Although it is now customary to explain functionalism in terms of causal-functional roles, as we have done, it will be instructive to begin our detailed discussion of functionalism by examining the Turing-machine version of functionalism. This will also give us the background needed for exploring the idea that the workings of the mind are best understood in terms of the operations of a computer, the so-called computational view of the mind (or computationalism, for short).

A Turing machine has these components:

- a *tape* divided into "squares" and unbounded in both directions
- a *scanner-printer* ("head") positioned at one of the squares of the tape at any given time
- a finite set of *internal states* (or *configurations*), $q_0, \ldots, q_n$
- a finite *alphabet* consisting of symbols, $b_1, \ldots, b_m$

One and only one symbol appears on each square (we may think of the blank as one of the symbols). The general operations of the machine are as follows:

A.   At each time, the machine is in one of its internal states, q_i, and its head is scanning a particular square on the tape.

B.   What the machine does at a given time t is completely determined by its internal state at t and the symbol its head is scanning at t.

C.   Depending on its internal state and the symbol being scanned, it does three things:

1.   its head replaces the symbol with another (possibly the same) symbol of the alphabet (to put it another way, it erases the symbol being scanned and prints a new one, which may be the same as the erased one)

2.   its head moves to the right or to the left by one square (or halt, with the computation completed)

3.   the machine enters into a new internal state.

Let's consider a Turing machine that adds positive integers in the unary notation (in this notation number n is represented as a sequence of n strokes, each stroke occupying one square). Consider the following picture in which the problem of adding 3 and 2 is presented to the machine, which is to be started off with its head in state q_0 and scanning the first digit:

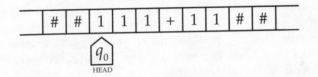

(The "scratch" symbol, #, marks the boundaries of the problem.) We want to "program" this Turing machine in such a way that when the computation is completed, the machine halts with a sequence of five consecutive strokes showing on the tape, like this:

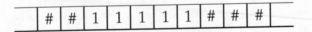

It is easy to see that there are various procedures by which the machine could accomplish this. One simple way is to have the machine (or its head) move to the right looking for the symbol +, replace it with a stroke, keep moving right until it finds the rightmost stroke, and when it does, erase it (i.e., replace it with the scratch symbol #) and then halt. The following simple "machine table" is a complete set of instructions that defines our adder (call it TM_1):

	q_0	q_1
1	$1Rq_0$	#Halt
+	$1Rq_0$	
#	$#Lq_1$	

Here is how we read this table. On the leftmost column you find the symbols of the machine alphabet listed vertically, and the top row lists the machine's internal states. Each entry in the interior matrix is an *instruction*: It tells the machine what to do when it is scanning the symbol shown in the leftmost column of that row and is in the internal state listed at the top of the column. For example, the entry $1Rq_0$, at the intersection of q_0 and 1, tells the machine: "If you are scanning the symbol 1 and are in internal state q_0, replace 1 with 1 (that is, leave it unchanged), move to the right by one square, and go into internal state q_0 (that is, stay in the same state)." The entry immediately below, $1Rq_0$, tells the machine: "If you are in state q_0 and scanning the symbol +, replace + with 1, move to the right by one square, and go into state q_0." The L in the bottom entry, $#Lq_1$, means "move left by one square"; the entry in the rightmost column, #Halt, means, "If you are scanning 1 and in state q_1, replace 1 with # and halt." It is easy to see (the reader is asked to figure this out on her own) the exact sequence of steps our Turing machine will follow to compute the sum 3 + 2.

The machine table of a Turing machine is a complete and exhaustive specification of the machine's operations. We may, therefore, identify a Turing machine with its machine table. Since a machine table is nothing but a set of instructions, this means that a Turing machine can be identified with a set of such instructions.

What sort of things are the "internal states" of a Turing machine? We will talk about this general question later, but with our machine TM_1, it can be helpful to think of the specific machine states in the following intuitive way: q_0 is a + and # searching state—it is a state such that when TM_1 is in it, it keeps going right, looking for + and #, ignoring any 1s it encounters. Moreover, if the machine is in q_0 and finds a +, it replaces it with a 1 and keeps moving to the right, while staying in the same state; when it scans a # (thereby recognizing the rightmost boundary of the given problem), it backs up to the left and goes into a new state q_1, the "print # over 1 and then halt" state. When TM_1 is in this state it will replace any 1 sign it finds with a # and then halt. Thus, each state "disposes" the machine to do a set of specific things depending on the symbol being scanned.

It is easy to see that we can design another Turing machine that will do the same job faster and more simply. For it is clear that to add unary numbers it is not necessary for the machine to determine the rightmost border of the given problem; all it needs to do is to erase the initial 1 and then replace the + sign with a 1. This is our TM_2, another adding machine:

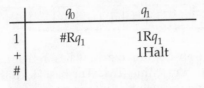

	q_0	q_1
1	#Rq_1	1Rq_1
+		1Halt
#		

We can readily build a third Turing machine, TM$_3$, that will do subtractions in the unary notation. Suppose the following subtraction problem is presented to the machine:

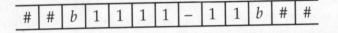

| # | # | b | 1 | 1 | 1 | 1 | – | 1 | 1 | b | # | # |

(The b is used to mark the boundaries of the problem.) Starting the machine in state q_0 scanning the initial 1, we can write a machine table that will compute $n - m$ by operating like this:

1. The machine starts off scanning the first 1 of n. It goes to the right until it locates m, the number being subtracted (how does it recognize it has located m?). It then erases the first 1 of this number (replacing it with a #), goes left and erases the last 1 of n (again replacing it with a #).
2. The machine then goes right and repeats the above process again and again, until it exhausts all the 1s in m (how does the machine "know" that it has done this?). We then have the machine move right until it locates the subtraction sign –, which it will erase (i.e., replace with a #) and then halt. (If you like tidy output tapes, you may have the machine erase the bs before halting.)
3. If the machine runs out of the first set of strokes before it exhausts the second set (this means that $n < m$), we can have the machine print a certain symbol, say ?, to mean that the given problem is not well defined. We must also provide for the case where $n = m$.

The reader is invited to write out a machine table that will implement these operations.

We can also think of a "transcription machine," TM$_4$, that will transcribe a given string of 1s to its right (or left). That is, if TM$_4$ is presented with the following tape to begin its computation:

| # | 1 | 1 | 1 | # | # | # | # | # | # | # | # |

it will end with the following configuration of symbols on its tape:

#	1	1	1	#	1	1	1	#	#	#	#	

The interest of the transcription machine lies in that it can be used to construct a multiplication machine, TM_5. The basic idea is simple: We can get $n \times m$ by transcribing the string of n 1s m times (that is, transcribing n repeatedly using m as a counter).

Since any arithmetical operation (e.g., squaring, taking the factorial, etc.) on natural numbers can be defined in terms of addition and multiplication, it follows that there is a Turing machine that will compute any arithmetical operation. In fact, it can be shown that any computation that can be done by any computer at all can be done by a Turing machine. That is, being computable and being computable by a Turing machine turn out to be equivalent notions.

We can think of a Turing machine with two separate tapes, one for input (on which the problem to be computed is presented) and the other for actual computation and the final output, and two separate heads, one for scanning and one for printing. This helps us to think of a Turing machine as receiving "sensory stimuli" (the symbols it scans on the input tape) through its scanner ("sense organ"), and emitting specific behaviors in response (the symbols printed on the output tape by its printer head). It can be shown that any computation that can be done by a two-tape machine, or a machine with any finite number of tapes, can be done by a one-tape machine. So adding more tapes does not strengthen the computing power of Turing machines or substantively enrich the concept of a Turing machine.

Turing also showed how to build a "universal machine," which is like a general-purpose computer in that it is not dedicated to the computation of a specific function but can be loaded with the machine table of the function you want to compute and the specific initial values ("arguments") for which you want to have the value of the function computed. On the input tape of this machine, you will specify two things: the machine table of the desired function in some standard notation that can be read by the universal machine and the values for which the function is to be computed. The universal machine is programmed to read the machine table of this function and carry out the necessary instructions until the computation is finished.

The notion of a Turing machine can be generalized to yield the notion of a *probabilistic automaton*. As you recall, each instruction of a Turing machine is *deterministic*: Given the internal state and the symbol being scanned, the immediate next operation is wholly and uniquely determined. An instruction of a probabilistic automaton will have the following form: Given internal state q_i and scanned symbol b_j

1. Print b_k with probability r_1, or print b_l with probability r_2, ..., or print b_m with probability r_n (where the probabilities add up to 1);
2   Move R with probability r_1, or move L with probability r_2 (where the probabilities add up to 1);
3. Go into internal state q_j; with probability r_1, or into q_k with probability r_2, ..., or into q_m with probability r_n (again the probabilities adding up to 1).

The operations of a probabilistic automaton, therefore, are indeterministic; the current internal state of the machine and the symbol it is scanning do not together uniquely determine what the machine will do. However, the behavior of such a machine is not random or arbitrary: There are fixed and stable probabilities that describe what the machine's outputs will be. If we are thinking of a machine that will describe the behavior of an actual psychological subject, a probabilistic machine may be more realistic than a deterministic one, although it is generally possible to construct a deterministic machine that will simulate the behavior of a probabilistic machine to any desired degree of accuracy.

"Physical Realizations" of Turing Machines

Suppose that we give the machine table for our simple adding machine, TM_1, to an engineering class as an assignment: Each student is to build an actual physical device that will do the computations as specified by its machine table. What we are asking the students to build, therefore, are "physical realizations" of TM_1, actual adding machines that will operate in accordance with the machine table of TM_1. We can safely predict that a huge, heterogeneous variety of machines will be turned in. Some of them may really look and work like the Turing machine as described: They may have a paper tape neatly divided into squares, with an actual physical "head" that can scan, erase, and print symbols. Some will perhaps use magnetic tapes and heads that read, write, and erase electrically. Some machines will have no "tapes" or "heads" but instead use spaces on a computer disk or memory locations in its cpu to do the computation. A clever student with a sense of humor (and lots of time and other resources) might try to build a hydraulically operated device with pipes and valves instead of wires and switches. The possibilities are endless.

But what exactly is the notion of a physical realization of a Turing machine? What makes a physical device a *realization of* a given Turing machine? First, the symbols of the machine's alphabet must be given concrete physical embodiments; they could be blotches of ink on paper, patterns of magnetized iron particles on plastic tape, electric charges in capacitors, or what have you. Whatever they are, the physical device that does the "scanning" must be able to "read" them—that is, differentially respond to them—with a high degree of reliability. This means that the physical properties of the symbols place a set of constraints on the physical design of the scanner, but these constraints need not, and usually will not, determine a unique design; a great multitude of physical devices are likely to be adequate to serve as a scanner for the given set of physically embodied symbols. The same considerations apply to the machine's printer and outputs as well: The symbols the machine prints on its output tape (we are thinking of a two-tape machine) must be given physical shapes, and the printer must be designed to produce them on demand. The printer, of course, doesn't have to "print" anything in a literal sense; the operation could be wholly electronic, or the printer could be a speaker that vocalizes the output or a cathode-ray monitor that visually displays it (then saves it for future computational purposes).

What about the "internal states" of the machine? How are they physically realized? Consider a particular instruction on the machine table of TM_1: If the machine is in state q_0 and scanning a +, replace that + with a 1, move right, and go into state q_1. Assume that P_0 and P_1 are the physical states realizing q_0 and q_1 respectively. P_0 and P_1, then, must satisfy the following condition: An occurrence of P_0, together with the physical scanning of +, must *physically cause* three physical events: (1) the replacement of the physical embodiment of + with that of 1, (2) an appropriate physical motion of the physical tape (or the head), and (3) an occurrence of state P_1 in the machine. In general, then, what needs to be done is to *replace the functional or computational relations* among the various abstract parameters (symbols, states, and motions of the head) mentioned in the machine table *with appropriate causal relations among the physical embodiments* of these parameters.

From the logical point of view, then, the internal states are only "implicitly defined" in terms of their relations to other parameters: q_j is a state such that if the machine is in it and scanning symbol b_k, the machine replaces b_k with b_l, moves R (that is, to the right), and goes into state q_h, and if the machine is scanning b_m, it does such and such, and so on. So q_j can be thought of as a function that maps symbols of the alphabet to the triples of the form $<b_k, R\ (or\ L),\ q_h>$. From the physical standpoint, P_j, which realizes q_j, can be thought of as a causal intermediary between the physically realized symbols and the physical realizations of the triples or, equivalently, as a *disposition* to emit appropriate physical outputs (i.e., the triples) in response to different physical stimuli (i.e., the symbols scanned). This means that the intrinsic physical natures of the Ps that realize the qs are of no interest to us as long as they have the right causal/relational properties; their intrinsic properties do not matter—or, more accurately, they matter only to the extent that they affect the causal powers of states and objects that have them. As long as these states perform their assigned causal work by making the right causal connections, they can be anything you please. And it is plausible to suppose that with a certain amount of engineering ingenuity, a machine could be rewired so that many physical states realizing distinct machine states could be interchanged without affecting the operation of the machine.

We see, then, a clear convergence between the functionalist conception of a mental state as a state occupying a certain causal role and the idea of a physical state realizing an internal state of a Turing machine. Just as, on the functionalist view, what makes a given mental state the kind of mental state it is is its causal role with respect to sensory inputs, behavior outputs, and other mental states, so what makes a physical state the realization of a given machine state is its causal relations to inputs, outputs, and physical states realizing other machine states. This is why it is natural for functionalists to look to Turing machines for a model of the mind.

Let S be a physical system (which may be an electromechanical device like a computer, a biological organism, a business organization, or anything else), and assume that we have adopted a vocabulary to describe its inputs and outputs. That is, we have a specification of what is to count as the inputs it receives from its surroundings and what is to count as its behavioral outputs. We will say that a Turing machine M is a *machine description* of system S, relative to a given input/output specification, just in case S realizes M relative to that input/output specification. Thus, the relation of *being a machine description of* is the converse of the relation of *being a realization of*. We can also define a weaker concept than machine description: Let us say that a Turing machine M is a *behavioral description* of S (again, relative to an input/output specification) just in case M provides a correct description of S's input-output correlations. Thus, every machine description of S is also a behavioral description, but the converse will not in general hold. M can give a true description of the input-output correlations characterizing S, but its machine states may not be realized in S, and S's inner workings may not correctly mirror the functional-computational relationships given by M's machine table. In fact, there may be another Turing machine M^*, distinct from M, which gives a correct machine description of S. It follows, then, that *two physical systems that are input-output equivalent may not be realizations of the same Turing machine*. (The pair of adding machines TM_1 and TM_2, is an instance of such a situation.)

Machine Functionalism: Its Motivation and Main Claims

Machine functionalists claim that we can think of the mind as a Turing machine (or a probabilistic automaton). This of course needs to be filled out, but from the preceding discussion it should be pretty clear how the story will go. The central idea is that what it is for something to have mentality—that is, to have a psychology—is for it to be a physically realized Turing machine of appropriate complexity, with its mental states (that is, mental-state types) identified with the internal states of the machine table. Another way of explaining this idea is to use the notion of machine description: An organism has mentality just in case there is a Turing machine of appropriate complexity that is a machine description of it, and its mental-state kinds are to be identified with the internal states of that Turing machine. All this is of course relative to an appropriately chosen input/output specification, since you must know, or decide, what is to count as the organism's inputs and outputs before you can determine what Turing machine (or machines) it can be said to instantiate.

Let us consider the idea that *the psychology of an organism* can be represented by a Turing machine, an idea that is commonly held by machine functionalists.[14] Let V be a complete specification of all possible inputs and outputs of a psychological subject S, and let C be all actual and possible input-output correlations of S (that is, C is a complete specification of which input applied to S elicits which output, for all inputs and outputs listed in V). In constructing a *psychology* for S, we are trying to formulate a *theory* that gives a perspicuous systematization of C by positing a set of internal states in S. Such a theory will *predict* for any input applied to S what output will be emitted by S and also *explain* why that particular input elicits that particular output. It is reasonable to suppose that for any minimally complex behavioral system this kind of systematization will not be possible unless we advert to its internal states; for we must expect that the same input applied to S will not always prompt S to produce the same output. The actual output elicited by a given input will depend, we must suppose, on the internal state of S at that time.

Before we proceed further, it is necessary to modify our notion of a Turing machine in one respect: The internal states, qs, of a Turing machine are *total* states of the machine at a given time, and the Ps that are their physical realizations, too, are *total physical states at a time* of the machine's physical realizer. This means that the Turing machines we are talking about are not going to look at all like the psychological theories we are familiar with; the states posited by these theories are seldom, if ever, total states of a subject at a time. But this is a technical problem, something that we will assume can be remedied with a finer-grained notion of an "internal state." We can then think of a total internal state to be made up of these "partial" states, which combine in different ways to yield different total states. This modification should not change anything essential in the original conception of a Turing machine. In the discussion to follow, we will be using this modified notion of an internal state in most contexts.

To return to the question of representing the psychology of a subject S in terms of a Turing machine: What Turing machine, or machines, will be adequate as a description of S's psychology? Evidently, any adequate Turing machine will have to be a behavioral description of S, in the sense defined above; that is, it must give a correct description of S's input-output correlations (as specified by V). But as we have seen, there is bound to be more than one Turing machine—in fact, there will be indefinitely many—that will give a correct representation of S's input-output correlations.

Since each of these machines is a correct behavioral description of our psychological subject S, they are all equally good as a *predictive instrument*: Although some of them may be easier to manipulate and calculationally more efficient, they will all predict the same behavior output for the same input conditions. This is a simple consequence of the notion of "behavioral description." In what sense, then, are they different Turing machines, and why do the differences matter?

It should be clear how behaviorally equivalent Turing machines, say M_1 and M_2, can differ from each other. To say that they are different Turing machines is to say that their machine tables are different—that is how Turing machines are individuated. This means that for the same input, M_1 and M_2 will likely go through *different computational processes* to arrive at the same output. Each machine has a set of internal states; let us say $<q_0, q_1, \ldots, q_n>$ for M_1 and $<r_0, r_1, \ldots, r_m>$ for M_2. Let us suppose further that M_1 is a machine description of our psychological subject S, but M_2 is not. That is, S is a physical realization of M_1 but not of M_2. This means that the computational relations represented in M_1, but not those represented in M_2, are mirrored in a set of causal relations among the physical states of S. So there are real physical (perhaps neurobiological) states in S, $<Q_0, Q_1, \ldots, Q_n>$, corresponding to M_1's internal states $<q_0, q_1, \ldots, q_n>$, and these Qs are causally hooked up to each other and to the physical scanner (sense-organs) and the physical printer (motor mechanisms) in a way that ensures that, for all computational processes generated by M_1, isomorphic causal processes occur in S. As we may say, S is a "causal isomorph" of M_1.

There is, then, a clear sense in which M_1 is, but M_2 is not, "psychologically real" for S, even though they are both accurate predictive theories of S's observable input-output behaviors. M_1 gives "the true psychology" of S in that, as we saw, S has a physical structure whose states constitute a causal system that mirrors the computational structure represented by the machine table of M_1 and that the physical/causal operations of S form an isomorphic image of the computational operations of M_1. This makes a crucial difference when what we want is an *explanatory* theory, a theory that *explains why S does what it does under the given input conditions.*

Suppose we say: When input *i* was applied to *S*, *S* emitted behavioral output *o* *because* it was in internal state *p*. This can count as an explanation, it seems, only if the state appealed to, namely, *p*, is in some sense a "real" state of the system. In particular, it can count as a *causal* explanation only if the state *p* is what, in conjunction with *i*, caused *o*, and this cannot happen unless *p* is actually a state of *S*. Now, it is clear that we can impute reality to *p* only if it is an internal state of M_1, a Turing machine realized by *S*, and not if *p* is a state of M_2, which is not realized by *S*. For in the former case, but not in the latter, there is a real physical state of *S*, namely, *P*, which realizes *p* and whose causal powers exactly match the functional-computational relations that characterize *p*. The explanatory force of "*S* emitted *o* when it received input *i* because it was in state *q*" derives from the causal relations involving *P* and the physical embodiments of *o* and *i*.

The philosophical issues here depend partly but crucially on the metaphysics of scientific theory you accept. If you think of scientific theories in general, or theories over some specific domain, merely as predictive instruments that enable us to infer or calculate further observations from the given ones, you will not attach any existential significance to its theoretical posits—like unobservable microparticles of theoretical physics and their (often quite strange) properties—and regard them only as calculational aids in deriving predictions. A position like this is called "instrumentalism" or "antirealism" about scientific theory.[15] On such a view, the "truth" of the theoretical principles does not matter, nor does the "reality" of the entities and properties posited by them; the only thing that matters is "the empirical adequacy" of the theory—how accurately the theory works as a predictive device and how comprehensive its coverage is. If you accept an instrumentalist stance toward psychological theory, therefore, any Turing machine that is a behavioral description of a psychological subject is good enough as its psychology, exactly as good as any other behaviorally adequate description of it, although some may be preferred over others on account of manipulative ease and calculational economy. If this is your view of the nature of psychology, the question which of the many behaviorally adequate psychologies is "really true" of the subject does not arise.

But if you adopt the viewpoint of "realism" about scientific theories, or at any rate about psychology, you will not think all behaviorally adequate descriptions are psychologically adequate. An adequate psychology for the realist must have "psychological reality": that is, the internal states it posits must be the real states of the organism with an active role as causal intermediaries between inputs and outputs, and this means that only a Turing machine that is a correct machine description of the organism is an acceptable psychological theory of it. The simplest and most elegant behavioral description may not be the one that correctly describes the inner processes that cause the subject's observable behavior; there is no a priori reason to suppose that our subject is put together according to the specifications of the most elegant theory (whatever the standards of simplicity and theoretical elegance might be). But why should one want to go beyond the instrumentalist position and insist on psychological reality? There are two related reasons: (1) psychological states, namely, the internal states of the psychological subject posited by a psychology, must be regarded as real, as we saw, if we expect the theory to generate explanations, especially causal explanations, of behavior. And this seems to be the attitude of the working psychologists: It is their common, almost universal, practice to attribute to their subjects internal states, capacities, functions, and mechanisms (e.g., information storage and retrieval, mental imagery, preference structure, etc.), referring to them in constructing what they regard as causal explanations of overt behavior. And (2) we expect to find actual biological mechanisms underlying the psychological states, capacities, and functions that are posited by correct psychological theories. Research in the neural sciences has had impressive successes—and we expect this to continue—in identifying physiological mechanisms that implement psychological functions and mechanisms. In fact, it is a reflection of our realistic stance about psychological theorizing that we expect, and perhaps should insist on, a physiological foundation for psychological theories. The requirement that the correct psychology of an organism be a machine description of it,[16] not merely a behaviorally adequate one, can be seen as an expression of a commitment to realism about psychological theory.

If the psychology of any organism can be represented as a Turing machine, it is natural to consider the possibility of using representability by a Turing machine to explicate, or define, what it is for something to have a psychology. As we saw, that precisely is what machine functionalism proposes: What it is for an organism, or system, to have a psychology—that is, what it is for an organism to have mentality—is for it to realize an appropriate Turing machine. It isn't merely that anything with mentality has an appropriate machine description; machine functionalism makes the stronger claim that its having a machine description of an appropriate kind is *constitutive of* its mentality. This is a philosophical thesis about the nature of mentality: Mentality, or having a mind, consists in realizing an appropriate Turing machine. What makes us creatures with mentality, therefore, is the fact that we are Turing machines. Functionalism will acknowledge that having a brain of certain structural complexity is important to mentality, but the importance of the brain lies exactly in that it is a Turing machine. It is our brain's computational properties, not its biological properties, that constitute our mentality. In short, our brain is our mind because it is a computer, not because it is the kind of organic, biological structure it is.

Machine Functionalism: Further Considerations

Suppose that two systems, S_1 and S_2, are *in the same mental state* (at the same time or different times). What does this mean on the functionalist conception of a mental kind? A mental kind, as you will remember, is supposed to be an internal state of a Turing machine (of an "appropriate kind"); so for S_1 and S_2 to be in the same state, there must be some Turing machine state q such that S_1 is in q and S_2 is in q. But what does this mean?

S_1 and S_2 are both physical systems, and we know that they could be systems of very different sorts (recall multiple realizability). As physical systems, they have physical states (that is, instantiate certain physical properties); to say that they are both in machine state q at time t is to say this: There are physical states Q_1 and Q_2, respectively, such that Q_1 realizes q in S_1, and Q_2 realizes q in S_2, and, at t, S_1 is in Q_1 and S_2 in Q_2. Multiple realizability tells us that Q_1 and Q_2 may not have very much in common as physical states; one could be a biological state and the other an electromagnetic one. What binds the two states together is only the fact that in their respective systems they implement the same internal machine state. That is to say, the two states play the same computational role in their respective systems.

But talk of "the same internal machine state q" makes sense only in relation to a given machine table. Internal states of a Turing machine are identifiable only relative to a given machine table: In terms of the layout of machine tables we used earlier, an internal state q is wholly characterized by the vertical column of instructions appearing under it. But these instructions will refer to other internal states, say, q_i, q_j, and q_k, and if you look up the instructions falling under these, you are likely to find references back to state q. So these states are interdefined. What all this means is that *the sameness or difference of an internal state across different machine tables has no meaning*. It makes no sense to say of an internal state q_i of one Turing machine and a state q_k of another that q_i is, or that it isn't, the same as q_k, nor does it make sense to say of a physical state Q_i of a physically realized Turing machine that it realizes, or doesn't realize, the same internal machine state q as does a physical state Q_k of another physical machine, unless the two physical machines are realizations of the same Turing machine.

It seems, then, that the machine-functionalist conception of mental kinds has the following consequence: For any two subjects to be in the same mental state, they must realize the same Turing machine. But if they realize the same Turing machine, their total psychology must be identical. That is, on machine functionalism, two subjects' total psychology must be identical if they are to share a single psychological state. This sounds absurd: It does not seem reasonable to require that for two persons to share a mental state, say, the belief that snow is white, the total set of psychological regularities governing their behavior be exactly identical. Before we discuss this issue further, we must attend to another matter, and this is the problem of how the inputs and outputs of a system are to be specified.

Suppose that two systems, S_1 and S_2, realize the same Turing machine; that is, the same Turing machine gives a correct machine description of each. We know that realization is relative to a particular input/output specification; that is, we must know what is to count as input conditions and what is to count as behavior outputs of the system involved before we can tell whether it realizes a given Turing machine. Let V_1 and V_2 be the two input/output specifications for S_1 and S_2, respectively, relative to which they share the same machine description. Since the same machine table is involved, V_1 and V_2 must be isomorphic: The elements of V_1 can be correlated, one to one, with the elements of V_2 in a way that preserves their roles in the machine table. And we are assuming, of course, that our Turing machine has the appropriate complexity to qualify as a psychological system.

But suppose that S_1 is a real psychological system, perhaps a human (say, "Larry"), whereas S_2 is a computer, an electromechanical device (call it "MAX"). So the inputs and outputs specified by V_2 are the usual inputs and outputs appropriate for a computing machine, perhaps strings of symbols entered on the keyboard and strings of symbols on the computer monitor or its printout. Now, whether MAX can be considered a psychological system at all is a question we will take up later, but it would seem that to grant it the full psychological status we grant Larry is in effect to *conflate a psychological subject with a computer simulation of one*—or at least to refuse to acknowledge a distinction between a real thing and a computer simulation of a real thing. No one is likely to confuse the operation of a jet engine or the spread of rabies in wildlife with their computer simulations. It's difficult to believe that this distinction suddenly vanishes when we perform a computer simulation of the psychology of a person.

One thing that obviously seems wrong about our computer, MAX, as a psychological system, when we compare it with Larry, is its inputs and outputs: While its input/output specification is isomorphic to Larry's, it seems entirely inappropriate for psychology. Although it may not be easy to characterize the differences precisely, we would not consider inputs and outputs consisting merely of strings of symbols as fitting for something with true mentality. Grinding out strings of symbols isn't like the full-blown behavior that we see in Larry. For one thing, MAX's outputs have nothing apparently to do with its survival or continued functioning, and its inputs don't have the function of providing MAX with information about its surroundings. And as a result of this, its outputs lack what may be called "teleological aptness" as a response to its inputs. All this makes it difficult to think of MAX's outputs as constituting real behavior or action, something that is necessary if we are to regard it as a genuine psychological system.

Qua realizations of a Turing machine, MAX and Larry are symmetrically related. If, however, we see here an asymmetry in point of mentality, it is clear that the nature of inputs and outputs is an important factor in this, and our considerations seem to show that for a system realizing a Turing machine to count as a psychological system, its input/output specification (relative to which it realizes the machine) must be *psychologically appropriate*. Exactly what this appropriateness consists in is an interesting and complex question that requires much further exploration. In any case, the machine functionalist must confront this question: Is it possible to give a characterization of this input/output appropriateness that is consistent with functionalism? Recall a similar point we discussed in connection with behaviorism: Not to beg the question, the behavior that the behaviorist is allowed to talk about in giving behavioristic definitions of mental states must be "physical behavior," not intentional action with an explicit or implicit mental component (e.g., buying a loaf of bread, greeting a friend, paying off a loan). If your project is to get mentality out of behavior, your notion of behavior must not presuppose mentality.

The same restriction applies to the machine functionalist: Her project is to define mentality in terms of Turing machines and input-output relations. The additional tool she can make use of, something not available to the behaviorist, is the concept of a Turing machine; but her input and output are subject to the same constraint—her input/output, like the behaviorist's, must be physical input/output. If this is right, it seems no easy task for the machine functionalist to distinguish, in a principled way, Larry's inputs/outputs from MAX's and hence genuine psychological systems from their simulations. We pointed out earlier that Larry's outputs, given his inputs, seem *teleologically appropriate*, whereas MAX's aren't. They have something to do with his proper functioning in his environment, his survival, and satisfaction of his needs and desires. But can this notion of teleology—purposiveness or goal-directedness—be explained in a psychologically neutral way, without begging the question? Perhaps, some biological/evolutionary story could be attempted, but it remains an open question whether such a bioteleological attempt will succeed. At any rate, this is a challenge that machine functionalism must confront.

Let us now return to the question whether machine functionalism is committed to the consequence that two psychological subjects can be in the same psychological state only if they have an identical total psychology. As we saw, the implication appears to follow from the fact that on machine functionalism, being in the same psychological state is being in the same internal machine state, and the sameness of a machine state makes sense only in relation to the same Turing machine. What is perhaps worse, it seems to follow that it makes no sense to say that two psychological subjects are *not* in the same psychological state unless they have an identical total psychology! But this conclusion must be slightly weakened in consideration of the fact that the input/output specifications of the two subjects realizing the same Turing machine may be different and that the individuation of psychologies may be sensitive to input/output specifications (we will shortly recur to this point). So let us speak of "isomorphic" psychologies for psychologies that are instances of the same Turing machine *modulo* input/output specification. We then have the following result: On machine functionalism, for two psychological subjects to share even a single mental state, their total psychologies must be isomorphic to each other. Recall Putnam's complaint against the brain-state theory: This theory makes it impossible for both humans and octopuses to be in the same pain state unless they shared the same brain state, an unlikely possibility. But it would seem that machine functionalism runs into an exactly analogous predicament: For an octopus and a human to be in the same pain state, they must share an isomorphic psychology—an unlikely possibility, to say the least! And for two humans to share a single mental state, they must have an exactly identical total psychology (since the same input/output specification presumably must hold for all or most humans). This consequence of machine functionalism clearly goes against our expectations.

However, things are perhaps not as bleak for machine functionalism as they might appear at first blush, for the following line of response seems available: For both humans and octopuses to be in pain, it is not necessary that *total* octopus psychology coincides with, or is isomorphic to, *total* human psychology. It is only necessary for there to be *some* Turing machine that is a correct machine description of both and in which pain figures as an internal machine state; it doesn't matter if this shared Turing machine falls short of the maximally detailed Turing machines that describe them (these machines represent their "total psychologies"). So what is necessary is that humans and octopuses share a partial, or abbreviated, psychology that encompasses pains. Whether or not pain psychology can so readily be isolated, or abstracted, from the total psychology is a question worth pondering, especially in the context of the functionalist conception of mental states, but there is another potential difficulty here that we should look at.

As we saw, all this talk of humans' and octopuses' realizing a Turing machine is relative to an input/output specification. Doesn't this mean that the input and output conditions characteristic of humans when they are in pain must be appropriately similar, if not identical, to the input/output conditions characteristic of octopuses' pains, if both humans and octopuses can be said to be in pain? Consider the output side:

Do octopuses wince and groan when in pain? Scream and yell? How similar is octopuses' escape behavior, from the purely physical point of view, to the escape behavior of, say, middle-aged, middle-class American males? Is there an abstract enough *nonmental* description of pain behavior that is appropriate for humans and octopuses and all other pain-capable organisms and systems? If there is not, machine functionalism seems to succumb again to the same difficulty that the functionalist has charged against the brain-state theory: An octopus and a human cannot be in the same pain state. At best they can, it seems, be in states that are psychologically isomorphic to each other. This is another aspect of the "appropriateness" problem we discussed earlier for input/output specifications.

But there is another "appropriateness" condition for Turing machines that we must now consider. You will remember that for a machine functionalist a system has mentality just in case it realizes an "appropriately complex" Turing machine. This proviso is necessary because there are all sorts of simple Turing machines (recall our sample machines) that clearly do not suffice to generate mentality. But how complex is complex enough? What is complexity anyway, and how is it measured? And what kind of complexity is "appropriate" for mentality? These are important but difficult questions, and machine functionalism, unsurprisingly, has not produced detailed general answers to them. What we have, though, is a concrete proposal, from Turing himself, of a test to determine whether a computing machine can "think." This is the celebrated "Turing test," and we now turn to Turing's proposal.

The Turing Test

Turing's proposal[17] is to bypass these general theoretical questions about appropriateness in favor of an "operational test" that looks at the performance capabilities of computing machines vis-à-vis average humans who, as all sides would agree, are fully mental. The idea is that if machines can do as well as humans on certain appropriate intellectual tasks, then they must be judged no less psychological ("intelligent") than humans. What, then, are these tasks? Obviously, they must be those that, intuitively, require intelligence and mentality to perform, and Turing describes a game, the "imitation game," to test for the presence of these capacities.

The imitation game is played as follows. There are three players: the interrogator, a man, and a woman, with the interrogator segregated from the other two in another room. The man and woman are known only as "X" and "Y" to the interrogator, whose object is to identify which is the man and which the woman by asking questions through a computer terminal. The man's object is to mislead the interrogator into making an er-

roneous identification, whereas the woman's job is to help the interrogator. There are no restrictions on the topics of the questions asked.

Suppose, Turing says, we now replace the man with a computing machine. Now the aim of the interrogator is to find out which is the human
and which the machine. The machine is programmed to fool the interrogator into thinking that it is a human. Will the machine do as well as the
man in the first game in fooling the interrogator into making wrong
guesses? Turing's proposal is that if the machine does as well as the man,
then we must credit it with all the intelligence that we would normally
confer on a human; it must be judged to possess the full mentality that
humans possess.

The gist of Turing's idea can be captured in a simpler test: By asking
questions (or just holding a conversation) via keyboard terminals, can we
find out whether we are talking to a human or a computing machine? If
there is a computer that can consistently fool us so that our success in
guessing its identity is no better than what could be achieved by random
guesses, we must concede, it seems, that this machine has the kind of
mentality that we grant to humans. There already are chess-playing computers that would fool most people this way, but only in playing chess:
Average chess players won't be able to tell if they are playing a human
opponent or a computer. But the Turing test covers all possible areas of
human concern: music and poetry, politics and the weather, how to fix a
leaking faucet or make a soufflé—no holds are barred.

The Turing test is designed so that the questions of intelligence and
mentality are separated from questions about the appearance of the machine (as Turing points out, it doesn't have to win beauty contests to qualify as a thinker), details of its composition and structure, whether it
speaks and moves about like a human, and so on. The test is to focus on a
broad range of rational, intellectual capacities and functions. But how
good is the test?

Some have pointed out that the test is both too tough and too narrow.
Too tough because something doesn't have to be smart enough to outwit
a human to have mentality or intelligence; in particular, the possession of
a language shouldn't be a prerequisite for mentality (think of mute animals). Human intelligence itself encompasses a pretty broad range, and
there appears to be no compelling reason to set the minimal threshold of
mentality at the level of performance required by the Turing test. The test
is perhaps also too narrow in that it seems at best to be a test for the presence of *humanlike* mentality, the kind of intelligence that characterizes humans. Why couldn't there be creatures, or machines, that are intelligent
and have a psychology but would fail the Turing test, which, after all, is
designed to test whether the computer can fool a *human* interrogator into

thinking it is a *human?* Furthermore, it is difficult to see it as a test for the presence of mental states like sensations and perceptions, although it may be an excellent test of broadly intellectual and cognitive capacities. To see something as a full psychological system we must see it in a real-life context, one might argue; we must see it coping with its environment, receiving sensory information from its surroundings and behaving appropriately in response to it.

Various replies can be attempted to counter these criticisms, but can we say, as Turing himself did, that the Turing test at least provides us with a *sufficient* condition for mentality, although, for the reasons just given, it cannot be considered a necessary condition? If something passes the test, it's at least as smart as we are, and since we have intelligence and mentality, it would be only fair to grant it the same status—or so one might argue. This reasoning seems to presuppose the following thesis:

> [Turing's thesis] If two systems are input-output equivalent, they have the same psychological status; in particular, one is mental just in case the other is.

We call it "Turing's thesis" because Turing seems to be committed to it. Why is Turing committed to it? Because the Turing test only looks at inputs and outputs: If two computers produce the same output for the same input, for all possible inputs—that is, if they are input-output equivalent—their performance on the Turing test will be identical, and one will be judged to have mentality if and only if the other is.

This means that if two Turing machines are correct behavioral descriptions of some system (relative to the same input/output specification), then they satisfy the "appropriateness" condition to the same degree (remember that "appropriateness" here refers to appropriateness for mentality). In this way the general philosophical stance implicit in Turing's thesis is more behavioristic than machine-functionalist. For machine functionalism is consistent with the denial of Turing's thesis: It will say that input-output equivalence, or behavioral equivalence, isn't sufficient to guarantee the same degree of mentality. What arguably follows from machine functionalism is only that systems that realize the same Turing machine—that is, systems for which an identical Turing machine is a correct machine description—enjoy the same degree of mentality.

It appears, then, that Turing's thesis is mistaken: Internal processing ought to make a difference to mentality. Imagine two machines, each of which does basic arithmetic operations for integers up to 100: Both give correct answers for any input of the form $n + m$, $n \times m$, $n - m$, and $n \div m$ for whole numbers n and m less than or equal to 100. But one of the machines calculates ("figures out") the answer by applying the usual algorithms we use for these operations, whereas the other has a file in which answers are stored for all possible problems of addition, multiplication, subtraction, and division for integers up to 100, and its computation consists in "looking up" the answer for any problem given to it. The second machine is really more like a filing cabinet than a computing machine; it does nothing that we would normally describe as "calculation" or "computation." Neither machine is complex enough to be considered for possible mentality; however, the example should convince us that we should consider the structure of internal processing, as well as input-output correlations, in deciding whether a given system has mentality.[18] If this is correct, it shows the inadequacy of a purely behavioral test, such as the Turing test, as a criterion of mentality.

So Turing's thesis seems incorrect; input-output equivalence doesn't give us equal mentality. But this doesn't necessarily invalidate the Turing test; for it may well be that given the inherent richness and complexity of the imitation game, any computing machine that can consistently fool humans—in fact, any machine that's in the ballpark for the competition—has to be running a highly sophisticated, unquestionably "intelligent" program, and there is no chance that this machine could be operating like a gigantic filing system with a superfast retrieval mechanism.[19]

The "Chinese Room" Argument

John Searle has constructed a much-debated thought experiment to show that mentality cannot be equated with a computing machine running a program, no matter how complex, "intelligent," and sophisticated.[20] Imagine someone (say, Searle himself) who understands no Chinese who is confined in a room ("the Chinese room") with a set of rules for systematically transforming strings of symbols to yield further symbol strings. These symbol strings are in fact Chinese expressions, and the transformation rules are purely *formal* in the sense that their application depends solely on the shapes of the symbols involved, not their meanings. Searle becomes very adept at manipulating Chinese expressions in accordance with the rules given to him (we may suppose that Searle has memorized the whole rule book) so that every time a string of Chinese characters is sent in, Searle quickly goes to work and promptly sends out an appropriate string of Chinese characters. From the perspective of someone outside the room, the input-output relationships are exactly the same as they would be if someone with a genuine understanding of Chinese, instead of Searle, were locked inside the room. And yet Searle does not understand any Chinese, and there is no understanding of Chinese going on anywhere inside the Chinese room. What goes on in the room is only manipulation of symbols on the basis of their shapes, or "syntax," but real understanding involves "semantics," knowing what these symbols represent, or mean. Although Searle's behavior is input-output equivalent to that of a speaker of Chinese, Searle understands no Chinese.

Searle's other premise is that what goes on inside a computer is exactly like what goes on in the Chinese room: rule-governed manipulation of symbols based on their shapes. There is no more understanding of Chinese in the computer than there is in the Chinese room. The conclusion to be drawn, Searle argues, is that mentality is more than rule-governed syntactic manipulation of symbols, and the Turing test, therefore, is invalid as a test of mentality.

It is not easy to assess the significance and force of Searle's argument, although its intuitive appeal and power cannot be denied. But we need to be careful: The appeal of Searle's example may be due to some misleading assumptions tacitly made in the way he describes what is going on in the Chinese room. We can agree with Searle that input-output equivalence does not constitute psychological equivalence and that the fact that the Chinese room or Searle is input-output equivalent with a speaker of Chinese doesn't show that the Chinese room or Searle is a system with a genuine understanding of Chinese. As has already been pointed out, we must attend to internal processing, the kind of program being run, when considering the question of mentality for the system. And here it may be seriously misleading to represent the man locked inside the room as merely "manipulating symbols." Given the sophisticated linguistic processing that has to be performed, we must expect that an extremely sophisticated and highly complex program, something that may far exceed any computer program that has yet been written, will be necessary. It is by no means clear that any human could manage to do what Searle imagines himself to be doing in the Chinese room—that is, short of throwing away the rule book and learning some real Chinese.

But Searle has a reply: Make the program as complex and intricate as you want; no amount of syntactic symbol-pushing will generate meaning, and mentality is not possible unless meanings are generated. Computation is syntax-driven: As long as the computer is given the same strings of 0s and 1s, it will generate certain further strings of 0s and 1s, no matter what these strings stand for—the prices of bags of potato chips or the addresses of a group of employees or the temperatures of the major cities in New England. The computer would move through exactly the same computational process even if the 0s and 1s meant nothing at all. Computational processes respond only to the shapes of symbols; their meanings, or what they represent, are computationally irrelevant. However, our intentional states, like beliefs and desires, are what they are because they mean, or represent, something. My belief that it is raining outside has the content "it is raining outside," and in virtue of having this content the belief represents, or purports to represent, a specific weather condition in my environment. Suppose this belief causes in me a desire to take an umbrella to work. This causal relation holds in part because the belief and the desire have the particular contents that they have; my belief didn't cause a desire to wear my best suit to work, and the belief that it is sunny outside wouldn't have caused me to want to take an umbrella with me. Mental processes are driven by representational contents, or meanings. Hence, they cannot be syntax-driven computational processes, and the mind cannot just be a computer running a program, no matter how complex and sophisticated the program may be. The mind is a "semantic engine"; the computer, in contrast, is only a "syntactic engine."

If this is the general argument underlying the Chinese room thought experiment, it clearly raises a legitimate and perplexing issue about meaning and mental causation. However, this is a general problem that arises for any materialist conception of mentality, quite apart from the specific issue of the computational account of mentality. For consider the position that Searle himself favors: Mentality can arise only in complex biological systems, like the human brain. It is plausible to think that the same neurobiological causal processes will go on no matter what the neural states involved represent about the world or whether they represent anything at all. Neural processes seem no more responsive to meaning and representational content than are computational processes. How meaning and understanding could arise out of molecules and cells is as much a mystery as how they could arise out of strings of 0s and 1s. Some of these issues will be discussed further in connection with mental causation (Chapter 6).

Further Readings

For a statement of machine functionalism, Hilary Putnam's paper "Psychological Predicates" (reprinted as "The Nature of Mental States") is recommended; see also his "Robots: Machines or Artificially Created Life?" and "The Mental Life of Some Machines," all reprinted in his *Mind, Language, and Reality: Philosophical Papers*, vol. 2 (Cambridge: Cambridge University Press, 1975). Ned Block's "Introduction: What Is Functionalism?" in his *Readings in Philosophy of Psychology*, vol. 1 (Cambridge: Harvard University Press, 1980), is a clear and concise introduction to the general topic of functionalism; so are his entries on "Functionalism" in *A Companion to Philosophy of Mind*, ed. Samuel Guttenplan (Oxford: Blackwell, 1994) and *A Companion to Metaphysics*, ed. Jaegwon Kim and Ernest Sosa (Oxford: Blackwell, 1995).

For a teleological approach to functionalism, see William G. Lycan, *Consciousness* (Cambridge: MIT Press, 1987), ch. 4. For general biological/evolutionary considerations in connection with issues about mentality, see Ruth G. Millikan, *Language, Thought, and Other Biological Categories* (Cambridge: MIT Press, 1984).

For issues involving the Turing test and the Chinese room argument, see Alan M. Turing, "Computing Machinery and Intelligence," *Mind* 59 (1950):433–460; John R. Searle, "Minds, Brains, and Programs," *Behavioral and Brain Sciences* 3 (1980):417–457; and Daniel C. Dennett, *Consciousness Explained* (Boston: Little, Brown, 1991), ch. 14.

For criticisms of machine functionalism (and functionalism in general), see Ned Block, "Troubles with Functionalism," in his *Readings in Philosophy of Psychology*, vol. 1.

Notes

1. Originally published in *Art, Philosophy, and Religion* (Pittsburgh: University of Pittsburgh Press, 1967), Hilary Putnam's "Psychological Predicates" was later reprinted under the new title "The Nature of Mental States" in various places, including *The Nature of Mind*, ed. David M. Rosenthal (New York: Oxford University Press, 1991).

2. Donald Davidson's argument for mental anomalism, as we shall see in Chapter 9, also played a significant part in the decline of reductionism.

3. At least some of them; for it might be argued that certain psychological states can be had only by materially embodied subjects, for example, feelings of hunger and thirst, bodily sensations like pain and itch, and sexual desire.

4. The term "realize" used in this principle has not been explained. As we make progress with this chapter, its meaning should become clearer; in the meantime, you will not go far astray if you read "*P* realizes *M*" as "*P* is a neural substrate, or correlate, of *M*."

5. This principle is closely related to the three principles stated in Chapter 1 as constituting "minimal physicalism."

6. See Ronald Melzack, *The Puzzle of Pain* (New York: Basic Books, 1973), pp. 15–16.

7. Some have argued that this function-versus-mechanism dichotomy is pervasively present at all levels, not restricted to the mental-physical case; see, for example, William G. Lycan, *Consciousness* (Cambridge: MIT Press, 1987).

8. As I take it, something like this is the point of Karl Lashley's principle of "equipotentiality"; see his *Brain Mechanisms and Intelligence* (New York: Hafner, 1963), p. 25.

9. To borrow Ned Block's formulation of the question in "Introduction: What Is Functionalism?" in his *Readings in Philosophy of Psychology*, vol. 1 (Cambridge: Harvard University Press, 1980), pp. 178–179.

10. As we shall see in connection with machine functionalism, there is another sense of "function," the mathematical sense, involved in "functionalism."

11. Strictly speaking, it is more accurate to say that *the capacity to sense pain* is being equipped with a tissue-damage detector and that pain, as an occurrence, is the activation of such a detector.

12. See, for example, B. F. Skinner, "Selections from *Science and Human Behavior*," in Block, *Readings in Philosophy of Psychology*, vol. 1.

13. A good treatment of mathematical theory of computability in terms of Turing machines can be found in Martin Davis, *Computability and Unsolvability* (New York: McGraw-Hill, 1958).

14. See, for example, Putnam, "Psychological Predicates."

15. For a recent statement and defense of a position of this kind, see Bas Van Fraassen, *The Scientific Image* (Oxford: Clarendon Press, 1980).

16. Is there, for any given psychological subject, a *unique* Turing machine that is a machine description (relative to a specification of input and output conditions), or can there be (perhaps there always must be) multiple, nontrivially different machine descriptions? Does realism about psychology require that there be a unique one? The reader is invited to reflect on these questions.

17. See A. M. Turing, "Computing Machinery and Intelligence," *Mind* 59 (1950):433–460.

18. For an elaboration of this point, see Ned Block, "Psychologism and Behaviorism," *Philosophical Review* 90 (1981):5–43.

19. See Daniel C. Dennett, *Consciousness Explained* (Boston: Little, Brown, 1991), pp. 435–440.

20. In John Searle, "Minds, Brains, and Programs," *Behavioral and Brain Sciences* 3 (1980):417–457; reprinted in Rosenthal, *The Nature of Mind*. (This paper was published together with twenty-eight responses by philosophers and cognitive scientists and Searle's replies.)

5
Mind as a Causal Structure: Causal-Theoretical Functionalism

In the preceding chapter we discussed the functionalist attempt to use the concept of a Turing machine to explicate the nature of mentality and its relationship to the physical. Here we will examine another formulation of functionalism in terms of "causal role." Central to any version of functionalism is the idea that a mental state can be characterized in terms of the input-output relations it mediates, where the inputs and outputs may include other mental states as well as sensory stimuli and physical behaviors. Mental events are conceived as nodes in a complex causal network that engages in causal transactions with the outside world by receiving sensory inputs and emitting behavioral outputs.

What, according to functionalism, distinguishes one mental kind (say, pain) from another (say, itch) is the distinctive input-output relationship associated with each kind. *Causal-theoretical functionalism* conceives of this input-output relationship as a causal relation, one that is mediated by mental events. Different mental events are different because they are implicated in different input-output causal relationships. Pain differs from itch in that each has its own distinctive causal role: Pains are typically caused by tissue damage and typically cause winces, groans, and escape behavior; analogously, itches are typically caused by skin irritation and typically cause scratching. But tissue damage causes pain only if certain other conditions are present, some of which are mental in their own right; not only must you have an intact and normally functioning nervous system, but you must also be normally alert and not engrossed in another task. Moreover, among the typical effects of pain are further mental events, such as a feeling of distress and a desire to be relieved of it. But this seems to involve us in a regress or circularity: To explain what a given mental state is, we need to refer to other mental states, and explaining these can only be expected to require reference to further mental states, and so on—a process that can go on in an unending regress, or loop back in a circle. Circularity threatens to arise at a more general level as well, in the functionalist conception of mentality itself: To be a mental state is to be an internal state serving as a causal intermediary between sensory inputs and mental states as causes, on the one hand, and behaviors and other mental states as effects, on the other. Viewed as an analysis of what it is to be a mental state, this is obviously circular. To circumvent the threatened circularity, machine functionalism exploits the concept of a Turing machine in characterizing mentality (Chapter 4). To achieve the same end, causal-theoretical functionalism attempts to use the entire network of causal relations involving all psychological states—in effect, a comprehensive psychological theory—to anchor the physical/behavioral definitions of individual mental properties.

The Ramsey-Lewis Method

Consider the following "pain theory," T:

(*T*) For any x, if x *suffers tissue damage* and **is normally alert,** x **is in pain**; if x *is awake*, x tends to be **normally alert**; if x **is in pain**, x *winces* and *groans* and **goes into a state of distress**; and if x **is not normally alert or is in distress**, x *tends to make more typing errors*.

We will assume that the statements that make up T describe lawful regularities (or causal relations). The italicized expressions are nonmental predicates designating observable physical, biological, and behavioral properties (or event and state kinds); the expressions in boldface are psychological expressions designating mental properties. T is of course much less than what we know or believe about pain and its relationship to other events and states, but let's assume that T encapsulates what is important about our knowledge of pain. What kind of "theory" T has to be if T is to serve as a basis of functional definitions of "pain" and other mental expressions appearing in it, is an important question that will be taken up in a later section. Here T serves chiefly as an example to illustrate the formal technique originally due to Frank Ramsey and adapted by David Lewis to formulate functional definitions of mental kinds.[1]

We first "Ramseify" T by "existentially generalizing" over each mental expression occurring in it, which yields this:

(T_R) There exist states M_1, M_2, and M_3 such that for any x, if x *suffers tissue damage* and is in M_1, x is in M_2; if x *is awake*, x tends to be in M_1; if x is in M_2, x *winces* and *groans* and goes into M_3; and if x is not in M_1 or is in M_3, x *tends to make more typing errors*.

It is evident that T logically implies T_R (essentially in the manner in which "x is in pain" logically implies "x is in some state or other"). Note that in contrast to T its Ramseification T_R contains no psychological expressions but only physical/behavioral expressions such as "suffers tissue damage," "winces," and so on. Where T "names names" for psychological states involved, T_R merely says that "some states," M_1, M_2, and M_3, are such that they are related among themselves and with physical/behavioral events as specified. Expressions like "M_1," "M_2," and the like are called "predicate variables," whereas expressions like "is normally alert" and "is in pain" are "predicate constants."

Ramsey, who invented the procedure now called "Ramseification," showed that, although T_R is weaker than T (since it is implied by, but does not imply, T), T_R is just as powerful as T, as far as physical/behavioral prediction goes; the two theories make exactly the same inferential connections between nonpsychological statements.[2] For example, both theories entail that if someone is awake and suffers tissue damage, she will probably wince and that if she doesn't groan, either she has not suffered tissue damage or is not awake. Since T_R is free of psychological expressions, it can serve as a basis for defining psychological expressions without circularity.

To make our sample definitions manageable, let us abbreviate T_R as "$\exists\ M_1, M_2, M_3\ [T(M_1, M_2, M_3)]$". (The symbol $\exists$, called the "existential quantifier," is read "there exist.") Consider, then:[3]

$$x \text{ is in pain} =_{\text{def.}} \exists\ M_1, M_2, M_3\ [T(M_1, M_2, M_3)\ \&\ x \text{ is in } M_2]$$

Note that "M_2" is the predicate variable that replaced "is in pain" in T. Similarly, we can define "is alert" and "is in distress" (although our little theory T was made up mainly to give us a reasonable definition of "pain"):

$$x \text{ is normally alert} =_{\text{def.}} \exists\ M_1, M_2, M_3\ [T(M_1, M_2, M_3)\ \&\ x \text{ is in } M_1]$$

$$x \text{ is in distress} =_{\text{def.}} \exists\ M_1, M_2, M_3\ [T(M_1, M_2, M_3)\ \&\ x \text{ is in } M_3]$$

Let's see what these definitions say. Consider the definition of "pain": it says that you are in pain just in case there are certain states M_1, M_2, and M_3 that are related among themselves and with such physical/behavioral states like tissue damage, wincing and groaning, and typing performance as specified in T_R *and* you are in M_2. It's clear that this definition gives us a concept of pain in terms of its causal/nomological relations and that among its causes and effects are other "mental states," although not specified as such but only as "some" states of the psychological subject, as well as physical and behavioral events and states. Notice also that there is a sense in which the three mental concepts are interdefined but without circularity; all the defined expressions are completely eliminable by the use of their definientia.

So the trick is to define psychological concepts en masse. Our T is a fragment of a theory, something made up to show how the method works; to generate more realistic functional definitions of psychological concepts, we will need a much more comprehensive underlying psychological theory encompassing many more psychological kinds and richer and more complex causal/nomological relationships to inputs and outputs. Such a theory will be analogous to a Turing machine that models a full psychology, and the resemblance of the present method to the approach of machine functionalism should be clear, at least in broad outlines. In fact, we can think of the Turing machine approach as a special case of the Ramsey-Lewis method, in which the psychological theory is presented in the form of the Turing machine table with the internal machine states, the qs, corresponding to the predicate variables, the Ms. We will discuss the relationship between the two approaches in more detail later in this chapter.

The Choice of an Underlying Psychological Theory

So what should the underlying psychological theory T be like if it is to yield, by the Ramsey-Lewis technique, appropriate functional definitions of psychological properties? To recover a psychological property from T_R by the Ramsey-Lewis method, the property must appear in T to begin with. So T must include all psychological properties. Moreover, T must carry enough information about each psychological property—about how it is nomologically connected with input conditions, behavior outputs, and other psychological properties—to circumscribe it closely enough to identify it as one that is distinct from other psychological properties. Given all this, there are two major possibilities to consider.

(1) *Commonsense psychology.* We might, with Lewis, consider using our shared commonsense psychological platitudes to form the underlying theory. The statements making up our "pain theory" T above are examples of such platitudes; there will be many more—about what makes people angry and how angry people behave, how wants and beliefs combine to generate further wants or actions, how perceptions cause beliefs and memories, how beliefs lead to further beliefs, and countless others. Few people will be able to articulate these principles of "folk psychology," but most mature people use them constantly in attributing mental states to people, making predictions about how people will behave, and understanding why people do what they do. We know these psychological regularities "tacitly," perhaps somewhat the way we "know" the language we speak without being able to state any explicit rules of grammar.

Without a suitably internalized commonsense psychology in this sense, we would hardly be able to manage our daily transactions with other people and enjoy the kind of communal life that we take for granted.[4] It is important that the vernacular psychology that serves as the underlying theory for functional definitions consists of *commonly known* generalizations. This is essential if we are to ensure that functional definitions yield the psychological concepts that all of us share. It is the shared funds of vernacular psychological knowledge that collectively define our commonsense mental concepts; there is no other conceivable source from which our mental concepts could magically have sprung.

(2) *Scientific psychology*. And yet we must remember that commonsense psychology is, well, only commonsensical: It is almost certainly incomplete and partial and likely contains serious errors. If mental concepts are to be defined in terms of causal/nomological relations, should we not use our best theory about how mental events and states are involved in causal/nomological relations among themselves and with physical and behavioral events and processes? Scientific psychology, after all, is in the business of investigating these regularities, and the best scientific psychology we could muster *is* the best overall theory about causal/nomological relations that involve mental events and states.

There are various problems and potential difficulties with either of these choices. Let us first note one important fact: If the underlying theory T is false, we cannot count on any mental concepts defined on its basis to have nonempty extensions—that is, to have instances to which they apply. For if T is false, its Ramseification, T_R, too, may well be false; in fact, if T has false nonmental consequences, T_R will be false as well (recall that T and T_R have the same physical/behavioral content). If T_R is false, every concept defined on its basis by the Ramsey-Lewis method will be vacuous—that is, it won't apply to anything. This is easy to see for our sample "pain theory" T above: Suppose this theory is false—in particular, suppose that what T says about the state of distress is false and that in fact there is no state that is related, in the way specified by T, with the other internal states and inputs and outputs. This will make our sample T_R false since there is nothing that can fill in for M_3. This would mean that "pain," as defined on the basis of T_R, can't be true of anything: Nothing satisfies the defining condition of "pain." The same goes for "normally alert" and "the state of distress." So if T, the underlying theory, is false, all mental concepts defined on the basis of T by the Ramsey-Lewis method are likely to turn out to have the same extension, namely, the empty extension!

This means that we had better make sure that the underlying theory is true. If our T is to yield our psychological concepts all at once, it is going to be a long conjunction of myriad psychological generalizations, and even a single false component will render the whole conjunction false. So we must face this question: What is going to be included in our T, and how certain can we be that T is true? Consider the case of scientific psychology: It is surely going to be a difficult, perhaps impossible, task to decide what parts of current scientific psychology are well enough established to be considered uncontroversially true. Psychology has been flourishing as a science for many decades now, but it is still comparatively young as a science, with its methodological foundations very much in dispute, and it is fair to say that it has yet to produce a robust enough common core of generally accepted laws and theories. In this respect, psychology has a long way to go before it reaches the status of, say, physics, chemistry, or even biology. These reflections lead to the following thought: On the Ramsey-Lewis method of defining psychological concepts, every dispute about underlying theory T is going to turn out to be a dispute about psychological concepts. This creates a seemingly paradoxical situation: If two psychologists should disagree about some psychological generalization that is part of theory T, which we could expect to be a very common occurrence, this would mean that they are using different sets of psychological concepts. But this would seem to imply that they could not really disagree, since the possibility of disagreement presupposes the sharing of the same concepts. How could I accept and you reject a given proposition unless we shared the concepts in terms of which the proposition is formulated?

Consider now the option of using commonsense psychology to generate psychological concepts. Can we be sure that all of our "psychological platitudes," or even any of them, are true? Consider the platitude, used as part of our "pain theory," that tissue damage causes pain in a normally alert person. It's clear that there are many exceptions to this regularity (that is why it is only a "platitude"): A normally alert person who is absorbed with another task will not feel pain when she suffers minor tissue damage. Truly massive tissue damage may well cause a person to go into a coma. And what is to count as "normally alert" in any case? Alert enough to experience pain when one is hurt? The platitudes of commonsense psychology serve us competently in our daily life, in anticipating the behavior of our fellow humans and making sense of it. But are we prepared to say that they are literally true? One reply to these considerations is to point out that we should think of our folk-psychological generalizations as hedged by generous escape clauses ("all other things being equal," "under normal conditions," "in the absence of interfering forces," etc.). Whether such weakened, noncommittal generalizations can introduce sufficiently restrictive constraints to yield well-defined psychological concepts is an open question.

In one respect, though, commonsense psychology seems to have an advantage over scientific psychology: its apparent greater stability. Theories and concepts of systematic psychology come and go; given what we know about the rise and fall of scientific theories, especially in the social and human domains, it is reasonable to expect that most of what we now consider our best theories in psychology will be abandoned and replaced sooner or later—probably sooner rather than later. Still, the rough regularities codified in commonsense psychology appear considerably more stable (perhaps because they are rough); can we really imagine giving up the virtual truism that a person's desire for something and her belief that doing a certain thing will secure it will tend to cause her to do it? This basic principle, which links belief and desire to action, is a central principle of commonsense psychology that underwrites the very possibility of making sense of why people do what they do. It's plausible to think that it was as central to the way the ancient Greeks or Chinese made sense of themselves and their fellow humans as it is to our own folk-psychological explanatory practices. Our shared folk-psychological heritage is what enables us to understand, and empathize with, the actions and emotions of the heroes and heroines in Greek tragedies and historical Chinese fiction. Indeed, if there were a culture, past or present, for whose members the central principles of our folk psychology, such as the one that relates belief and desire to action, did not hold true, its institutions and practices would hardly be intelligible to us, and its language would be untranslatable into our own. The source and nature of this relative permanence and commonality of folk-psychological platitudes are phenomena that are in need of explanation, but it seems clear that folk psychology enjoys a degree of stability and universality that eludes scientific psychology.

We should note, though, that vernacular psychology and scientific psychology need not be thought to be in competition with each other. One could say that vernacular psychology is the appropriate underlying theory for the functional definition of vernacular psychological concepts, while scientific psychology is the appropriate one for scientific psychological concepts. If you believe, however, that scientific psychology shows, or has shown, vernacular psychology to be seriously flawed (for example, that many of its central generalizations are in fact false[5]), you would have to reject the utility of the concepts generated from it by the Ramsey-Lewis method, for as we saw these concepts would then apply to nothing. One could still insist that even so, the Ramsey-Lewis method does yield appropriate definitions of these concepts, noting that it's just a fact about the concepts of a seriously flawed theory (e.g., the concepts of phlogiston, magnetic effluvium, and caloric fluid) that they have no applications in the real world. The difficulty with the Ramsey-Lewis method, however, is that vernacular psychology does not have to be "seriously flawed" to render its concepts empty; a single false psychological platitude will be enough to bankrupt the whole system.

One final point to note about our sample functionalist definitions is this: They can accommodate the phenomenon of multiple realization of mental states. This is easily seen. Suppose that the original psychology, T, is true of both humans and Martians, whose physiology, let us assume, is very different from ours (it is inorganic, say). Then T_R, too, would be true for both humans and Martians: It is only that the triple of physical states $<H_1, H_2, H_3>$, which realizes the three mental states <pain, normal alertness, distress> and which therefore satisfies T_R, is different from the triple $<I_1, I_2, I_3>$, which realizes the mental triple in Martians. But in either case there exists a triple of states, as T_R demands, which are connected in the specified ways. So when you are in H_1 you are in pain, and when Mork the Martian is in I_1, he is in pain, since each of you satisfies the functionalist definition of pain as stated.

Functionalism as Physicalism

Let us return to scientific psychology as the underlying theory to be Ramseified. As we noted, we want this theory to be a true theory. Now, there is another question about the truth of psychological theories that we need to discuss. Let us assume that psychological theories posit internal states to systematize correlations between sensory inputs and behavioral outputs. These internal states are the putative psychological states of the organism. Suppose now that each of two theories, T_1 and T_2, gives a correct systematization of inputs and outputs for a given psychological subject S but that each posits a different set of internal states. That is, T_1 and T_2 are both *behaviorally adequate* psychologies for S, but each attributes to S a different internal psychological mechanism that connects S's inputs to its outputs. Is there some further fact about these theories, or about S, that will determine which (if any) is the correct psychology of S and hence the theory to be Ramseified to yield causal-functional definitions of mental states?

If psychology is a truly autonomous special science, under no methodological, theoretical, or ontological constraints from any other science, we would have to say that the only ground for preferring one or the other of two behaviorally adequate theories consists in broad formal considerations of simplicity, calculational efficiency, ontological parsimony, and the like. There could be no further hard, factual reasons favoring one theory over the other. As you will recall, behaviorally adequate psychologies for subject S are analogous to Turing machines that are "behavioral descriptions" of S (see Chapter 4). You will also recall that according to machine functionalism, not every behavioral description of S is a correct psychology of S and that a correct psychology is one that is a machine description of S, namely, a Turing machine that is physically realized by S (relative to an appropriate input/output specification). This means that there are internal physical states of S that realize the internal machine states of the Turing machine in question—that is, there are in S "real" internal physical states that are (causally) related to each other and to sensory inputs and behavioral outputs as specified by the machine table of the Turing machine.

It is clear, then, that causal-theoretical functionalism, formulated on the Ramsey-Lewis model, does not as yet have a physicalist requirement built into it. According to machine functionalism as it was formulated in the preceding chapter, for subject S to be in any mental state, S must be a *physical realization* of an appropriate Turing machine; causal-theoretical functionalism as developed thus far in this chapter, in contrast, requires only that there be "internal states" of S that are connected among themselves and to inputs and outputs as specified by S's psychology, without saying anything about the nature of these internal states. What we saw in connection with machine functionalism is that it is the further physicalist requirement, to the effect that the states of S that realize the machine's internal states be physical states, which makes it possible to pick out S's correct psychology, that is, its machine description. In the same way, the only way to discriminate between behaviorally adequate psychologies is to explicitly introduce a similar physicalist requirement, perhaps through a statement like this:

(P) The states that the Ramseified psychological theory T_R affirms to exist are physical states; that is, the variables, $M_1, M_2, \ldots$ of T_R and in the definitions of specific mental states (see our sample definitions of "pain," etc.) range over physical states.

A functionalist who accepts (P)—that is, a physicalist functionalist—will interpret the ontology of our original, un-Ramseified psychological theory in an analogous way: The internal states posited by a correct psychological theory are physical states. These considerations have the following implications for psychology: Unless these physicalist constraints are introduced, there appears to be no way of discriminating among behaviorally adequate psychologies. Conversely, the fact that we do not think all behaviorally adequate psychologies are "correct" or "true" signifies our commitment to the reality of the internal, theoretical states posited by our psychologies, and the only way this psychological realism is cashed out is to regard them as internal physical states of the organism involved. This is equivalent in substance to the physical realization principle discussed in the preceding chapter, the thesis that all psychological states must be physically realized.

   This appears to reflect the actual research strategies in psychology and the methodological assumptions that underlie them: The correct psychological theory must, in addition to being behaviorally adequate, have "physical reality" in the sense that the psychological capacities, dispositions, and mechanisms it posits have a physical (presumably neurobiological) basis. The psychology that gives the most elegant and simplest systematization of human behavior may not be the true psychology, any more than the simplest artificial intelligence (AI) program (or Turing machine) that accomplishes a certain intelligent task (e.g., proving logic theorems) accurately reflects the way we humans actually perform it. The psychological theory that is formally the most elegant may not describe the way humans (or other organisms or systems involved) actually process their sensory inputs and produce behavioral outputs. There is no reason, either a priori or empirical, to believe that the mechanism that underlies our psychology, something that has evolved over many millions of years in the midst of myriad unpredictable natural forces, must be in accord with our notion of what is simple and elegant in a scientific theory. The psychological capacities and mechanisms posited by a true psychological theory must be real, and the only reality to which one can appeal is physical reality.

   Of course, the antiphysicalist would argue that psychological capacities and mechanisms have their own separate, nonphysical reality. But it is difficult to imagine what they could be like when divorced from any physical underpinnings; perhaps they are some ghostly mechanisms in a Cartesian mental substance. This may be a logically possible position, but, as we earlier noted, physicalism in a broad sense is the framework of our discussion.

Objections and Difficulties

   In this section we will review several points that are often thought to be major obstacles to the functionalist program. Some of the problematic features of machine functionalism discussed in the preceding chapter apply to functionalism generally, and we will not take them up again here.

Qualia

You will recall this question: What do all instances of pain have in common in virtue of which they are all pains? You will remember the functionalist's answer: their characteristic causal role—their typical causes (e.g., tissue damage, trauma) and effects ("pain behavior"). But isn't there a more obvious answer: What all instances of pain have in common by virtue of which they are all cases of pain is that they all *hurt*? Pains hurt, itches itch, tickles tickle: Can there by anything more obvious than that?

Sensations have characteristic *qualitative* features; these are also called "phenomenal" or "phenomenological" or "sensory" qualities—"qualia" for short. Seeing a ripe tomato has a certain distinctive sensory quality, a quality that is unmistakably different from the sensory quality of seeing a bunch of spinach leaves. We are familiar with the smell of a rose and of ammonia, can tell the sound of a chirping canary apart from that of a Chinese gong, and can imagine the feel of a cool, smooth marble tabletop as we run our hands over it. Our waking life is a continuous feast of qualia—colors, smells, sounds, and all the rest. When we are temporarily unable to taste or smell because of a medical condition so that eating favorite food is like chewing cardboard or sawdust, we become acutely aware of what is missing from our experience.

But by identifying sensory events with causal roles, functionalism appears to miss their qualitative aspects altogether. For it seems quite possible that causal roles and phenomenal qualities come apart, and the possibility of "qualia inversion" seems to prove it. It would seem that the following situation is perfectly conceivable: When you look at a ripe tomato, your color experience is like the color I experience when I look at a bunch of spinach, and vice versa. That is, your experience of red might be qualitatively like my experience of green, and your experience of green is like my experience of red. Such differences need not show up in any observable behavioral differences: We both say "red" when someone asks us what color ripe tomatoes are, and we are equally good at picking tomatoes out of a mound of lettuce leaves. In fact we can imagine, some have argued, that your color spectrum is systematically inverted with respect to mine, without this being manifested in any behavioral differences between us. Moreover, we can imagine a system, like an electromechanical robot, that is functionally—that is, in terms of inputs and outputs—equivalent to us but to which we have no good reason to attribute any qualitative experiences. This is called the "absent qualia problem."[6] If inverted qualia, or absent qualia, are possible in functionally equivalent systems, qualia are not capturable by functional definitions, and functionalism cannot be an account of all psychological states and properties. This is the qualia argument against functionalism.

Can the functionalist offer the following reply? On the functionalist account, mental states are realized by internal physical states of the psychological subject; so for humans the experience of red, as a mental state, is realized by a certain specific neural state. This means that you and I cannot differ in respect of the qualia we experience as long as we are in the same neural state; given that both you and I are in the same neural state, something that is in principle ascertainable by observation, either both of us experience red or neither does.

But this reply falls short for two reasons. First, even if it is correct as far as it goes, it does not address the qualia issue for physically different systems (say, you and the Martian) that realize the same psychology. Nothing it says makes qualia inversion impossible for you and the Martian; nor does it rule out the possibility that qualia might be absent from the Martian experience. Second, the reply assumes that qualia supervene on physical/neural states, but this supervenience assumption is what is at issue. However, the issue about qualia supervenience concerns the broader issues about physicalism and not specifically a problem with functionalism.[7]

This issue concerning qualia has been controversial, with some philosophers doubting the coherence of the very idea of inverted or absent qualia.[8] We will return to the issue of qualia in connection with the more general question of consciousness (Chapter 7).

The Cross-Wired Brain

Let us consider the following very simple, idealized model of how our mechanisms for pain and itch work: Each of us has a "pain box" and an "itch box" in our brains. We can think of the pain box as consisting of a bundle of neural fibers ("nociceptive neurons") somewhere in the brain that gets activated when we experience pain, and similarly for the itch box. When pain sensors in our tissues are stimulated, they send neural signals up the pain input channel to the pain box, which then gets activated and sends signals down its output channel to our motor systems to cause appropriate pain behavior (winces and groans). The itch mechanism works similarly: When a mosquito bites you, your itch receptors send signals up the itch input channel to your itch box and so on, finally culminating in your itch behavior (scratching).

Suppose now that a mad neurophysiologist rewires your brain by crisscrossing both the input and output channels of your pain and itch centers. That is, the signals from your pain receptors now go to your (former) itch box and the signals from this box now trigger your motor system to emit winces and groans; similarly, the signals from your itch receptors now go to your (former) pain box, which sends its signals to the motor system that causes scratching behavior. Even though your brain is cross-wired with respect to mine, we both realize the same functional psychology; we both scratch when bitten by mosquitoes and groan when our fingers are burned. From the functionalist point of view, we instantiate the same pain-itch psychology.

Suppose that we both step barefoot on an upright thumbtack; both of us give out a sharp shriek of pain and hobble to the nearest chair. I am in pain. But what about you? The functionalist says that you are in pain also. What makes a neural mechanism inside the brain a pain box is exactly the fact that it receives input from pain receptors and sends output to cause pain behavior. With the cross-wiring of your brain, your former itch box has now become your pain box, and when it is activated, you are in pain. At least that is what the functionalist conception of pain implies. But is this an acceptable consequence?

This is a version of the inverted qualia problem: Here the qualia that are inverted are pain and itch (or the painfulness of pains and the itchiness of itches), where the supposed inversion is made to happen through anatomical intervention. Many will feel a strong pull toward the thought that if your brain has been cross-wired as described, what you experience when you step on an upright thumbtack is an itch, not a pain, in spite of the fact that the input-output relation that you exhibit is one that is appropriate for pain. The appeal of this hypothesis is, at bottom, the appeal of the brain-state theory. We seem to have a strong, if not overwhelming, inclination to think that types of conscious experience, such as pain and itch, supervene on the *local* states and processes of the brain no matter how they are hooked up with the rest of the body or the external world, and that the qualitative character of our mental states is conceptually and causally independent of their causal roles in relation to sensory inputs and behavioral outputs. Such an assumption is implicit, for example, in the popular philosophical thought experiment with "the brain in a vat," in which it is supposed that a disembodied but live brain in a vat of liquid is maintained in a normal state of consciousness by being fed with appropriate electric signals generated by a supercomputer. The qualia we experience are causally dependent on the inputs: As our neural system is presently wired, pinpricks cause pains, not itches. But this is a contingent fact about our neural mechanism; it seems perfectly conceivable (even technically feasible at some point in the future) to reroute the causal chains involved so that pinpricks cause itches, not pains, and skin irritations cause pains, not itches, without disturbing the overall functional organization of our behavior.

Functional Properties, Disjunctive Properties, and Causal Powers

The functionalist claim is often expressed by assertions like "Mental states are causal roles" and "Mental properties are functional properties." We should get clear about the logic and ontology of such claims. Let us begin with an example: For something, S, to be in the state of pain (that is, for S to have, or instantiate, the property of being in pain) is, according to functionalism, for S to be in some state (or instantiate some property) with causal connections to appropriate inputs (e.g., tissue damage, trauma) and outputs ("pain behavior"). To bring out the ontological structure of such a claim more perspicuously, let us talk uniformly in terms of *properties* rather than *states*. We may then say: The property of being in pain is the property of having some property with a certain causal specification (that is, in terms of its causal relations to certain inputs and outputs). Thus, in general, we have the following canonical expression for all mental properties:

Mental property M is the property of having a property with causal specification H.

The functionalist as a rule believes in the multiple realizability of mental properties: For every mental property M, there will in general be many (in fact, indefinitely many) properties, $Q_1, Q_2, \ldots$, meeting the causal specification H, and anything will count as instantiating M just in case it instantiates one or another of these Qs. A property defined the way M is defined is often called a "second-order property" (since it "quantifies over" properties); in contrast, the Qs, their realizers, are called "first-order properties." (This of course is relative: The Qs may in turn be second-order with respect to another set of properties.) If M is pain, then, its first-order realizers will be physiological properties, at least for organisms, and we expect them to vary from one species to another.

This construal of mental properties as second-order properties, which is common among the functionalists, seems to create some puzzles. If M is the property of having some property meeting specification H, where $Q_1, Q_2, \ldots$, are exactly those properties satisfying H, it would seem that M is identical with the *disjunctive* property of having Q_1 or Q_2 or. ... For isn't it evident that to have M just *is* to have either Q_1 or Q_2 or . . . ? Now, most philosophers who believe in the multiple realizability of mental properties will deny that mental properties are disjunctive properties—disjunctions of their realizers—for the reason that the first-order realizing properties are extremely diverse and heterogeneous, so much so that their disjunctions cannot be considered well-behaved properties with the kind of systematic unity required for propertyhood. As you may recall, the rejection of such disjunctions as legitimate properties was at the heart of the multiple realization argument against the brain-state type physicalism. Functionalists have often touted the phenomenon of multiple realization as a basis for the claim that the properties studied by cognitive science are formal and abstract—abstracted from the material compositional details of the cognitive systems. What our considerations appear to show is that cognitive science properties so conceived threaten to turn out to be heterogeneous disjunctions of properties after all. And these disjunctions seem not to be suitable as nomological properties, properties in terms of which laws and causal explanations can be formulated. If this is right, it would disqualify mental properties, construed as second-order properties, as serious scientific properties.

But the functionalist may stand her ground, refusing to identify second-order properties with the disjunctions of their realizers, and she may reject disjunctive properties in general as bona fide properties, on the ground that from the fact that both P and Q are properties, it doesn't follow that there is a disjunctive property, that of having P or Q. From the fact that being round and being green are properties, it doesn't follow, some have argued, that there is such a property as being round or green; things that have this "property" (say, a red, round table and a green, square doormat) seem to have nothing in common in virtue of having it. However, we need not embroil ourselves in this dispute about disjunctive properties, for the issue here is independent of the question about disjunctive properties.

For there is another line of argument, based on broad causal considerations, that seems to lead to the same conclusion. It is a widely accepted assumption, or at least a desideratum, that mental properties have causal powers; that is, instantiating a mental property can, and does, cause other events to occur (that is, cause other properties to be instantiated). In fact, it is the founding premise of causal-theoretical functionalism. Unless mental properties have causal powers, there would be little point in worrying about them. The possibility of invoking mental events in explaining behavior, or any other events, would be lost if mental properties should turn out to be causally inert. But on the functionalist account of mental properties, just where does a mental property get its causal powers? In particular, what is the relationship between mental property M's causal powers and the causal powers of its realizers, the Qs?

It is difficult to think that M's causal powers could magically materialize on their own; it is much more plausible to think—it probably is the only plausible thing to think—that M's causal powers arise out of those of its realizers, the Qs. In fact, not only do they "arise out" of them, but the causal powers of any given instance of M must be the same as those of the particular Q_i that realizes M on that occasion. Carburetors[9] can have no causal powers beyond those of the physical structures that serve as one, and an individual carburetor's causal powers must be exactly those of the particular physical device in which it is realized (if for no other reason than the simple fact that this physical device *is* the carburetor). To believe that it could have excess causal powers beyond those of the physical realizer is to believe in magic: Where *could* they possibly come from?

Let us consider this issue in some detail by reference to machine functionalism. A psychological subject, on this version of functionalism, is a physical/biological system that realizes an appropriate Turing machine (relative to some input/output specification). And for it to be in mental state M is for it to be in a physical state P where P realizes M—that is, P is a physical state that is causally connected in appropriate ways with other internal physical states and physical inputs and outputs. In this situation, all that there is, when the system is in mental state M, is its physical state P; being in M has no excess reality over and beyond being in P, and whatever causal powers that accrue to the system in virtue of being in M must be those of state P. This instance of M can have no causal powers over and beyond those of P.

But we must remember that M is multiply realized—say, by P_1, P_2, and P_3 (the finitude assumption will make no difference). If "multiplicity" means anything here, these Ps must be importantly different, and we must suppose that the differences must largely consist in *causal* differences. That is, these physical realizers of M count as different physical kinds because they have different, perhaps extremely diverse, causal powers. For this reason, it is not possible to associate a unique set of causal powers with M; each instance of M, of course, is an instance of either P_1 or P_2 or P_3 and as such represents a unique set of causal powers, but M taken as a kind or property does not. In view of this, it is difficult to regard M as a property with any causal/nomological unity, and we have to think that M has little chance of entering into significant lawful relationships with other properties. All this makes the scientific usefulness of M highly problematic. Moreover, it has been suggested that kinds in science are individuated on the basis of causal powers; that is, to be recognized as a useful property in a scientific theory, a property must possess (or be) a determinate set of causal powers.[10] To put it another way, the resemblance that defines kinds in science is primarily *causal/nomological resemblance*: Things that are similar in causal powers and play similar roles in laws are classified as falling under the same kind. Such a principle of individuation for scientific kinds will disqualify M and other multiply realizable properties as scientific kinds. This surely makes the science of the Ms, namely, psychology, a dubious prospect.

These are somewhat surprising conclusions, not the least because most functionalists are ardent champions of psychology, and of cognitive science, as forming an irreducible and autonomous domain in relation to the underlying physical/biological sciences, and this arguably is the received view concerning the nature and status of cognitive science. But if our reasoning here is at all in the right direction, the conjunction of functionalism and the multiple realizability of the mental apparently leads to the conclusion that psychology is in danger of losing its unity and integrity as a science. On functionalism, then, mental kinds are in danger of fragmenting into their multiply diverse physical realizers and ending up without the kind of causal/nomological unity required of scientific kinds.[11] In the section to follow, we will look further into the nature of psychology under the functionalist conception of mentality.

Concepts and Properties: The Functionalist
Conception of Psychology

The attentive reader will have noticed that our discussion of functionalism thus far has sometimes spoken of "concepts" (as in "mental concepts," "functional concepts") and sometimes of "properties," "states," and "kinds." Putnam originally formulated functionalism as a theory about the meanings of psychological predicates (as the title of his first paper on functionalism, "Psychological Predicates," indicates). And as you may recall, the central claim of another important functionalist, Armstrong, was put forth as a thesis about mental concepts (as in "the concept of pain is the concept of a state typically caused by . . . and apt for causing . . ."). Concepts belong with such things as meanings, ideas, and predicates and are part of the conceptual-linguistic framework that we use to represent our beliefs about the world. Properties, states, and kinds are usually thought of as being "out there" in the world, constituting part of the world that we depict by the use of our conceptual-linguistic apparatus. Most important, they are what gives the world its causal structure, and if we have done our job right, the concepts of our best scientific theories will represent causally important properties of the natural world, and the laws of our theories will depict the causal regularities that hold in the world. But concepts and theories are our own creations; if there were no intelligent, language-using creatures, there would be no language, meanings, or concepts, but there would still be a world with its objects, their properties, and a network of causal relations. Roughly, that is the way we think of concepts, meanings, and the like on the one hand and properties, states, and kinds on the other.

Going back to the functionalist account of pain, we may take Armstrong's word at face value and think of it as an account of the concept of pain, or the meaning of the predicate "is in pain," not an account of the property of being in pain or pain as a state or event. Investigating the nature of pain and giving an account of it are properly jobs for the scientist (probably a physiological psychologist or neurophysiologist), not a philosopher; as philosophers, we can try to give an account of the pain concept, and the functionalist account may well be the right one—or at least close to being the right one. But it may well turn out that empirical scientific investigation shows, or will show, that no single unitary property or state answers to our concept of pain (as functionally conceived)—and that is the real implication of multiple realizability. Rather, there is a multiplicity of them, one property for humans, one property for octopuses, and still another for Martians. And neurophysiology is coming ever closer to giving an account of what this pain property is in humans and other higher organisms. This is in contrast to two other kinds of cases: (1) the concept of magnetism and (2) the concept of phlogiston. Scientific investigation has shown that there is a unique determinate property, or state, of being magnetic; there is a certain determinate microstate of metals (having to do with molecular alignments) that answers to our concept of magnetism. But the concept of phlogiston turned out to be an empty concept having no application to the real world; scientific inquiry showed that there was nothing in the real world answering to this concept. Similarly for the concepts of caloric fluid, magnetic effluvium, entelechy, witch, and all the rest that have fallen by the wayside. These were intelligible and in some ways interesting concepts; it's just that nature didn't cooperate—nothing in nature turned out to satisfy them.

The concept of pain and other concepts of sensations have fared better than the concept of phlogiston. Pain is a real state of organisms, but if its multiple realization is seriously taken, it turns out to be different states in different organisms. What binds these states together is a certain structural similarity of their causal positions in the networks of causal relations in which they are embedded, but their causal powers are exactly as dissimilar and heterogeneous as those of their physical realizers. So suppose that $<P_1, P_2, \ldots, P_n>$ is the n-tuple of physical states that realize a psychology, T, for humans and that a quite diverse n-tuple of physical states, $<Q_1, Q_2, \ldots, Q_n>$, realizes T for Martians. We are supposing, then, that humans and Martians realize the same psychology, T, which posits an n-tuple of mental states $<M_1, M_2, \ldots, M_n>$. What makes instances of P_i "the same mental state" as instances of Q_i, according to functionalism, is that they fill "the same causal role" in respect of other mental states and inputs and outputs. But the inputs and outputs of the Martians can be (and must be expected to be) quite different from human inputs and outputs. (Remember two things: First, realization is always relative to an input/output specification, and, second, inputs and outputs must be physical events and processes, not covertly psychological ones.) This means that "the same causal role" only means similarity of causal structure, not sameness of causal powers. That is, it isn't the case that when a human is in P_i and a Martian is in Q_i, they both respond in the same way to the same inputs and emit the same outputs; rather, it's only that a human in P_i, when input i is applied to him, emits output o just in case a Martian in Q_i emits output $m(o)$ when input $m(i)$ is applied to it, where $m(o)$ and $m(i)$ are respectively the Martian counterparts of i and o. But i and o must be presumed to be (at least they can be) physically very unlike $m(i)$ and $m(o)$, and P_i and Q_i presumably must have quite dissimilar causal powers to fill their assigned causal roles.

This makes cross-inductions between human psychology and Martian psychology extremely risky. Psychological regularities in humans, although they bear a formal structural similarity with those in Martians, are

subserved by a physical mechanism that is entirely different (we are supposing) from the physical mechanism that subserves Martian psychology,
and this means that the fact that a certain psychological regularity holds
for humans cannot by itself serve as evidence that a similar regularity
holds in the case of Martians or any other species of creatures with a com-
parably rich mentality. Moreover, the structural microexplanation of why
a given psychological regularity holds would be quite different for humans and Martians. Thus, in spite of their superficial similarity when
viewed top-down, human psychology and Martian psychology are independent of each other in causal/explanatory structure and sources of evidence and must be considered, to all intents and purposes, distinct scientific theories.

The moral of the foregoing can be summed up briefly. The idea that
psychology is *physically realized* is the idea that what does the pushing
and the pulling in the psychological realm is the underlying physical
structure, and the idea that psychology is *multiply realized* is the idea that
the physical mechanisms that do the pushing and the pulling can be, and
in fact often are, extremely heterogeneous in different psychological systems. The two ideas together lead to the consequence that the apparent
generality of psychology (or cognitive science) and its autonomy from the
underlying physical/biological sciences, which for many functionalists is
of the essence of psychology, may indeed be only apparent. It is not the
kind of generality that translates into generality of explanation or shared
evidence. The multiple realization of psychological properties implies
that psychology itself is multiply realized. And our considerations make
it highly dubious that one can both insist on an autonomous psychology
and want it to generate causal laws and causal explanations valid for all
psychological systems.

Further Readings

For statements of causal-theoretical functionalism, see David
Lewis's "Psychophysical and Theoretical Identifications" and David
Armstrong's "The Nature of Mind," both reprinted in *Readings in Philosophy of Psychology*, vol. 1, ed. Ned Block (Cambridge: Harvard University
Press, 1980). Sydney Shoemaker's "Some Varieties of Functionalism," in
his *Identity, Cause, and Mind* (Cambridge: Cambridge University Press,
1984), is also recommended.

Hilary Putnam, who was the first to articulate functionalism, has become one of its more severe critics; see his *Representation and Reality*
(Cambridge: MIT Press, 1988), especially chs. 5 and 6. For other criticisms
of functionalism, see Ned Block, "Troubles with Functionalism," in his
Readings in Philosophy of Psychology; Christopher S. Hill, *Sensations: A*

Defense of Type Materialism (Cambridge: Cambridge University Press, 1991), ch. 3; John R. Searle, *The Rediscovery of the Mind* (Cambridge: MIT Press, 1992). On the problem of qualia, see Chapter 7 and the suggested readings therein. On the causal powers of functional properties, see Ned Block, "Can the Mind Change the World?" in *Meaning and Method*, ed. George Boolos (Cambridge: Cambridge University Press, 1990).

On functionalism and the multiple realization argument, see Jaegwon Kim, "Multiple Realization and the Metaphysics of Reduction," in Jaegwon Kim, *Supervenience and Mind* (Cambridge: Cambridge University Press, 1993).

Notes

1. See David Lewis, "How to Define Theoretical Terms," in his *Philosophical Papers*, vol. 1 (New York: Oxford University Press, 1983), and "Psychophysical and Theoretical Identifications," reprinted in *Readings in Philosophy of Psychology*, vol. 1, ed. Ned Block (Cambridge: Harvard University Press, 1980).

2. Ramsey's original construction was in a more general setting of "theoretical" and "observational" terms rather than "psychological" and "physical/behavioral" terms. See Lewis, "Psychophysical and Theoretical Identifications," for details.

3. Here we follow Ned Block's method (rather than Lewis's) in his "Introduction: What Is Functionalism?" in Block, *Readings in Philosophy of Psychology*, vol. 1.

4. These remarks are generally in line with the "theory" theory of commonsense psychology. There has recently appeared a competing account, the "simulation" theory, according to which our use of commonsense psychology is not a matter of possessing a theory and applying its laws and generalization but our "simulating" the behavior of others, using ourselves as models. See Robert M. Gordon, "Folk Psychology as Simulation," *Mind and Language* 1 (1986):159–171; Alvin I. Goldman, "Interpretation Psychologized," reprinted in Goldman, *Liaisons* (Cambridge: MIT Press, 1992). This approach has not yet been worked out in sufficient detail to be examined for its implications for functionalism, although it is clear that it will create prima facie difficulties for the use of commonsense psychology as an underlying theory for the Ramsey-Lewis definitions of mental concepts.

5. Although it is difficult to imagine how the belief-desire-action principle *could* be shown to be empirically false. It is important to keep in mind that not all principles of vernacular psychology need to be thought to enjoy the same status, epistemic or otherwise.

6. See Ned Block, "Troubles with Functionalism," in Block, *Readings in Philosophy of Psychology*, vol. 1.

7. This issue is discussed elsewhere in this book; see, for example, Chapters 3 and 7.

8. See Sydney Shoemaker, "Functionalism and Qualia," in his *Identity, Cause, and Mind* (Cambridge: Cambridge University Press, 1984); Ned Block, "Are Absent Qualia Impossible?" *Philosophical Review* 89 (1980):257–274.

9. Being a carburetor is a functional property defined by a job description ("mixer of air and gasoline vapors" or some such), and a variety of physical devices can serve this purpose.

10. See, for example, J.A. Fodor, *Psychosemantics* (Cambridge: MIT Press, 1987), ch. 2.

11. For more details, see Jaegwon Kim, "Multiple Realization and the Metaphysics of Reduction," in Kim, *Supervenience and Mind* (Cambridge: Cambridge University Press, 1993).

6
Mental Causation

Causal relations involving mental events are among the familiar facts of everyday experience. My fingers are busily dancing about on the computer keyboard because I want to write about mental causation. The word "because" connecting my want and the movements of my fingers is naturally taken to express a causal connection: My want causes my fingers to move. And we can causally explain the movements of my fingers—for example, why they hit the keys "m," "e," "n," "t," "a," and "l" in succession—by invoking my desire to type the word "mental." This is a case of *mental-to-physical* causation. There are two other kinds of causal relations in which mental events figure: *physical-to-mental* and *mental-to-mental* causation. Sensations are among the familiar examples that involve causal relations of the physical-to-mental kind: Severe burns cause pains, irradiations of the retinas cause visual sensations, and food poisoning can cause sensations of nausea. Instances of mental-to-mental causation are equally familiar. We often believe one thing (say, that we had better take an umbrella to work) because we believe another thing (say, that it is going to rain later today). This is a case in which a belief causes another belief. The belief that you have won a fellowship to graduate school may cause a feeling of joy and satisfaction, which may in turn cause you to want to call your parents. On a grander scale, it is human knowledge and desire that built the pyramids of Egypt and the Great Wall of China; produced the glorious music, literature, and other artworks of our forebears; built our great cities; detonated nuclear bombs; and caused holes in the ozone layer. Our mental events are intricately woven into the complex mosaic of causal relations of our world. At least that is the way things seem.

But how is it possible for the mind to cause a change in a material body? Through what mechanism or process does a mental event manage to initiate, or insert itself into, a causal chain of physical events? How is it

possible that a chain of physical and biological events and processes ter-
minates, suddenly and magically, in a full-blown conscious experience,
with its vivid colors, smells, and sounds? Think of your total sensory experience right now—visual, tactual, auditory, olfactory, and so on: How is
it possible for all this to arise out of the electrochemical processes in the
gray matter of your brain?

Agency and Mental Causation

An agent is someone with the capacity to perform *actions*. In
this sense, we are all agents: We do such things as turning on the stove,
heating water in the kettle, making coffee, and entertaining a friend.
These are actions that we perform; they are unlike "mere happenings"
that involve us, like sweating on a hot day in the sun, shuddering because
of the cold, and growing hair and fingernails.

What do these actions involve? Consider my heating water in the kettle. This must at least involve my *causing* the water in the kettle to rise in
temperature. It probably involves more than that: If I ask you to heat the
stew pot and you then inadvertently turn on the wrong burner and heat
the water in the kettle, it would be correct to say that I caused the temperature of the water to rise but incorrect (or at least odd) to say that I heated
the water. In any case, why did I heat the water? I did so to make coffee.
That is, I *wanted* to make coffee and *believed* that I needed hot water to
make coffee (and, to be boringly detailed, I believed that by heating the
water in the kettle I could get hot water). Our beliefs and desires guide
our actions, and we appeal to them to explain why we do what we do.

We may consider the following schema as the fundamental principle
that connects desire, belief, and action:

[The desire-belief-action principle (DBA)] If *S* desires something and
believes that doing *A* will help secure it, *S* will do *A*.

As stated, DBA is too strong. For one thing, we often choose not to act on
our desires, and sometimes we change or get rid of them when we realize
that pursuing them is too costly, leading to consequences that we do not
want. For example, you wake up in the middle of the night and want a
glass of milk, but the thought of getting out of bed in the chilly winter
night talks you out of it. For another, even when we try to act on our desires and relevant beliefs about the means needed to realize them, we
may find ourselves physically incapable of doing *A*; it may be that when
you have finally overcome your aversion to getting out of your bed, you
find yourself chained to your bed! To save DBA, various things can be
done to weaken it; we can add further conditions to the antecedent of
DBA (e.g., the condition that there are no other conflicting desires) or

weaken the consequent (e.g., by turning it into a probability or tendency statement¹ or adding the all-purpose hedge "ceteris paribus").

The belief-desire pair that is related to an action in accordance with DBA can be called a "reason" for that action. What the exceptions to DBA we have just considered show is that an agent may have a reason, a "good" reason, to do something but fail to do it. Sometimes there may be more than one belief-desire pair that is related to a given action, as specified by DBA: In addition to your desire for a glass of milk, you heard a suspicious noise from downstairs and wanted to check it out. Let us suppose that you finally did get out of your bed to venture down the stairway. Why did you do that? What explains it? It is possible that you went downstairs because you thought you really ought to check out the noise and that your desire for a drink of milk had no role in it. If so, it is your desire to check the source of the noise, not your desire for milk, that explains why you went downstairs in the middle of the night. It would be correct for you to say, "I went downstairs because I wanted to check out the noise" but incorrect to say, "I went downstairs because I wanted a glass of milk." We can also put the point this way: Your desire to check out the noise and your desire for milk were both *reasons for* going downstairs, but the first, not the second, was the *reason for which* you did what you did, namely, a *motivating reason*. And it is "reason for which," not mere "reason for," that explains the associated action. But what precisely is the difference between them? That is, what distinguishes explanatory reasons from nonexplanatory reasons?

An influential answer defended by Donald Davidson² is the simple thesis that a reason for which an action is done is one that *causes* it. That is, what makes a reason for an action an explanatory reason is its role in the causation of that action. Thus, on Davidson's view, the crucial difference between my desire to check out the noise and my desire for a glass of milk lies in the fact that the former, not the latter, caused my action of going downstairs. This makes explanation of action by reasons, namely, "rationalizing explanation," a species of causal explanation: Reasons explain actions in virtue of being their causes.

If this is correct, it follows that agency is possible only if mental causation is possible. For an agent is someone who is able to act for reasons and whose actions can be explained and evaluated in terms of the reasons for which he acted. And this entails that reasons, that is, mental states like beliefs, desires, and emotions, must be able to cause us to do what we do. Since what we do includes bodily motions, this means that agency—at least human agency—presupposes the possibility of mental-to-physical causation. Somehow your beliefs and desires must cause your limbs to move in appropriate ways so that in half a minute you find your whole body displaced from your bedroom to the kitchen downstairs.

Mental Causation, Mental Realism, Epiphenomenalism

As already noted, sensations involve the causation of mental events by physical processes. In fact, the very idea of perceiving something—say, seeing a tree—involves the idea that the object seen is a cause of an appropriate perceptual experience. For suppose that there is a tree in front of you and that you are having a visual experience of the sort you would be having if your retinas were stimulated by the light rays reflected by the tree. But you would not be seeing *this* tree if there were a holographic image of a tree interposed between you and the tree that was exactly as the tree would look from where you stand. You would be seeing the holographic image of a tree, not the real tree. This difference, too, seems to be a causal one: Your perceptual experience is caused by the holographic image, not by the tree.

Perception is our only window to the world; without it we could know nothing about what goes on around us. If, therefore, perception necessarily involves mental causation, there could be no knowledge of the world without mental causation. Moreover, a significant part of our knowledge of the world is based on experimentation, not mere observation. Experimentation differs from passive observation in that it requires our active intervention in the natural course of events; we carefully design and deliberately set up the experimental conditions and then observe the outcome. This means that experimentation presupposes mental-to-physical causation and is impossible without it. Much of our knowledge of causal relations—in general, knowledge of what happens under what conditions—is based on experimentation, and such knowledge is crucial not only as a basis for our theoretical knowledge of the world but also as a guide to our practical decisionmaking. We must conclude, then, that if the mind cannot causally affect physical events and processes, neither practical knowledge required to inform our decisions nor theoretical knowledge that yields an understanding of the world is likely to be available.

Mental-to-mental causation, too, is involved in human knowledge. Consider the process of inferring one proposition from another. Suppose someone asks you, "Is the number of planets odd or even?" If you are like most people, you would probably proceed as follows: "Well, how many planets are there? Nine, and nine is an odd number. So there are an odd number of planets." You have just inferred the proposition that there are an odd number of planets from the proposition that there are nine planets and have accepted the former on the basis of this inference. This process evidently involves mental causation: Your belief that the number of planets is odd was caused by your belief that there are nine planets. Inference is one way in which beliefs can generate other beliefs. A brief reflection makes it evident that most of our beliefs are generated by other beliefs we hold, and "generation" here could only mean causal generation. It follows, then, that all three types of mental causation—mental-to-physical,

physical-to-mental, and mental-to-mental—are implicated in the possibility of human knowledge.

Epiphenomenalism is the thesis that although all mental events are caused by physical events, mental events are only "epiphenomena," that is, events without powers to cause any other event. Mental events are effects of physical processes, but they do not in turn cause anything else, being powerless to affect physical events or even other mental events; they are the absolute termini of causal chains. Think of a moving car and the series of shadows it casts as it moves: The shadows are caused by the moving car but have no effect on the car's motion. Nor are the shadows at different instants causally connected: The car shadow at a given instant *t* is caused not by the car shadow an instant earlier but by the car itself at *t*. A person who can only observe the moving shadows but not the car may very well be led to impute causal relations between the successive shadows, but he would be mistaken. Similarly, you may think that the pain in your tooth has caused your desire to take aspirin, but that, according to epiphenomenalism, would be a mistake: Your toothache and your desire for aspirin are both caused by brain events, which themselves may be causally connected, but the two mental events are not related as cause to effect any more than two successive car shadows. The apparent regularities that we observe in mental events, the epiphenomenalist will argue, do not represent genuine causal connections; like the regularities characterizing the moving shadows of a car or the successive symptoms of a disease, they are merely reflections of the real causal processes at a more fundamental level.

These are the claims of epiphenomenalism. Few philosophers have been self-professed epiphenomenalists, although there are those whose views appear to lead to such a position. We are more likely to find epiphenomenalist thinking among the scientists who do research in neurophysiology. They are apt to treat mentality, especially consciousness, as a mere shadow or afterglow thrown off by the complex neural processes going on in the brain; these physical/biological processes are what at bottom do all the pushing and pulling to keep the human organism properly functioning. How should we respond to this epiphenomenalist stance on the status of mind? Samuel Alexander, a noted emergentist during the early twentieth century, commented on epiphenomenalism with the following biting remark:

> [Epiphenomenalism] supposes something to exist in nature which has nothing to do, no purpose to serve, a species of noblesse which depends on the work of its inferiors, but is kept for show and might as well, and undoubtedly would in time, be abolished.[3]

Alexander is saying that if epiphenomenalism is true, mentality has no work to do and hence is entirely useless, and this renders it pointless to recognize it as something real. Our beliefs and desires would have no role in causing our decisions and actions and would be powerless to explain them; our perception and knowledge would have nothing to do with our artistic creations and technological inventions. *Being real and having causal powers go hand in hand; to deprive the mental of causal potency is in effect to deprive it of its reality.*

It is important to see that what Alexander has said is not an *argument against* epiphenomenalism: It only points out, in a stark and forceful way, what accepting epiphenomenalism means. We should also remind ourselves that the epiphenomenalist does not reject the reality of mental causation altogether; she only denies mind-to-body and mind-to-mind causation, not body-to-mind causation. In this sense, she gives the mental a well-defined place in the causal structure of the world; the mental, for her, is causally integrated into the world. But one who denies mental causation *tout court* treats the mental as both causeless and effectless. To a person holding such a view, mental events are in total causal isolation from the rest of the world, even from other mental events; each mental event is a solitary island unto itself, with no connection to anything else. Its existence would be entirely inexplicable since it has no cause, and it would make no difference to anything else since it has no effect. It would be a mystery how the existence of such things could be known to us. As Alexander declares, they could just as well be "abolished"—that is, regarded as nonexistent. On this line of reasoning, therefore, the reality of mental causation is equivalent to the reality of the mental itself.

Cartesian Interactionism

So why not grant the mind full causal powers, among them the power to influence bodily processes? This would save the reality of the mental and recognize what after all is so manifestly evident to common sense. And that is just what Descartes tried to do with his thesis that minds and bodies, even though they are substances of very different sorts, are in intimate causal commerce with each other. In fact, he thought that there was a specific site within the human body where the mind was in direct causal interaction with the body; in the *Sixth Meditation* he wrote:

> The mind is not immediately affected by all parts of the body, but only by the brain, or perhaps just by one small part of the brain. . . . Every time this part of the brain is in a given state, it presents the same signals to the mind, even though the other parts of the body may be in a different condition at the time. . . . For example, when the nerves in the foot are set in motion in a violent and unusual manner, this motion, by way of the spinal cord, reaches the inner parts of the brain, and there gives the mind its signal for having a certain sensation, namely the sensation of a pain as occurring in the foot. This stimulates the mind to do its best to get rid of the cause of the pain, which it takes to be harmful to the foot.[4]

In the *Passions of the Soul*, Descartes identified the pineal gland as the "seat of the soul," the locus of direct mind-body interaction. This gland, Descartes maintained, could be moved directly by the soul, thereby moving the "animal spirits," which would then transmit the causal influence to appropriate parts of the body:

> And the activity of the soul consists entirely in the fact that simply by willing something it brings it about that the little gland to which it is closely joined moves in the manner required to produce the effect corresponding to this desire.[5]

In the case of physical-to-mental causation, this process is reversed: Disturbances in the animal spirits surrounding the pineal gland make the gland move, which in turn causes the mind to experience appropriate sensations and perceptions. For Descartes, then, each of us is a "union" or "intermingling" of a mind and a body in direct causal interaction.

Few will quarrel with Descartes's acknowledgment of the reality of mind-body interaction or his wish to give an account of it. The only question, one that has troubled many thoughtful readers of Descartes for centuries, is how such interaction is possible—how the "mingling" or "union" of an immaterial soul with some bodily organ is possible—within the framework of Descartes's substance dualism. Descartes was immediately challenged by Pierre Gassendi, among others:

> But you still have to explain how that "joining and, as it were, intermingling" . . . can apply to you if you are incorporeal, unextended and indivisible. If you are no larger than a point, how are you joined to the entire body, which is so large? How can you be joined even to the brain, or a tiny part of it, since . . . no matter how small it is, it still has size or extension? If you wholly lack parts, how are you intermingled . . . with the particles of this region? For there can be no intermingling between things unless the parts of each of them can be intermingled. And if you are something separate, how are you compounded with matter so as to make up a unity?[6]

The Cartesian soul has no extension in space: Either it is entirely outside space, or, at best, it occupies a geometric point in space. How, Gassendi is asking, can such a thing "mingle" or "unite" with a material object, something with countless spatial parts? Could the two things mingle in the sense that they causally interact? But as Princess Elizabeth of Bohemia wondered, how can "man's soul, being only a thinking substance, . . . determine animal spirits so as to cause voluntary actions"?[7]

You want to raise your arm, and your arm goes up. Presumably, nerve impulses reaching appropriate muscles in your arm made those muscles contract, and that's how the arm went up. And these nerve signals presumably originated in the activation of certain neurons in your brain. What caused these neurons to fire? We now have a quite detailed understanding of the process that leads to the firing of a neuron, in terms of complex electrochemical processes involving ions in the fluid inside and outside a neuron, differences in voltage across cell membranes, and so forth. All in all we seem to have a pretty good picture of the processes at this microlevel on the basis of the known laws of physics, chemistry, and biology. If the immaterial mind is going to cause a neuron to emit a signal (or prevent it from doing so), it must somehow intervene in these electrochemical processes. But how could that happen? At the very interface between the mental and the physical where direct and unmediated mind-body interaction takes place, the nonphysical mind must somehow influence the state of some molecules, perhaps by electrically charging them or nudging them this way or that way. Is this really conceivable? Surely the working neuroscientist does not believe that to have a complete understanding of these complex processes she needs to include in her account the workings of immaterial souls and how they influence the molecular processes involved. Perhaps we will never fully understand all the details of these processes, but our ignorance surely must be ignorance of further physical/biological facts, not of some facts about the operations of an immaterial soul. Even if the idea of a soul's influencing the motion of a molecule (let alone a whole pineal gland) were coherent, the postulation of such a causal agent would seem neither necessary nor helpful in understanding why and how our limbs move.

Psychophysical Laws and "Anomalous Monism"

The expulsion of minds as substantival entities perhaps makes it easier to understand the possibility of mental causation. For we would no longer have to contend with the question how immaterial souls with no physical characteristics—no bulk, no mass, no energy, no electric charge, perhaps no location in space—could causally influence, and be influenced by, material objects and processes. As we saw, few people now regard minds as substances of a special nonphysical sort, and mental events and processes are now standardly viewed as occurring in certain complex physical systems like biological organisms, not immaterial minds. The problem of mental causation, therefore, is now formulated in terms of two kinds of events, mental and physical, not in terms of two types of substances: How is it possible for a mental event to cause, or to be caused by, a physical event? Or in terms of properties: How is it possible for an instantiation of a mental property to cause a physical property to be instantiated, or vice versa?

But why is this supposed to be a "problem"? We don't usually think that there is a special philosophical problem about, say, chemical events causally influencing biological processes or a nation's economic and political conditions causally influencing each other. So what is it about mentality and physicality that makes causal relations between them a philosophical problem? For substance dualism, it is, at bottom, the extreme heterogeneity of minds and bodies that makes causal relations between them prima facie problematic. Given that mental substances have now been expunged, aren't we home free with mental causation? The answer is that certain other assumptions that demand our respect present prima facie obstacles to the possibility of mental causation.

One such assumption centers on the question whether there are *laws connecting mental phenomena with physical phenomena* that are needed to underwrite causal connections between them. Donald Davidson's celebrated "anomalism of the mental" states that there can be no such laws.[8] A principle connecting laws and causation that is widely, if not universally, accepted is this: *Causally connected events must instantiate a law.* If heating a metallic rod causes its length to increase, there must be a general law connecting events of the first type and events of the second type; that is, there must be a law stating that the heating of a metallic rod is generally followed by an increase in its length. But if causal connections require laws and there are no laws connecting mental events with physical events, it would seem to follow that there could be no mental-physical causation. This line of reasoning will be examined in more detail below. But is there any reason to doubt the existence of laws connecting mental and physical phenomena?

In earlier chapters we often assumed that there are lawlike connections between mental and physical events; you surely recall the stock example of pains and C-fiber excitations. The psychoneural identity theory, as we saw, assumes that each type of mental event is lawfully correlated with a type of physical event. Talk of "physical realization" of mental events, too, presupposes that there are lawlike connections between a mental event of a given kind and its diverse physical realizers; for a physical realizer of a mental event must at least be lawfully sufficient for the occurrence of that mental event. Now, Davidson's claim about the nonexistence of psychophysical laws is restricted to intentional mental events and states ("propositional attitudes"), those with propositional content, like beliefs, desires, and intentions, and doesn't touch nonintentional mental events and states, like pains, itches, and mental images. Why does Davidson think that there can be no laws connecting, say, beliefs with physical events? Doesn't—in fact, shouldn't—every mental event have a neural substrate, that is, a neural state that, as a matter of law, suffices for its occurrence?

Before we take a look at Davidson's argument, let us consider some examples. Take the belief that it's inappropriate for the president to get a $200 haircut. How reasonable is it to expect to find a neural substrate for this belief? Is it at all plausible to think that all and only people who have this belief share a certain specific neural state? It makes perfectly good sense to try to find neural correlates for pains, hunger sensations, visual images, and the like, but somehow it doesn't seem to make much sense to look for the neural correlates of mental states like our sample belief or for such things as your sudden realization that your philosophy paper is due tomorrow, your hope that airfares to California will be lower after Christmas, and the like. Is it just that these mental states are so complex that it is very difficult, perhaps impossible, for us to discover their neural bases? Or is it the case that they are simply not the sort of state for which neural correlates could exist and that it makes no sense to look for them?

There is another line of consideration for being skeptical about psychophysical laws, and this has to do with the way we individuate mental states. If you are like most people, you don't know the difference between birches and beeches—that is, when you are confronted by a birch (or a beech), you cannot tell whether it is a birch or a beech. But you've heard your gardener talk about the birches in your backyard, and you believe what he says. And you are apt to utter sentences like "The birches in my yard are pretty in the fall," "Birches are nice trees to have if you have a large yard," and the like. On the basis of these utterances, we may attribute to you the belief that there are birches in your backyard, that birches are pretty in the fall, and so on. Now imagine the following counterfactual situation: Everything is identical with the story that was just told except that in this contrary-to-fact situation the words "birch" and "beech" have exchanged their meanings. That is, in the counterfactual situation, "birch" means beech, and "beech" means birch; and when your gardener, in the counterfactual situation, talks to you about the trees he calls "birches," he is talking about beeches. Now, when you utter sentences like "The birches in my yard are pretty in the fall" in this counterfactual situation, we must attribute to you not the belief that the birches in your yard are pretty in the fall but rather the belief that the beeches in your yard are pretty in the fall. That is so not because you in the counterfactual world are different from you in the actual world in any intrinsic respect but because in that other world the linguistic practice in your community is different. Since "birch" means beech in that world, when you utter the word "birch" in that world, we must take you to be talking about beeches, even though nothing about you is different. (Remember that you learned to use the word "birch" from your gardener.) What all this means is that what content a given belief of yours has—for example, whether your belief is about beeches or birches—depends, at least in part but crucially, on external factors, conditions outside your skin—in this instance the linguistic practices of the community of which you are a member. That is, belief content is individuated externally, not purely internally. This in turn implies that it will not be possible to find regular, lawlike relationships between your brain states, which are entirely internal to your body, on the one hand, and beliefs as individuated by their content, on the other. If this is the case, it would be fruitless to try to discover neural correlates for beliefs (for further discussion of content, see Chapter 8).

These considerations are not intended as conclusive arguments for the impossibility of psychophysical laws but only to dispel, or at least weaken, the strong presumption we are apt to hold that there must "obviously" be such laws since mentality depends on what goes on in the brain. It is now time to turn to Davidson's famous but difficult argument against psychophysical laws, which will be presented here only in outline; for a full appreciation of the argument, you are urged to consult the original sources.[9]

A crucial premise of Davidson's argument is the thesis that the ascription of intentional states, like beliefs and desires, is regulated by certain *principles of rationality*, principles to ensure that the total set of such states ascribed to a subject will be as rational and coherent as possible. This is why, for example, we refrain from attributing to a person flatly and obviously contradictory beliefs—even when the sentences uttered have the surface logical form of a contradiction. When someone replies, "Well, I do and don't" when asked, "Do you like Ross Perot?" we do not take her to be expressing a literally contradictory belief, the belief that she both likes and does not like Perot; rather, we take her to be saying something like "I like some aspects of Perot (say, his economic agenda), but I don't like certain other aspects (say, his international policy)." If she were to insist: "No, I don't mean that; I really both do and don't like Perot, period," we wouldn't know what to make of her utterance; perhaps her "and" doesn't mean what the English "and" means. We cast about for some consistent interpretation of her meaning because an interpreter of a person's speech and mental states is under the mandate that an acceptable interpretation must make her come out with a consistent and reasonably coherent set of beliefs—as coherent and rational as evidence permits. When we fail to come up with a consistent interpretation, we are likely to blame our unsuccessful interpretive efforts rather than accuse our subject of harboring explicitly inconsistent beliefs. We also attribute to a subject beliefs that are obvious logical consequences of beliefs already attributed to him. For example, if we have ascribed to a person the belief that Boston is less than 50 miles from Providence, we would, and should, ascribe to him the belief that Boston is less than 60 miles from Providence, the belief that Boston is less than 70 miles from Providence, and countless others. We do not need independent evidence for these further belief attributions; if we are not prepared to attribute any one of these further beliefs, we should be prepared to withdraw the original belief attribution as well. Our concept of belief does not allow us to say that someone believes that Boston is within 50 miles of Providence but doesn't believe that it is within 60 miles of Providence—unless we are able to give an intelligible explanation of how this could happen in the particular case involved. This principle, which requires that the set of beliefs be "closed" under obvious logical entailment, goes beyond the simple requirement of consistency in a person's belief system; it requires the belief system to be coherent as a whole—it must in some sense hang together, without unexplained gaps. In any case, Davidson's thesis is that the requirement of rationality and coherence[10] is of the essence of the mental—that is, it is constitutive of the mental in the sense that it is exactly what makes the mental mental.

But it is clear that the physical domain is subject to no such requirement; as Davidson says, the principle of rationality and coherence has "no echo" in physical theory. But suppose that we have laws connecting beliefs with brain states; in particular, suppose we have laws that specify a neural substrate for each of our beliefs—a series of laws of the form "N occurs to a person at t if and only if B occurs to that person at t," where N is a neural state and B is a belief with a particular content (e.g., the belief that there are birches in your yard). If such laws were available, we could attribute beliefs to a subject, *one by one*, independently of the constraints of the rationality principle. For in order to determine whether she has a certain belief B, all we need to do would be to ascertain whether B's neural substrate N is present in her; there would be no need to check whether this belief makes sense in the context of her other beliefs or even what other beliefs she has. In short, we could read her beliefs off her brain. Thus, neurophysiology would preempt the rationality principle, and the practice of belief attribution would no longer need to be regulated by the rationality principle. By being connected by law with neural state N, belief B becomes hostage to the constraints of physical theory. On Davidson's view, as we saw, the rationality principle is constitutive of mentality, and beliefs that have escaped its jurisdiction can no longer be considered mental states. If, therefore, belief is to retain its identity and integrity as a mental phenomenon, its attribution must be regulated by the rationality principle and hence cannot be connected by law to a physical substrate.

Let us assume that Davidson has made a plausible case for the impossibility of psychophysical laws (we may call his thesis "psychophysical anomalism") so that it is worthwhile to explore its consequences. One question that was raised earlier is whether it might make mental causation impossible. Here the argument could go like this: Causal relations require laws, and this means that causal relations between mental events and physical events require psychophysical laws, laws connecting mental and physical events. But psychophysical anomalism holds that there can be no such laws, whence it follows that there can be no causal relations

between mental and physical phenomena. Davidson, however, is a believer in mental causation; he explicitly holds that mental events sometimes cause, and are caused by, physical events. This means that
Davidson must reject the argument just sketched that attempts to derive
the nonexistence of mental causation from the nonexistence of psychophysical laws. How could he do that?

What Davidson disputes in this argument is its first step, namely, the
inference from the premise that *causation requires laws* to the conclusion
that *psychophysical causation requires psychophysical laws.* Let's look into this
in some detail. To begin, what is it for one event c to cause another event
e? This holds, on Davidson's view, only if the two events instantiate a law,
in the following sense: c falls under a certain event kind (or description) F,
e falls under an event kind G, and there is a law connecting events of kind
F with events of kind G (as cause to effect). This is in essence the widely
accepted nomological model of causation: Causal connections must be
supported, or subsumed, by laws. Suppose, then, that a particular mental
event, m, causes a physical event, p. This means, according to the nomological conception of causation, that for some event kinds, C and E, m falls
under C and p falls under E, and there is a law that connects events of
kind C with events of kind E. This makes it evident that laws connect individual events only as they fall under kinds (or descriptions). Thus,
when psychophysical anomalism says that there are no psychophysical
laws, what it says is that there are no laws connecting mental *kinds* with
physical *kinds.* So what follows is only that *if mental event m causes physical
event p, the kinds, C and E, under which m and p respectively fall and that are
connected by law, must both be physical kinds.* In particular, C, under which
mental event m falls, cannot be a mental kind or description; it must be a
physical one. This means that m is a physical event! For an event is mental
or physical according to whether it falls under a mental kind or a physical
kind. But this "or" is not exclusive; m, being a mental event, must fall
under a mental kind, but that does not prevent it from falling under a
physical kind as well. This argument applies to all mental events that are
causally related to physical events, and there appears to be no reason not
to think that every mental event has some causal connection, directly or
via a chain of other events, with a physical event. All such events, on
Davidson's argument, are physical events.[11]

That is Davidson's "anomalous monism." It's a monism because it
claims that all events, mental events included, are physical events (you
will recall this as "token physicalism"). Moreover, it is physical monism
that does not require psychophysical laws; in fact, as we just saw, it is
based on the nonexistence of such laws. Davidson's world, then, looks
like this: It consists exclusively of physical objects and physical events,
but some physical events (and presumably some physical objects, too)

also fall under mental kinds (or have mental properties) and therefore are mental events. Laws connect physical kinds and properties, thereby generating causal connections among individual events, and these causal nexus are what gives structure to the world.

Property Epiphenomenalism and the Causal Efficacy of Mental Properties

One of the premises from which Davidson derives anomalous monism is the claim that mental events are causes and effects of physical events. On anomalous monism, however, to say that a mental event m is a cause of a physical event p (p may be mental or physical) amounts only to this: m has a physical property Q such that an appropriate law connects Q (or events with property Q) with some physical property P of p. Since no laws exist that connect mental and physical properties, purely physical laws must do all the causal work, and this means that individual events can enter into causal relations only because they possess physical properties that figure in laws. Consider an example: Your desire for a drink of water causes you to turn on the tap. On the nomological model of causation, this requires a law that subsumes the two events, your desire for a drink of water and your turning on the tap. However, psychophysical anomalism says that this law must be a physical law, since there are no laws connecting mental-event kinds with physical-event kinds. Hence, your desire for a drink of water must be redescribed physically—that is, an appropriate physical property of your desire must be identified—before it can be brought under a law. In the absence of psychophysical laws, therefore, it is the physical properties of mental events that determine, wholly and exclusively, what causal relations they enter into. In particular, the fact that your desire for a drink of water is a desire for a drink of water—that is, the fact that it is an event of this mental kind—seems to have no bearing at all on its causation of your turning on the tap. What actually does the causal work is its physical properties—perhaps the fact that it is a neural event of a certain kind.

It seems, then, that under anomalous monism mental properties are causal idlers with no work to do. To be sure, anomalous monism is not epiphenomenalism in the classic sense, since mental events are allowed to be causes of other events. The point is that it is an epiphenomenalism about *mental properties*—we may call it "mental property epiphenomenalism"[12]—in that it renders mental properties and kinds causally irrelevant. At least it has nothing to say about how mental properties might be causally relevant, while affirming that every event that enters into a causal relation does so on account of its physical properties. To make this vivid: If you were to redistribute mental properties over the events of this world any way you please—you might even remove them entirely from all events, making them purely physical—that would not alter the network of causal relations of this world in the slightest way; it would not add or subtract a single causal relation anywhere in the world!

This shows the great importance of properties in the debate over mental causation: It is the causal efficacy of mental properties that we need to vindicate and give an account of. With mental substances out of the picture, there are only mental properties left to play any causal role, whether these are construed as properties of events or of objects. If mentality is to do any causal work, it must be the case that having a given mental property rather than another, or having it rather than not having it, must make a causal difference; it must be the case that an event, because it has a certain mental property (e.g., being a desire for a drink of water), enters into a causal relation (e.g., it causes you to look for a water fountain) that it would otherwise not have entered into.

Thus, the challenge posed by Davidson's psychophysical anomalism is to answer the following question: How can anomalous mental properties, properties that are not fit for laws, be causally efficacious properties? It would seem that there are only two ways of responding to this challenge: First, we may try to reject its principal premise, namely, psychophysical anomalism, by finding faults with Davidson's argument and then offering plausible reasons for thinking that there are indeed laws connecting mental and physical properties; second, we may try to show that the nomological conception of causality—in particular as it is understood by Davidson—is not the only concept of causality and that there are alternative conceptions of causation on which mental properties, though anomalous, could still be causally efficacious. Let us explore the second possibility.

Can Counterfactuals Help?

There indeed is an alternative approach to causation that on the face of it does not seem to require laws, and this is the counterfactual account of causation. According to this approach, to say that event *c* caused event *e* is to say that if *c* had not occurred, *e* would not have occurred. The idea that a cause is the *sine qua non* condition, or *necessary* condition, of its effect is a similar idea. This approach has much intuitive plausibility. The overturned space heater caused the house fire. Why do we say that? Because if the space heater had not overturned, the fire would not have occurred. What is the basis of saying that the accident was caused by a sudden braking on a rain-slick road? Because we think that if the driver had not suddenly stepped on his brakes on the wet road, the accident would not have occurred. In such cases we seem to depend on counterfactual ("what if") considerations rather than laws. Especially if you insist on exceptionless "strict laws," as Davidson appears to, we obviously are not in possession of such laws to support these perfectly ordinary and familiar causal claims. The situation seems the same when mental events are involved: There is no mystery about why I think that my desire for a drink of water caused me to step into the dark kitchen last night and stumble over the sleeping dog. I think that because I believe the evidently true counterfactual "If I had not wanted a drink of water last night, I wouldn't have gone into the kitchen and stumbled over the dog." In confidently making these ordinary causal or counterfactual claims, we seem entirely unconcerned about the question whether there are laws about wanting a glass of water and stumbling over a sleeping dog. Even if we were to reflect on such questions, we would be undeterred by the unlikely possibility that such laws exist or can be found. To summarize, then, the idea is this: We know that mental events, in virtue of their mental properties, can, and sometimes do, cause physical events because we can, and sometimes do, know appropriate psychophysical counterfactuals to be true. And mental causation is possible because such counterfactuals are sometimes true.

Does this solve the problem of mental causation? Before you embrace it as a solution, you should consider the following line of response. If "*c* caused *e*" just *means* "If *c* had not occurred, *e* would not have occurred," neither could "ground" the other; that is, neither could be offered as an explanation of how the other can be true. That George is an unmarried adult male cannot in any sense be a ground for, or explain, George's being a bachelor. Here there is a single fact expressed in two trivially equivalent ways. The same goes, on the counterfactual approach, for "My desire for a drink of water caused my walking into the kitchen" and "If I had not wanted a drink of water, I would not have walked into the kitchen." If we are concerned about how the first could be true, then we should be equally concerned about how the second could be true. For the two sentences express the same fact. So at this stage the counterfactual approach itself amounts to nothing more than a reaffirmation of faith in the reality of mental causation.

The counterfactualist will likely retort as follows: The counterfactual account goes beyond a mere reaffirmation of mental causation, for it opens up the possibility of accounting for mental causation in terms of an account of how mental-physical counterfactuals can be true. To show that there is a special problem about mental causation, you must show that there is a special problem about the truth of these counterfactuals. Moreover, by adopting the counterfactual strategy, we divorce mental causation from contentious questions about psychophysical laws.

This reply is fair enough. So are there special problems about these psychophysical counterfactuals? There are many philosophical puzzles and

difficulties surrounding counterfactuals, especially about their "semantics"—that is, conditions under which counterfactuals can be evaluated as
true or false. There are two main approaches to counterfactuals: (1) the
nomic-derivational approach and (2) the possible-world approach. On
the nomic-derivational approach, a counterfactual conditional, "If P were
the case, Q would be the case," is true just in case the consequent, Q, of
the conditional can be logically derived from its antecedent, P, when
taken together with laws and, possibly, auxiliary statements of conditions
holding on the occasion.[13] Consider an example: "If this match had been
struck, it would have lighted." This counterfactual is true since (let us assume) its consequent "the match lighted" can be derived from its antecedent "the match was struck" in conjunction with the law "Whenever
a dry match is struck in the presence of oxygen it lights" taken together
with the auxiliary statements "The match was dry" and "There was oxygen present."

It should be immediately obvious that on this analysis of counterfactuals, the counterfactual account of mental causation won't make the problem of mental causation go away. For the truth of the psychophysical
counterfactuals, like "If I had not wanted to check out the strange noise, I
would not have gone downstairs" and "If Jones's C-fibers had been activated, she would have felt pain," would require laws that would enable
the derivation of the physical consequents from their psychological antecedents (or vice versa), and it is difficult to see how any laws could serve
this purpose unless they were psychophysical laws, laws connecting mental with physical phenomena. On the nomic-derivational approach, therefore, the problem of psychophysical laws arises all over again.

So let us consider the possible-world approach to counterfactuals. In a
simplified form, it says this: The counterfactual "If P were the case, Q
would be the case" is true just in case Q is true in the world in which P is
true and that, apart from P's being true there, is as much like the actual
world as possible (to put it another way: Q is true in the closest P-
world).[14] In other words, to see whether or not this counterfactual is true,
we go through the following steps: Since this is a counterfactual, its antecedent, P, is false in the actual world. We must go to a possible world
("world" for short) in which P is true and see if Q is also true there. But
there are many worlds in which P is true—that is, there are many P-
worlds—and in some of these Q will be true and in others false. So which
P-world should we pick in which to check on Q? The answer: Pick that P-
world which is the most similar, or the closest, to the actual world. The
counterfactual "If P were true, Q would be true" is true if Q is true in that
world; it is false otherwise.

Let's see how this works with the counterfactual "If this match had
been struck, it would have lighted." In the actual world, the match wasn't
struck; so suppose that the match was struck (this means, go to a world in

which the match was struck), but keep other conditions the same as much as possible. Certain other conditions must also be altered under the counterfactual supposition that the match was struck: For example, in the actual world the match lay motionless in the matchbox and there was no disturbance in the air in its vicinity, so these conditions have to be changed to keep the world consistent as a whole. However, we need not, and should not, change the fact that the match was dry and the fact that sufficient oxygen was present in the ambient air. So in the world we have picked, the following conditions, among others, obtain: The match was struck, it was dry, and oxygen was present in the vicinity. The counterfactual is true if and only if the match lighted in that world. Did the match light in that world? In asking this question, we are asking which of the following two worlds is closer to the actual world:[15]

W_1: The match was struck; it was dry; oxygen was present; the match lighted.

W_2: The match was struck; it was dry; oxygen was present; the match did not light.

We would judge, it seems, that of the two W_1 is closer to the actual world. But why do we judge this way? Because, it seems, we believe that in the actual world there is a lawful regularity to the effect that when a dry match is struck in the presence of oxygen it ignites, and W_1, but not W_2, respects this regularity. So in judging that this match, which in fact was dry and bathed in oxygen, would have lighted if it had been struck, we seem to be making crucial use of the law just mentioned. If in the actual world dry matches, when struck, seldom or never light, there seems little question that we would go for W_2 as the closer world and declare the counterfactual "If this match had been struck, it would have lighted" to be false. It is difficult to see what else could be involved in our judgment that W_1, not W_2, is the world that is closer to the actual world other than these considerations of lawful regularities.

Consider a psychophysical counterfactual: "If Brian had not wanted to check out the noise, he wouldn't have gone downstairs." Suppose that we take this counterfactual to be true, and on that basis we judge that Brian's desire to check out the noise caused him to go downstairs. Consider the following two worlds:

W_3: Brian didn't want to check out the noise; he didn't go downstairs.

W_4: Brian didn't want to check out the noise; he went downstairs anyway.

If W_4 is closer to the actual world than W_3 is, that would falsify our counterfactual. So why should we think that W_3 is closer than W_4? In the actual world, Brian wanted to check out the noise and went downstairs. As far as these two particular facts are concerned, W_4 evidently is closer to the actual world than W_3 is. So why would we hold W_3 to be closer and hence the counterfactual to be true? The only plausible answer, again, seems to be this: We know, or believe, that there are certain lawful regularities and propensities governing Brian's wants, beliefs, and so on, on the one hand and his behavior patterns, on the other, and that given the absence of a desire to check out a suspicious noise in the middle of the night, along with other conditions prevailing at the time, his not going downstairs at that particular time fits these regularities better than the supposition that he would have gone downstairs at that time. We consider such regularities and propensities to be reliable and lawlike and commonly appeal to them in assessing counterfactuals, even though we have only the vaguest idea about the details that we would need to know to state them in an explicit and precise way.

Again, the centrality of psychophysical laws to mental causation is apparent. Although there is room for further discussion on this point, it seems at least plausible that considerations of lawful regularities governing mental and physical phenomena are crucially involved in the evaluation of psychophysical counterfactuals of the sort that can ground causal relations between the mental and the physical. We need not know the details of such regularities, but we must believe that they exist and know their rough content and shape to be able to evaluate these counterfactuals as true or false. So are we back where we started, with Davidson and his argument for the impossibility of psychophysical laws?

Not exactly, fortunately. Because the laws involved need not be laws of the kind Davidson has in mind—what he sometimes calls "strict laws." These are exceptionless, explicitly articulated laws that form a closed and comprehensive theory, like the fundamental laws of physics. Rather, the laws involved in evaluating these counterfactuals—indeed, laws on the basis of which we make causal judgments in much of science as well as in daily life—are rough-and-ready generalizations tacitly qualified by escape clauses ("ceteris paribus," "under normal conditions," "in the absence of interfering conditions," etc.) and apparently immune to falsification by isolated negative instances. Laws of this type, often called ceteris paribus laws, seem to satisfy the usual criteria of lawlikeness: As we saw, they seem to have the power to ground counterfactuals, and our credence in them is enhanced as we see them confirmed in more and more instances. Their logical form, verification conditions, and their efficacy in explanations and predictions are not well understood, but it seems beyond question that they are the essential staple that sustains and nourishes our causal discourse.

Does the recognition that causal relations involving mental events are supported by these "nonstrict," ceteris paribus laws solve the problem of mental causation? It does enable us to get around the anomalist difficulty raised by Davidsonian considerations—at least temporarily. We can see, though, that even this difficulty has not been fully resolved. For it may well be that these nonstrict laws are possible only if strict laws are possible and that where there are no underlying strict laws that can explain them or otherwise ground them, they remain only rough, fortuitous correlations, their lawlike appearance perhaps only illusory.

We have thus far discussed various issues about mental causation that arise from the widely accepted thesis that causal relations require backing by laws and the apparent implication of this requirement that if there is to be mind-body causation, there must be laws connecting mental and physical properties. This, however, is not the only source of difficulties for mental causation. We turn to others in the sections to follow.

The Extrinsicness of Mental States

Computers compute with 0s and 1s. Suppose you have a computer running a certain program, say, a program that monitors the inventory of a supermarket. Given a string of 0s and 1s as input (a can of Campbell's tomato soup has just been scanned by the optical scanner at a checkout station), the computer will go through a series of computations and emit an output (the count of Campbell's tomato soup cans in stock has been adjusted, etc.). Thus, the input string of 0s and 1s represents a can of Campbell's tomato soup being sold, and the output string of 0s and 1s represents the amount of Campbell's tomato soup still in stock. When the manager checks the computer for a report on the available stock of Campbell's tomato soup, the computer "reports" that the present stock is such and such, and it does so *because* "it has been told" (by the checkout scanners) that twenty-five cans have been sold so far today. And this "because" is naturally understood as signifying a causal relation.

But we also know that it makes no difference to the computer what the strings of 0s and 1s *mean*. If the input string had meant the direction and speed of wind at the local airport or the identification code of an employee or even if it had meant nothing at all, the computer would have gone through exactly the same computational process and produced the same output string. In this case the output string, too, would have meant something else, but what is clear is that the "meanings," or "representational contents," of these 0s and 1s are in the eye of the computer programmer or user, not something that is involved in the computational process. Give the computer the same string of 0s and 1s as input, and it will go through the same computational process every time and give you the same output. The semantics of these strings is irrelevant to computation; what matters is their shape, that is, their syntax. The computer is a "syntactic engine," not a "semantic engine"; it's driven by the shapes of symbols, not their meanings.

According to an influential view of psychology (known as the "computational theory of mind" or "computationalism"), mental processes are best viewed as computational processes on internal mental representations (see Chapter 4). On this view, constructing a psychological theory is like writing a computer program; such a theory will specify for each appropriate input (say, a sensory stimulus) the computational process that a cognizer will undergo to produce a certain output (say, the visual detection of an edge). But what the argument of the preceding paragraph seems to show is that on the computational view of psychology, the meanings, or contents, of internal representations make no difference to psychological processes. Suppose a certain internal representation, i, represents the state of affairs S (say, that there are horses in the field); having S as its representational content, or meaning, is the semantics of i. But if we suppose, as is often done on the computational model, that internal representations form a languagelike system, i must also have a syntax, or formal structure. So if our considerations are right, it is the syntax of i, not its semantics, that determines the course of the computational process involving i. The fact that i means that there are horses in the field rather than, say, that there are lions in the field, is of no causal relevance to what other representations issue from i. The computational process that i initiates will be wholly determined by i's syntactic shape. But this is to say that the *contents* of our beliefs and desires and of other propositional attitudes have no causal relevance for psychology; it is only their syntax that makes a difference to what they cause.

This difficulty is independent of computationalism and can be seen to arise for any broadly physicalist view of mentality. Assume that beliefs and desires and other intentional states are neural states (this only assumes token physicalism, the thesis that every instance, or "token," of a mental state is a physical "token" state, and not the reductionist type physicalism). Each such state, in addition to being a neural state with biological/physical properties, has a specific content (e.g., that water is wet or that Bill Clinton is left-handed). That a given state has the content it has is a *relational*, or *extrinsic*, *property* of that state; for the fact that your belief is about water or about Clinton is in part determined by your causal-historical association with water and Clinton. Let us consider what this means and why it is so.

Suppose there is in some remote region of this universe another planet ("twin earth") that is exactly like our earth except for the following fact: On twin earth there is no water, that is, no H_2O, but an observably indistinguishable chemical substance, XYZ, fills the lakes and oceans there, comes out of the tap in twin-earthian homes, and so on. Each of us has a doppelganger there who is an exact molecular duplicate of us (let us ignore the inconvenient fact that your twin there has XYZ molecules in her body where you have H_2O molecules in your body). On twin earth, people speak twin English, which is just like English, except for the fact that the twin-earthian "water" means XYZ, not water, and when twin earthians utter sentences containing the expression "water," they are talking about XYZ, not water. Thus, twin earthians have thoughts about XYZ, where earthians have thoughts about water, and when you believe that water is wet, your twin-earthian doppelganger has the belief that XYZ is wet, even though you and she are molecule-for-molecule duplicates. And when you think that Bill Clinton is left-handed, your twin thinks that the twin-earthian Bill Clinton (he is the president of the twin-earth United States) is left-handed. And so on. The differences in earthian and twin-earthian beliefs (and other intentional states) are due not to internal physical or mental differences but rather to their relationship to the different objects and conditions in their environment, including their past interactions with them (see discussion of "wide content," Chapter 8). Content properties, therefore, are extrinsic, not intrinsic, properties of your internal states; they depend on your causal history and your relationships to the particular objects and events in your surroundings. States that have the same intrinsic properties—the same neural/physical properties—may have different contents if they are embedded in different environments. Further, an identical internal state that lacks an appropriate relationship to the external world may have no representational content at all.

But isn't it plausible to suppose that behavior causation is "local" and depends only on the intrinsic neural/physical properties of these states, not their extrinsic relational properties? Someone whose momentary neural/physical state is exactly identical with yours will emit the same behavior, say, raise the right arm, whether or not her brain state has the same content as yours or even if it had no content at all, as long as her state is identical with yours in all intrinsic neural/physical details. This raises doubts about the causal relevance of contents: The properties of our mental states involved in behavior causation are plausibly expected to be local and intrinsic, but contents of mental states are relational and extrinsic (and perhaps also historical). This, then, is another problem of mental causation; it challenges us to answer the question "How can extrinsic mental properties be causally efficacious in behavior causation?"

Various attempts have been made to reconcile the extrinsicness of contents with their causal efficacy, but it is fair to say that none of the available proposals offers a perspicuous and wholly adequate solution to this problem (see the readings recommended at the end of this chapter). The problem has turned out to be a highly complex one involving many issues in metaphysics, philosophy of language, and philosophy of science. We now turn to our third, and last, problem of mental causation.

The Causal Closure of the Physical Domain

Suppose, then, that we have somehow overcome the difficulties arising from the possible anomalousness and extrinsicness of mental properties. We are still not home free: There is a further challenge to mental causation that we must confront, one that arises from the principle, embraced by most physicalists, that the physical domain is *causally closed*. What does this mean? Pick any physical event, say, the decay of a uranium atom or the collision of two stars in distant space, and trace its causal ancestry or posterity as far as you would like; the principle of causal closure of the physical domain says that this will never take you outside the physical domain. Thus, no causal chain involving a physical event will ever cross the boundary of the physical into the nonphysical: If x is a physical event and y is a cause or effect of x, then y, too, must be a physical event. Another (somewhat weaker) way of putting the point would be this: If a physical event has a cause at time t, it has a physical cause at t. Thus, if the closure principle, in either form, holds, to explain the occurrence of a physical event we never need to go outside the physical domain.

Contrast this with the Cartesian picture: According to Cartesian interactionist dualism, a causal chain starting with a physical event could very well leave the physical domain and enter the mental domain (physical-to-mental causation), meander there for a while (mental-to-mental causation), and then return to the physical domain (mental-to-physical causation). This means that mental and physical events occur as links in the same causal chain and that to give a full causal explanation of why a physical event occurred, we sometimes have to go outside the physical domain and look for its mental cause. It follows, then, that *on Cartesian dualism there can be no complete physical theory of the physical domain*. To explain some physical events, you must go outside the physical realm and appeal to nonphysical causal agents and laws governing their behavior! Complete physics would in principle be impossible, even as an idealized goal. On the Cartesian model, the mental domain would not be closed either, and neither physics nor psychology could be pursued independently of the other.

Most physicalists will find the Cartesian model unacceptable if not incoherent; they accept the causal closure of the physical not only as a fundamental metaphysical doctrine but as an indispensable methodological presupposition of the physical sciences. If you reject it, you are buying into the Cartesian picture, a picture that no physicalist could tolerate. For it depicts the mental domain as an ontological equal of the physical domain; the two domains coexist side by side, causally interacting with each other, and there is no reason to call such a position physicalism rather than mentalism. Any physicalist must acknowledge the primacy of the physical in some robust sense, and the violation of the physical causal closure undermines that primacy.

If the causal closure of the physical domain is to be respected, it seems prima facie that mental causation must be ruled out—unless mental events and properties are somehow brought into the physical domain. But if they are part of the physical domain, doesn't that mean that they *are* physical properties and events? If so, that would be reductionism pure and simple. But this is a prospect that most philosophers, including many physicalists, find uncomfortable; they want to hold that although only physical things and events exist in this world, certain complex physical systems (e.g., biological organisms) and events (e.g., neural events) can have physically irreducible mental properties (see Chapter 9). Is there, then, a way of bringing the mental close enough to the physical so that the causal closure principle is not violated and yet not fully into it, so that the dreaded reductionism is avoided?

Mind-Body Supervenience and Causal/Explanatory Exclusion

As we have seen, functionalists think of mental properties as "physically realized," and that makes mental properties almost physical but not quite (or so functionalists think). We also saw how the functionalist conception of mental properties as second-order properties having physical properties as their realizers gives rise to difficulties in explaining the causal powers of mental properties (Chapter 5). Let us here focus on another aspect of the functionalist conception shared by many nonfunctionalists as well: the idea that mental properties are *supervenient* on physical properties. As we saw (Chapter 1), mind-body supervenience is the thesis that any two things, or events, that are exactly alike in all physical respects cannot differ in mental respects. That is to say, there can be no mental difference unless there is a physical difference. The idea that each mental-event or -state kind has a neural substrate or correlate, too, is a form of mind-body supervenience: It assumes that if two organisms are in identical neural states, they cannot be in different mental states. We can think of the neural substrate of mental property M as its "supervenience base" or "base property," that is, the physical base on which it supervenes (for more details on supervenience, see Chapter 9). Note the following points about supervenience thus conceived: (1) If N is a neural state on which mental property M supervenes, then N is a sufficient condition for the occurrence of M (that is, as a matter of law, whenever an organism is in N, it is in M);[16] (2) M can have multiple supervenience bases, $N_1, N_2, \ldots,$ each of which is sufficient to give rise to M (this is analogous to the functionalist idea of multiple realizability of the mental); (3) M is distinct from each of its many bases, $N_1, N_2, \ldots$.

According to some philosophers, mind-body supervenience gives us the right kind of physicalism: It respects the primacy of the physical by giving a clear sense to the idea that the physical determines the mental. Without the instantiations of appropriate physical properties, no mental property can be instantiated, and what particular mental properties are instantiated depends wholly on what physical properties happen to be instantiated. And yet, in view of (3) above, mental properties remain distinct from their physical base properties. But does mind-body supervenience help with mental causation? Does it bring the mental close enough to the physical to allow mind-body causation and yet manage to avoid mind-body reductionism?

The sharp and sudden pain I felt in my elbow caused me to wince. Mind-body supervenience says that the pain has a supervenience base, a certain neural state N. (We can also think of N as the pain's neural substrate or realizer.) So the situation looks like this:

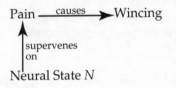

If neural state N is a supervenience base for pain, it is lawfully sufficient for pain. If, therefore, pain is a sufficient cause of wincing, there seems ample reason to conclude that N, too, is causally sufficient for wincing (by the transitivity of nomic/causal sufficiency). That is, there seems to be an excellent reason for thinking that N is a cause of wincing. On the standard nomological conception of causation, this conclusion is inescapable. Thus, we now have the following picture:

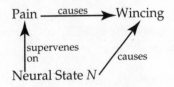

Does this mean that the wincing has *two distinct causes*, the pain and neural state N? This seems not credible. For that would mean that the wincing is *causally overdetermined*; in fact, it would follow that all cases of mental causation are cases of overdetermination, which is difficult to believe. And it doesn't make sense to think of the pain as an intermediate link in a causal chain starting from N and terminating at the wincing; for the pain and the occurrence of N are perfectly simultaneous, and it makes no sense to think of a causal chain or mechanism leading from N to the pain. The former supervenes on, or is realized by, N, not caused by it.

In this situation, moreover, the causal role of the pain is in danger of preemption by N. This is "the problem of causal/explanatory exclusion": For any single event, there can be no more than a single sufficient cause, or causal explanation, unless it is a case of causal overdetermination.[17] If we trace the causal chain backward from the wincing, we are likely to reach N first, not the pain. It is incoherent to think that the pain somehow directly, without an intervening chain of physiological processes, acted on certain muscles, causing them to contract; that would be telekinesis, a strange form of action at a distance! If the pain is to have a causal role here, it must somehow ride piggyback on the causal chain from N to the wincing. It is implausible in the extreme to think that there might be two independent causal paths here, one from N to the wincing and the other from the pain to the wincing.

Given these considerations, how could we fit the pain into this causal picture? We now see that the diagram above presents an unstable picture: The causal relations it depicts are not together coherent, and we must somewhat redraw the diagram to get a coherent picture of the situation. What are the options?

(1) *The epiphenomenalist model.* This treats the pain as an epiphenomenon of neural state N, denying it a causal role in the production of the wincing. N taken by itself is a full cause of it. The following diagram represents this proposal.

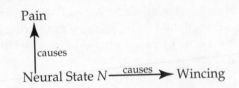

We have already discussed the viability of epiphenomenalism as a solution to the mind-body problem.

(2) *The model of supervenient causation.* This approach views the pain's claim as a cause of the wincing *as consisting in* its supervenience on neural

state N, which causes a certain physiological event on which the wincing supervenes. More generally, it takes causal processes at the microlevel as fundamental and considers causal processes at the macrolevel as dependent, or supervenient, on those at the microlevel. The following diagram represents this approach:

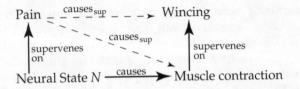

In this diagram "causes$_{sup}$" is to be read "superveniently causes" or "is a supervenient cause of"; the broken arrows represent this relation. As the diagram indicates, the pain supervenes on N and the wincing supervenes on the contraction of a certain group of muscles; the pain's causation of wincing consists in its supervenience base N's causing the muscle contraction, which is the supervenience base of the wincing. The latter causal relation is fully physical, and we are supposing here that there is no special problem about physical causation. Further, we may speak of the pain as a supervenient cause of the wincing as well, since its supervenience base causes it. In general, then, an instantiation of a property is a supervenient cause of an event in virtue of the fact that its supervenience base causes that event.

How does this differ from the epiphenomenalist model? What is the difference between saying that the pain is an epiphenomenon of N and saying that the pain is a supervenient cause? An advocate of the present approach will point out, first of all, as has been noted, that it is wrong to think of pain as a causal effect of N; although the pain depends on N for its existence, this dependence is not happily viewed as causal—it isn't as though the pain is brought about by N through an intervening causal chain (what would such a causal chain look like?). The dependence involved is more like the way the rigidity of a steel rod depends on its molecular structure than the way the expansion of its length depends on its being heated. Second, it will be pointed out that this model of supervenient causation applies to all macrocausal relations, not just those involving mental causes. Heating this kettle of water causes the water to boil. How does this happen? The increase in the water temperature is supervenient on certain molecular processes (something like the water molecules' moving with increasing velocities), and these molecular processes causally lead to violent ejections of water molecules into the air, upon which the macrophenomenon, the boiling, supervenes. This means that mental events as supervenient causes are as causally robust as macrophysical phenomena, that is, the familiar physical phenomena of daily experience. The fact that macrocausation is implemented at the microlevel doesn't show, the advocate of this approach will argue, that macrophenomena are robbed of their causal efficacy. If the mental can be shown to have a causal status equal to that of macrophysical phenomena, why isn't that a sufficient vindication of their causal relevance and efficacy?[18]

(3) *The reductionist model.* The simplest solution, and in many ways the most elegant one, is reductionism. The reductionist identifies pain with neural state N. Since pain $= N$, there is here only one cause of the wincing, and all the puzzles with our original triangular diagram vanish. And pain of course has all the causal powers of N, and its causal powers are fully vindicated. The following diagram represents the reductionist proposal:

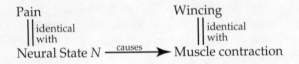

The fact that reductionism delivers the simplest solution to the problem of mental causation is probably the best argument in favor of it. But it may not be a sufficient argument, for reductionism has been rejected by a majority of philosophers of mind for what they take to be compelling reasons. We will look into the issues concerning reductive and nonreductive physicalism in a later chapter (Chapter 9) as well as some further issues involving mental causation.

Further Readings

Donald Davidson's "Mental Events," "Psychology as Philosophy," and "The Material Mind," all reprinted in his *Essays on Actions and Events* (New York: Oxford University Press, 1980), are the sources of anomalous monism. See Jaegwon Kim, "Psychophysical Laws," in Kim, *Supervenience and Mind* (Cambridge: Cambridge University Press, 1993), for an explication and analysis of Davidson's argument for the anomalism of the mental. On the problem of mental causation associated with anomalous monism, see Ernest Sosa, "Mind-Body Interaction and Supervenient Causation," *Midwest Studies in Philosophy* 9 (1984):271–281; Louise Antony, "Anomalous Monism and the Problem of Explanatory Force," *Philosophical Review* 98 (1989):153–158. Davidson's response is contained in his "Thinking Causes," in *Mental Causation*, ed. John Heil and Alfred Mele (Oxford: Clarendon Press, 1993). This volume also contains rejoinders to Davidson by Kim, Sosa, and Brian McLaughlin, as well as a number of other interesting papers on mental causation.

For counterfactual-based accounts of mental causation, see Ernest LePore and Barry Loewer, "Mind Matters," *Journal of Philosophy* 84 (1987):630–642; Terence Horgan, "Mental Quausation," *Philosophical Perspectives* 3 (1989):47–76.

On mental causation and wide and narrow content, see Fred Dretske, *Explaining Behavior* (Cambridge: MIT Press, 1988); Tyler Burge, "Individualism and Causation in Psychology," *Pacific Philosophical Quarterly* 70 (1989):303–322.

On supervenience and mental causation, see Jaegwon Kim, "Epiphenomenal and Supervenient Causation," in Kim, *Supervenience and Mind;* Brian McLaughlin, "Event Supervenience and Supervenient Causation," *Southern Journal of Philosophy* 22 (1984), the Spindel Conference Supplement:71–92; Peter Menzies, "Against Causal Reductionism," *Mind* 97 (1988):551–574; Gabriel Segal and Elliott Sober, "The Causal Efficacy of Content," *Philosophical Studies* 63 (1991):1–30; Stephen Yablo, "Mental Causation," *Philosophical Review* 101 (1992):245–280; Cynthia Macdonald and Graham Macdonald, "Introduction: Supervenient Causation," in *Philosophy of Psychology,* ed. Cynthia Macdonald and Graham Macdonald (Oxford: Blackwell, 1995). Yablo's paper is also useful on the issue of the causal/explanatory exclusion. John Heil's *The Nature of True Minds* (Cambridge: Cambridge University Press, 1992), ch. 4, includes an interesting and wide-ranging discussion of mental causation.

Notes

1. For a systematic development of this approach, see J. W. Atkinson and D. Birch, *The Dynamics of Action* (New York: Wiley, 1970).

2. In Donald Davidson, "Actions, Reasons, and Causes," reprinted in his *Essays on Actions and Events* (New York: Oxford University Press, 1980). For important noncausal approaches, see G. H. von Wright, *Explanation and Understanding* (Ithaca: Cornell University Press, 1971); George M. Wilson, *The Intentionality of Human Action* (Stanford: Stanford University Press, 1989); Carl Ginet, *On Action* (Cambridge: Cambridge University Press, 1990).

3. Samuel Alexander, *Space, Time, and Deity* (London: Macmillan, 1920), vol. 2, p. 8.

4. René Descartes, *The Philosophical Writings of Descartes,* vol. 1, eds. John Cottingham, Robert Stoothoff, and Dugald Murdoch (Cambridge: Cambridge University Press, 1985), pp. 59–60.

5. René Descartes, *The Passions of the Soul* I, 41, in ibid., vol. 2, p. 343.

6. Ibid., p. 238.

7. *The Essential Descartes,* ed. Margaret Wilson (New York: New American Library, 1969), p. 373.

8. More precisely, Davidson's claim is that there are no "strict laws" connecting psychological and physical phenomena. He now explicitly allows the existence of

nonstrict psychophysical laws, qualified by ceteris paribus clauses. See his "Thinking Causes" in *Mental Causation,* ed. John Heil and Alfred Mele (Oxford: Clarendon Press, 1993). The present discussion is not intended as an exact exegesis of Davidson's position.

9. See Davidson's "Mental Events," "Psychology as Philosophy," and "The Material Mind," all reprinted in *Essays on Actions and Events.* For an interpretive reconstruction of Davidson's argument, see Jaegwon Kim, "Psychophysical Laws," in Kim, *Supervenience and Mind* (Cambridge: Cambridge University Press, 1993).

10. This is a form of what is often called "the principle of charity"; Davidson also requires that an interpretation of a person's belief system must make her beliefs come out largely *true.* See the discussion of interpretation theory in Chapter 8.

11. In "Mental Events" Davidson defends the stronger thesis that there are no laws at all about mental phenomena, whether psychophysical or purely psychological, and it is his view that the laws (or "strict laws," as he calls them) can be found only in basic physics. A sharp-eyed reader will have noticed that Davidson's argument here requires this stronger thesis, since the argument as it stands leaves open the possibility that the two causally connected events m and p instantiate a purely psychological law.

12. Brian McLaughlin calls it "type epiphenomenalism" in his "Type Epiphenomenalism, Type Dualism, and the Causal Priority of the Physical," *Philosophical Perspectives* 3 (1989):109–136.

13. See Ernest Nagel, *The Structure of Science* (New York: Harcourt, Brace & World, 1961), ch. 4; J. L. Mackie, "Counterfactuals and Causal Laws," in *Analytic Philosophy,* ed. R. J. Butler (Oxford: Blackwell, 1962).

14. For fuller statements of this approach, see Robert Stalnaker, "A Theory of Conditionals," reprinted in *Conditionals,* ed. Frank Jackson (Oxford: Oxford University Press, 1991); David Lewis, *Counterfactuals* (Cambridge: Harvard University Press, 1973).

15. These worlds are very much underdescribed, of course; we are assuming that the worlds are roughly the same in other respects.

16. If some mental states are "extrinsic" in the sense of the preceding section, they are likely to fail to supervene on local neural states. The present discussion may be considered restricted to those mental states that do supervene on neural states. For further discussion of these and other relevant issues, see Chapter 8.

17. See Jaegwon Kim, "Mechanism, Purpose, and Explanatory Exclusion," in Kim, *Supervenience and Mind.*

18. For further discussion, see Jaegwon Kim, "Epiphenomenal and Supervenient Causation," in Kim, *Supervenience and Mind*; also Brian McLaughlin, "Event Supervenience and Supervenient Causation," *Southern Journal of Philosophy* 22 (1984), the Spindel Conference Supplement:71–92; Peter Menzies, "Against Causal Reductionism," *Mind* 97 (1988):551–574; Gabriel Segal and Elliott Sober, "The Causal Efficacy of Content," *Philosophical Studies* 63 (1991):1–30.

7

Consciousness

At first blush, nothing could be more obvious and familiar to us, it seems, than the phenomenon of consciousness. It is familiar and obvious because we are conscious at every moment of our waking lives; it is a ubiquitous and unsurprising feature of everyday existence—except when we are in deep sleep, in a coma, or otherwise, well, unconscious. In one of its senses, "conscious" is just another word for "awake," and we know what it is to be awake, or to awaken from sleep, anesthesia, or a momentary loss of consciousness caused by trauma to the head. Moreover, consciousness seems to be a central and crucial feature of our mentality—or at any rate the kind of mentality we have; without consciousness we would no longer be creatures with mentality, or so it may seem to many of us. A brain-dead person has presumably suffered an irrevocable loss of consciousness; most of us would be inclined to feel that for all human intents and purposes such a person is entirely gone from us. For Descartes, being conscious (or "thinking," in his broad usage of this term) is the essence of mentality. It is self-evident, according to him, that "there can be nothing in the mind, in so far as it is a thinking thing, of which it is not aware" and that "we cannot have any thought of which we are not aware at the very moment when it is in us."[1] Thus, on the Cartesian conception, our mental life is exhausted by the contents of our awareness—that is, things of which we are conscious. So why has consciousness baffled so many thinkers throughout history, driving Schopenhauer to despairingly call it "the world knot," something that we could never hope to untie? Why was consciousness shunned by both psychologists and philosophers during much of this century? Why are there still serious philosophers who argue that consciousness doesn't really exist, that it is merely a piece of bad philosophical fiction? It is not an exaggeration to say that the so-called mystery of the mind is largely the mystery of consciousness.

Before we take up substantive issues, it will be useful to clarify our terminology. "Conscious," as an adjective, applies both to persons (and organisms and perhaps other systems) and to their states (or events, processes, and the like). Thus, you and I are conscious creatures, but amoebas and trees aren't. But this of course doesn't mean that we are conscious at every moment of our existence; we are conscious when we are awake and alert and not conscious while in a deep sleep or coma. We are also conscious, or aware, *of* things, states, or facts (e.g., the large new McDonald's sign at the street corner, a nagging pain in the back, being tailed by a highway patrol car). In cases of this sort, "conscious" and "aware" have roughly the same meaning. But we also apply "conscious" to events, states, and processes. Familiar sensory states and events, such as pains, itches, and mental images, are conscious states and events. Emotions, like anger, joy, and sadness, can also be conscious, and many of our beliefs, desires, hopes, and memories are also conscious. I have the conscious belief that it's time to finish up my work and head home and the conscious hope that I can finish writing this section before I have to leave. And so on.

What is the relationship between these two uses of "conscious," as applied to persons ("subject consciousness," as we might call it) and as applied to their states ("state consciousness")? Can we say something like this: A state of a person is a conscious state just in case that person is aware, or conscious, of it? It seems true that if a given state is a conscious state, the person whose state it is must be aware of it. Yet it is clearly not true that if you are aware of a state, then that state is a conscious state. You may be aware of your age and weight or conscious of the flickering of a fluorescent light bulb that is about to burn out, but that isn't to say that your age and weight or the flickering light are conscious states. More to the point, you are normally conscious of your posture and orientation (e.g., whether you are standing or lying down, whether your left elbow is bent), and this kind of proprioceptive awareness is in some sense direct and immediate; but surely these bodily states are not conscious states. The suggested relationship between state consciousness and subject consciousness makes better sense when restricted to mental states: A mental state is a conscious mental state just in case the subject whose state it is is conscious, or in some special way aware, of it (we will further consider this issue below).

Aspects of Consciousness

In philosophical and psychological discussions of consciousness, we can discern several related but distinguishable aspects, or components, of consciousness, one or another of which may be the focus of attention in a given discussion. Thus it often happens that when someone claims to have a "solution" to the problem of consciousness or an explanation, or a "model," of consciousness, what is being offered concerns only one of the several distinguishable features of consciousness and is completely silent on the rest. As a result, those who profess to be discussing "the problem of consciousness" sometimes don't even appear to be talking about the same topic. So it will be useful to begin with a survey of some prominent aspects of the phenomena that collectively go under the name "consciousness."

Phenomenal Properties, or "Qualia"

When you look at a ripe tomato, you sense its color in a certain way, a way that is different from the way you sense the color of a bundle of lettuce leaves. If you crush the tomato and bring your nose close to it, it smells in a certain way, which is different from the way a crushed lemon smells. Sensory mental events and states, like seeing a ripe red tomato, smelling gasoline, experiencing a shooting pain in the arm, and the like, have distinctive "phenomenal" (or "phenomenological") characters, that is, felt or sensed qualities, by means of which they are usually identified as sensations of a certain type. It has become customary to refer to these sensory qualities of mental states as "raw feels" or "qualia."[2] Sometimes the notion of a quale is explained by saying that when you are in a mental state with a qualitative character there is *something that it is like to be in that state.* You know what it is like to see a vivid yellow patch against a green background, but a person who is yellow-green color-blind presumably doesn't know what it is like for you to have this experience. Conversely, normally sighted persons don't know, at least firsthand, what it is like for the color-blind person to see yellow against green. Moreover, it is also said that for any conscious creature, say, a bat (an example made famous by Thomas Nagel), there is *something that it is like to be that creature,* whereas there is nothing it is like to be, say, a table or a flowerpot. Nagel has famously argued that we cannot know what it is like to be a bat; nor can we know, according to him, what it is like to echolocate an insect by using bat sonar—what the sensory representation of such an activity is like to the bat.[3]

Such qualitative sensory characters seem present also in mental states not normally classified as sensations. Anger, joy, remorse, envy, pride, and other emotions appear to have certain distinctive qualitative feels to them, although they are not type-classified (as, e.g., anger, envy, etc.) solely, or even primarily, on the basis of their qualitative character. For example, it may be difficult, or impossible, to categorize an emotion as one of anger, envy, jealousy, or any combination of the three on the basis of its felt qualities alone. Nor does every instance of an emotion need to be accompanied by a distinctive felt character; you are unhappy with the continuing budget deficits of the federal government, but is your unhappiness—must it be—accompanied by some felt quality? Probably not. Being in such a state seems more a matter of having certain beliefs and attitudes (e.g., that large and continuing budget deficits are bad for the country's economy, that the government should soon take drastic measures to correct the situation, etc.) than having an experience with a distinctive sensory quality.

But might it be the case that all beliefs share a special distinctive phenomenal feel? The answer must be no—for the rather uninteresting reason that the existence of unconscious mental states, including beliefs, of which the subject is not aware, is now widely recognized. Freudian depth psychology, parts of which have by now almost achieved the status of folk psychology of the sophisticates, has told us about the psychological mechanism by which we repress beliefs and desires that are repugnant to our conscious minds. Nowadays we routinely hear news of people whose repressed memories of childhood abuse are recovered through psychotherapy. But we don't have to go to such controversial cases for beliefs of which the subject is unaware. Suppose I ask you, "Do you believe that some neurosurgeons wear hats?" You would probably say yes, you do believe that some neurosurgeons wear hats. This is a belief you have always had (you would have said yes if I had asked you two years ago), and not a new belief that you have just now acquired, although you have just become aware that you have this belief. My question made an unconscious belief an "occurrent" one. Obviously, there are countless other such beliefs that you hold. Beliefs that are not occurrent are sometimes called "dispositional" beliefs. It is clear that dispositional beliefs cannot have any phenomenal character, for the simple reason that their subjects are not aware of them.

So the question about the phenomenal character of mental states becomes interesting only if it is restricted to conscious mental states, states of which their subjects are aware. Take beliefs as a start: Are all conscious instances of the belief that George Washington was the first president of the United States, in different persons or for the same person at different times, characterized by a special qualitative character unique to beliefs with this content? The answer to this question must be no: One person having such a belief might have a mental image of George Washington (as on the dollar bill), another may simply have the words "George Washington" hovering in her mind, and still another may have no particular mental image or any other sort of phenomenal occurrence at all when she has this thought. But there is also a more general question: Do all occurrent beliefs, beliefs we are actively entertaining, share some specific belieflike phenomenal character? Some have claimed that when we are aware of a thought as a belief, there is a certain feel of assertoric or affirmative judging, a sort of "Oh, yes!" feeling. Similarly, one might claim that an occurrent disbelief is accompanied by a directly experienced feel of denial and that remembering is accompanied by a certain feeling of déjà vu. Perhaps wants and desires are accompanied by a sense of yearning or longing combined with a sense of present deprivation.

But such claims are difficult to assess. The "Oh, yes!" feeling may be nothing more than our coming to be aware that we believe a certain proposition. Such an awareness does not seem to be accompanied by a particular kind of sensory quality. When you want to find out how your bruised elbow is coming along, you can focus your attention on the elbow and try to see whether the pain is still there. Here there clearly is a special kind of sensory feel, a quale, that you are looking for and can identify in your experience. However, when you are unsure whether you really believe some proposition, say, that euthanasia is morally permissible, that Mozart is a greater composer than Beethoven, or that Clinton will win in 1996, you don't look for a sensory quale of a special type. It seems absurd to suggest that there is some sensory quality Q such that if you find Q attached to your thought that euthanasia is morally permissible, then you say "Aah! Now I know I believe that euthanasia is morally permissible," and if you don't find Q, you say, "Oh, no! I don't have the belief!"

If there are no distinctive phenomenal qualities associated with types of intentional mental states—beliefs, desires, intentions, and the rest—we face the following interesting question. How do you find out that you *believe*, rather than, say, *doubt* or merely *hope*, that it will rain tomorrow? Such knowledge, at least in most instances, seems direct and immediate in the sense that it is not based on evidence or observation and that the only possible answer to the question, "How do you know?" seems to be "I just do." One thing that is certain is that we don't find out whether we believe or hope by looking inward to detect special qualia. But it is not clear either that we know that we are angry or embarrassed by detecting a special phenomenal quality. How, then, do we know that we are angry rather than embarrassed? Or embarrassed rather than ashamed? Sometimes we find that it is not possible to classify our feeling, say, as either one of embarrassment or shame or perhaps as both. But then how do we know *that*? There do not appear to be any simple answers to these questions.

In any case it is evident that there are conscious mental states with no special phenomenal character. In general, mental occurrences that we call "experiences" appear to be those that possess phenomenal properties. If this is so, the idea of phenomenal character and the idea of there being something it is like come apart. For it certainly seems that there is something it is like to believe something, to suspend judgment about something, to wonder about something, to want something, and so on. But as we saw, at least many instances of these states don't have any phenomenal, sensory quality.

Subjectivity: Privacy and Special Epistemic Access

Subjectivity is often claimed to be of the essence of consciousness.[4] One sense of subjectivity is epistemological, having to do with the supposed special character of knowledge of conscious states. The main idea is that one has a special epistemic access to one's own current conscious states; we seem to be "immediately aware," as Descartes said, of our own feelings, thoughts, and perceptions and enjoy a special sort of first-person authority with regard to them. A precise explanation of just what this "immediate" or "direct" access consists in is a controversial question.[5] For our purposes, it will suffice to note the following three features: (1) Such knowledge is not based on evidence about other things—observation of what we say or do, what others tell us, physical or physiological cues, and the like. Your knowledge that you have a toothache, that you are thinking about what to do this weekend, and such, is direct and immediate in this sense. So the first feature of our knowledge of our own conscious states is that it is not based on evidence about some other thing you know or believe. (2) Second, your knowledge of your own current mental states carries special authority in the sense that your claim to have such knowledge cannot, except in special circumstances, be overridden by third-person testimony. Concerning such matters as the queasy feelings you are experiencing in your stomach, your afterimages, the itchy spot on your shoulder, what you are thinking about, and other such matters, *what you say goes, at least in normal circumstances*, and others must defer to your avowals. As the qualifying proviso implies, first-person authority need not be thought to be absolute and unconditional; under special circumstances, your claim to know might be overridden. What might such special circumstances be? One obvious and uninteresting case is one in which you misdescribe your sensation (suppose that there is independent evidence that your grasp of the language in which you make the report is less than perfect, and that behavioral and physiological evidence indicates that you are almost certainly experiencing another kind of sensation). Or one might argue that our neurophysiological knowledge could at some point reach a state in which it becomes possible to check, and correct, first-person testimony against physiological data concerning the subject's brain activities (say, from a magnetic resonance imaging of her brain). In any case, whatever the degree or firmness of first-person authority, it is evident that the subject does occupy a specially privileged position in regard to her own current conscious states. (3) As these remarks indicate, there is an asymmetry between first- and third-person knowledge of conscious states. Neither of the two foregoing points applies to third-person knowledge, that is, knowledge of another person's conscious states. She alone enjoys immediate and specially authoritative access to her conscious states; we have to listen to what she has to say or observe her behavior or examine her brain. The idea that knowledge of one's own conscious states is "private" reflects this epistemic asymmetry between first and third person.

In recognizing the subject's special epistemic position in relation to her own current conscious states, we need not adopt the model of complete and perfect "transparency"—nor the stronger claim that the subject's mind, while wholly transparent to herself, is totally opaque and impenetrable to others. In particular, the thesis does not include the claim that the subject is either infallible or omniscient in regard to her present conscious states. Infallibility would mean that whatever she believes about such states must be true. Point (1) says only that her knowledge, or belief, concerning such states is not based on, or inferred from, evidence. That doesn't mean that what she believes is necessarily true. Point (2) says that whatever she believes and says about her present conscious states "goes"—that is, it enjoys immunity against third-person challenges—not that it must be true. Nor do these points add up to the claim that she has omniscient knowledge about her conscious mind—that is, she knows every aspect of her conscious states. It is important to keep in mind that recognition of first-person authority does not necessarily lead to the extreme Cartesian thesis[6] of the complete transparency of the conscious mind. Such a position may well be false; however, that should not blind us to the very important epistemic properties of conscious states—in particular, the asymmetry between first- and third-person knowledge of such states.

A related but distinct sense of "access" used in connection with consciousness is currently on the scene, and we should at least briefly note it here. The access we have been discussing is epistemic access in the sense of the subject's *being aware of*, or *coming to know*, something. The second sense of access, introduced by Ned Block,[7] who wants to contrast it with consciousness of qualia (what he calls "phenomenal consciousness"), concerns the availability of the content of a conscious state for the subject's verbal reports and for her "executive module" to guide her behavior and action. Suppose your sensory system registers a piece of information with content p (say, that there is a green couch in front of you). The state with this information is "access-conscious" in case information p is available for verbal reports (e.g., when appropriately prompted, you respond, "I see a green couch in front of me" or "There is a green couch over there"), and this information can be used by you to guide your action (e.g., you walk around the couch on the way to the door rather than bumping into it). This is a very rough characterization of a concept intended to do explanatory-theoretical work in psychology, but it isn't without ties to the commonsense psychological framework in which our discussion is couched. We can see some ways in which this idea of access is related to our notion of epistemic access: If the content, or information, carried in a mental state is epistemically accessible to us, we can, in normal circumstances, report that we are in such a state, and this knowledge can guide our actions. Is the converse of this also true—that is, if a state is access-conscious, does it follow that the subject has the kind of special epistemic access we have discussed? How is consciousness of qualia related to access consciousness in Block's sense? These questions involve complex issues, and we must set them aside.[8]

Subjectivity: "Point of View"

Some philosophers have introduced the notion of a special first-person *point of view*, or *perspective*, as an essential characteristic of consciousness. Nagel writes:

> If physicalism is to be defended, the phenomenological features must themselves be given a physical account. But when we examine their subjective character it seems that such a result is impossible. The reason is that *every subjective phenomenon is essentially connected with a single point of view*, and it seems inevitable that an objective, physical theory will abandon that point of view.[9]

And in a later essay:

> *Yet subjective aspects of the mental can be apprehended only from the point of view of the creature itself* . . . , whereas what is physical is simply there, and can be externally apprehended from more than one point of view.[10]

Nagel is saying that the subjectivity of mental phenomena is essentially connected with—perhaps consists in—there being "a single point of view" from which these phenomena are apprehended. This fits in with the claim discussed earlier that conscious states have phenomenal (or phenomenological) features in the sense that there is something it is like to be in such states. For, as Nagel emphasizes, there is no impersonal "what it's like"; it is always what it is like *for a given subject* (for you, for humans, for bats) to see yellow, to taste pineapple, to echolocate a moth. Things don't look, or appear, this way or that way, period; they look a certain way to one perceiving subject and perhaps a different way to another. There can be no "looks" or "appearances" in a world devoid of subjects capable of having experiences.

Understood this way, the talk about "points of view" appears to have two parts. First, there is the idea that for any conscious state there is a subject whose state it is and that the content of consciousness consists in how things look or appear to that subject. Second, there is the idea that for each conscious state there is a *unique* subject, a single person, whose consciousness it is or, as Nagel puts it, who "apprehends" it. But these points are not new to us. That any "state" must be a state *of* some thing appears to be a general point about all states, mental or otherwise. That a conscious state must be a state of some subject whose experience it constitutes is a point presupposed in our earlier discussion concerning phenomenal characters and direct awareness. And we have already discussed the idea of a "single subject" involved in consciousness, namely, the supposed privacy of consciousness and the first- and third-person asymmetry.

There is another way in which "the first-person point of view" has been associated with the notion of subjectivity. Consider the following sentences:

(S) The shortest spy believes that he (himself) is clever.

(P) The shortest spy believes that the shortest spy is clever.

In (S) a person, the shortest spy, is referring to himself *qua himself* in attributing the property of being clever. In contrast, in (P) that person is attributing cleverness to himself, not qua himself but qua third person. For we may suppose that the person has been told by a source he trusts that the shortest spy is clever but has no idea who the shortest spy is (it turns out, unbeknownst to him, that he is the shortest spy).

We can see, then, that (S) and (P) are logically independent of each other; that is, neither implies the other. For even if (S) is true, (P) can be false, if the shortest spy does not know, or believe, that he is the shortest spy. Conversely (P) can be true and yet (S) false, if the person who in fact is the shortest spy thinks that someone else is the shortest spy and has a low self-esteem about his own intelligence. So we see that the following two general locutions are not equivalent:

(S*) x believes himself/herself to be F.

(P*) x believes x to be F.

These points remain true when other intentional mental verbs are substituted for "believes"; you may want to verify this with verbs such as "doubts," "hopes," "wants," and the like.

But apparently this phenomenon is unique to psychological cases; for consider the following sentences that do not involve psychological verbs:

(1) x causes himself/herself/itself to be F.

(1a) x causes x to be F.

(2) x is as tall as himself/herself/itself.

(3) x is as tall as x.

The two sentences in each of these pairs are equivalent. The difference introduced by the use of a reflexive pronoun ("himself," "itself," etc.), or reflexive reference to the subject, seems unique to first-person mental ascriptions to the self. For this reason, some have proposed that the subjectivity of the mental—at least one essential aspect of it—consists in this special kind of reflexivity of first-person reference to the self.[11]

In our discussion of consciousness, however, we may set aside this aspect of subjectivity; for the phenomenon, while it raises some deeply interesting philosophical issues, arises for intentional mental states in general and does not specifically concern *conscious* mental states as such, although of course this does not necessarily rule out the existence of some possibly interesting connections at a deeper level.

Consciousness as Inner Awareness

One idea that often turns up in philosophical accounts of consciousness is that consciousness is a kind of inner awareness—that is, awareness of one's own mental states. The model is that of a kind of internal scanner or monitoring device that keeps tabs on the internal goings-on of a system. When you are driving alone on an uncrowded, monotonous expressway, you sometimes go on a sort of automatic pilot: You perceive the conditions of the road and make the necessary adjustments to the steering wheel and accelerator to keep the car going at a steady speed in your lane, but there is a sense in which your perceptions are not fully conscious. That is, you are not actively aware of what you see and hear, although you do see and hear (otherwise you would go off the road!), and you may be unable to recall much about the conditions of the traffic or the highway for the last few minutes. Or consider pains: We are told that in the heat of competition or combat, an injured athlete or wounded soldier can be entirely unaware of his pain. His attention is preoccupied with another task, and he is not conscious of his pain. In such a case we seem to have an instance of pain that isn't a conscious state.

Wanting to give a physicalistically acceptable model of consciousness, David Armstrong has proposed an account of this kind. According to Armstrong, consciousness can be thought of as "perception or awareness of the state of our own mind."[12] When you go on automatic pilot while driving, you perceive the conditions around you, but you do not perceive, or are unaware of, your perceivings. The injured athlete does not perceive her pain, and this is exactly what makes her pain unconscious. When she comes to be aware of the pain, it becomes a conscious pain.

In a similar vein, David Rosenthal has suggested that "a mental state's being conscious consists in one's having a thought that one is in that very mental state."[13] On this account, then, a mental state is a conscious state just in case there is a "higher-order" thought, or awareness, that one is in that state. So consciousness is a sort of "metapsychological" state, that is, a psychological state about another psychological state. A creature, on this account, is a conscious creature just in case it is capable of having higher-order mental states in this sense. A view like this typically allows the existence of mental states, even sensory states, that are not conscious—that is, those not accompanied by higher-order thoughts. And this for good reason: Otherwise there would be an infinite progression of higher and still higher mental states, without end.

How plausible is this view of consciousness? There is no question that it has a certain initial plausibility and nicely fits some typical cases of mental states that we recognize as conscious. And the Armstrong-style view seems to open the door to a functionalist explanation of consciousness: On the functionalist view, first-order perceptions receive an account in terms of their causal roles or functions—in terms of their typical stimulus causes and behavioral/psychological effects—and if this is right, one might plausibly attempt a similar functional account of consciousness as an internal monitoring device on these first-order perceptions and other mental states. Perhaps such an account could explain the role of consciousness in organizing and coordinating disparate perceptions—say, perceptions coming through different sensory channels—and even yield a functionalist account of "the unity of consciousness." At every moment of our waking lives, we are bombarded by sensory stimuli of all sorts. The role of consciousness in appropriately coordinating and integrating an organism's myriad sensations and perceptions and selecting some of them for special attention is probably crucial to its ability to cope with the constantly changing forces of its environment, and this means that an approach such as Armstrong's may fit in well with an evolutionary explanation of the emergence of consciousness in higher organisms.

But a functional account like this suffers from implausibilities when examined from the subjective point of view. It may be plausible enough to say that a pain is a conscious pain just when you are aware of it. But what is it that you are aware of when you are aware of a pain? According to functionalism, pain is a causal-functional role: To be in pain is to be in a state apt to be caused by tissue damage and apt for causing pain behaviors. To be aware of your pain, then, would be to be aware that you are in such a functional state. But this seems plainly wrong; when you are aware of pain, you are aware of its hurtfulness—you are aware that your knee hurts! Note, however, that if this is a difficulty, it is a difficulty for the functionalist version of the higher-order approach to consciousness, not necessarily for the general approach in terms of higher-order states.

What, then, of the general model of consciousness as consisting in having higher-order thoughts concerning other mental states? We should immediately notice that according to this approach only creatures with the capacity for such thoughts can be conscious, and this may rule out most of the animal kingdom, including human infants, from the realm of consciousness. Higher-order thoughts supposedly implicated in consciousness have the form "I am aware that I am in state M," where "M" refers to a type of mental state (e.g., pain, the belief that the car brakes have just locked). Having such a thought would require, at minimum, an ability to refer to oneself, and this in turn seems to entail the possession of some notion of self, the idea of oneself as distinct from other things and subjects. Admittedly, all this is a complex and speculative affair, but anyhow it isn't clear what sorts of general conceptual, cognitive, and other psychological capacities are involved in having higher-order thoughts of the required kind. Moreover, doesn't such a thought (the thought that you are in state of kind M) require the possession of the concept of M? (If you have the thought that you are in pain, don't you have to have the concept of pain—an idea of what it is to be in pain?) It would seem, at least intuitively, that some lower forms of animals, perhaps reptiles and fish, have sensations and perceptions and that their sensations and perceptions are phenomenally represented to them. But how plausible is it to suppose that these animals have the cognitive capacity to form self-regarding thoughts of the sort required by the higher-order thought account of consciousness? In fact, it isn't clear that we would want to attribute any intentional states, like beliefs and thoughts, to such creatures. Would we for that reason deny consciousness to such animals? Don't infants not yet capable of self-referential thoughts experience pains when they have colic? It may be one thing to have *conscious* sensations and quite another to have *thoughts about* such sensations. On the face of it, the latter requires a much higher and more complex set of cognitive capacities than the former. The gist of the difficulty, then, is this: The higher-order thought account of consciousness makes the capacity for intentional states—of a fairly sophisticated sort—a prerequisite for having conscious states, and that seems wrong.

When we reflect on these and related issues, the higher-order thought model seems to fare better as an account of *self-consciousness* rather than consciousness itself.[14] It is clear that self-consciousness requires an ability to form thoughts involving oneself, to take the first-person point of view and attribute properties to oneself qua oneself. In this sense, the view of consciousness under discussion seems better suited for the second and third aspects of consciousness delineated above, namely, direct and unmediated awareness of one's own mental states and the idea of first-person perspective; it appears to have little to say about the phenomenal aspect of consciousness. Moreover, not every mental state of which we are aware—of which we have a second-order thought—needs to be a conscious state. For example, if after several sessions with your therapist you come to be aware of your hidden hostile feelings toward your roommate, that need not make your hostility a conscious state. You now believe, and perhaps know, that you harbor hostile feelings toward him, but this need not turn your feelings into conscious feelings. For this to happen, you must, in some sense, begin to "feel" these feelings. Consciousness of a mental state includes an awareness of it, but a special kind of awareness seems required if the awareness is to count as an instance of conscious awareness.

Various organisms and man-made systems have sensory receptors or scanners through which they acquire information about their environment, process and store the information in various ways, and use it to guide their behavior. Birds, bees, and even the lowliest insects do it, as do electromechanical robots and even simple burglar alarm systems. And in some of the more sophisticated systems of this kind, there may be, as Armstrong says, an internal monitoring center that keeps an eye on the flow and processing of information through the system and uses this information for a more efficient coordination and integration of the total information available to the system. Whether some such model is realized in a particular system, say, in humans, and if so how, are empirical questions on which philosophers don't have much to say. However, the idea of a system's acquiring and using information about the status of its first-order information processing is not something that on the face of it presents us with any special mystery. It is not in itself a philosophically perplexing idea.

Moreover, it does not seem necessary to suppose that there is a *single* monitoring mechanism in humans, one central agent in charge of overseeing all first-order cognitive processes going on in us. For all we know, there may be many such monitoring centers more or less loosely allied and cooperating with one another, exchanging information and coordinating their activities, without there being a single supermonitor, a central authority, overseeing all these subsystems. The idea that there must be a single central monitoring mechanism corresponds to the idea that there is in each of us an "ego" or self, a single subject of all our conscious states.[15]

But don't we all believe in a single subject of consciousness? Isn't this an evident fact when you think about your own mental life? When you look inward to your present conscious experiences, isn't it evident that there is a certain unified awareness (if not the elusive self that Hume said he could not find) that comprises a visual awareness of these words on the page, an auditory awareness of the music from your radio overlaid with the whirring noise of the air conditioner, a tactual awareness of the pressure of the chair against your back, and the thought that consciousness is indeed an elusive thing? If there is one single scanner that monitors all our cognitive and information-processing states and processes, that might physically validate our subjective view of the self as a unity. But should the latter constrain in any way what we might find in our brains? Should we say that if neurophysiology finds nothing in our brains that performs the function of central monitoring, then that would show the falsity of physicalism? Or on the contrary, would that show that there really is no such thing as a unified subject of consciousness? These are good philosophical questions to think about.

Does Consciousness Supervene on Physical Properties?

The subjectivity of consciousness, in the sense of awareness of our own psychological states, seems, as we have seen, explicable in principle in terms of some internal monitoring mechanism, and this provides us with a basis for a possible physical/neural explanation of self-awareness. The "directness" and "immediacy" of such awareness, too, perhaps can be explained in terms of a direct coupling of such a scanning device to a speech center, a mechanism responsible for verbal reports.[16] The first- and third-person asymmetry of access seems no particular mystery: It arises from the simple fact that my scanning device (and its associated speech center), not yours, is directly monitoring my internal states. These ideas are rough and may ultimately fail. However, what they show is the possibility of understanding the subjectivity of consciousness in the sense of direct first-person access to one's own mental states; for at least we can imagine a *possible mechanism* that can implement it at the physical/physiological level. That is, we could see what it would be like to have an explanation of the subjectivity of consciousness. That shows that at least we understand the problem.

On this view of consciousness as direct awareness of internal states, consciousness would be supervenient on the basic physical/biological structure and functioning of the organism. The fact that an organism is equipped with the capacity directly to monitor its current internal states is a fact about its physical/biological organization and must be manifested through the patterns of its behavior in response to environmental conditions. This means that if two organisms are identical in their physical/biological makeup, they cannot differ in their capacity for self-monitoring capability. In that sense, consciousness as special first-person epistemic authority may well be supervenient on physical and biological fact.[17]

What, then, of the phenomenal aspect of consciousness? Do qualia supervene on the physical/biological constitution of organisms? You feel pain when your C-fibers are stimulated; is it necessarily the case that your physical duplicate feels pain when her C-fibers are stimulated? In our world pains and other qualitative states exist, and we suppose them to depend, in regular lawlike ways, on what goes on in the physical/biological domain. Is there a possible world that is a total physical duplicate of this world but in which there are no phenomenal mental states? Many philosophers think that qualia do not supervene on physical/biological fact. For example, Kripke writes:

> What about the case of the stimulation of C-fibers? To create this phenomenon, it would seem that God need only create beings with C-fibers capable of the appropriate type of physical stimulation; whether the beings are conscious or not is irrelevant here. It would seem, though, that to make the C-fiber stimulation correspond to pain, or be felt as pain, God must do something in addition to the mere creation of the C-fiber stimulation; He must let the creatures feel the C-fibers as *pain*, and not as a tickle, or as warmth, or as nothing, as apparently would also have been within His powers.[18]

Kripke contrasts this situation with one involving molecular motion and heat: After God created molecular motion, he did not have to perform an additional act to create heat. When molecular motion came into being, heat, too, came into being.

If Kripke is right, there are two kinds of possible worlds that, though identical with our world in all physical respects, are different in mental respects: First, there are worlds with different physical/phenomenal correlations (e.g., C-fiber stimulation correlates with itches rather than pains) and, second, those in which there are no phenomenal mental events at all, "zombie worlds." In the latter there are people exactly like you and me, behaving just as we do (including saying things like "That toothache kept me awake all night, and I feel too tired and sleepy to work on the paper right now"), but they are zombies with no experience of pain, sleepiness, itch, fatigue, or any of the rest.

But is Kripke right? How is it possible for God to create C-fiber stimulation but not pain? Let us look at various considerations against qualia supervenience:

1. There is no conceptual connection between the concept of pain and that of C-fiber stimulation (that is, no connection of meaning between "pain" and "C-fiber stimulation"), and therefore there is no contradiction

in the supposition that an organism has its C-fibers stimulated without experiencing pain or any other sensation. This argument, however, is not entirely persuasive; for there is no conceptual connection between heat and molecular motion either, nor between water and H_2O, and yet there is no possible world in which molecular motion exists but not heat or a world that contains H_2O but no water. In considering this reply, we must ask whether the case of pain and C-fiber excitation is relevantly similar to cases like heat–molecular motion and water-H_2O.

2. "Inverted spectra" are possible: It is perfectly conceivable that there are worlds that are just like ours in all physical respects but in which people, when looking at the things we look at, experience colors that are complementary to the colors we experience.[19] In such worlds cabbages are really green and tomatoes are really red; however, people there experience red when they look at cabbages and green when they look at tomatoes, although they call cabbages "green" and tomatoes "red." Such worlds seem perfectly conceivable, with no hidden contradictions. In fact, why isn't it conceivable that there be a world in which colors are sensed the way sounds are sensed by us and vice versa—worlds with inverted sense modalities? (Arthur Rimbaud, the French poet, saw colors in vowels, like this: "A black, E white, I red, U green, O blue."[20])

3. In fact, why couldn't there be people in the actual world, perhaps among our friends and relatives, whose color spectra are inverted with respect to ours, although their relevant neural states are the same? As was just noted, they call tomatoes "red" and cabbages "green" as we do, and all our observable behaviors coincide perfectly. However, their color experiences are different from ours.[21] We normally do not imagine such possibilities; we think that when you and I are in relevantly similar neurophysiological states, we experience the same sensation. But such an assumption is precisely the assumption that sensory states supervene on physical conditions, which is what is at issue. Also, to assume that there are lawlike regularities between neural states and qualia is to assume qualia supervenience. Why should we think there are such laws, and if there are, how could we know them?

4. Implicit in these remarks is the point that qualia do not supervene on functional properties of organisms either.[22] A functional property is, roughly, a property in virtue of which an organism responds to a given sensory input by emitting some specific behavioral output. You and your physical duplicate must share the same functional properties; that is, functional properties supervene on physical properties. So if qualia should supervene on functional properties, they would supervene on physical properties. This means that to question the supervenience of qualia on physical properties is ipso facto to question their supervenience on functional properties.[23]

The main argument for the failure of the physical supervenience of qualia, then, is the apparent conceivability of zombies and qualia inversions in organisms physically indistinguishable from us.[24] Conceivability may not in itself imply real possibility, and the exact relationship between conceivability and possibility is a difficult issue. And we could make errors in judging what's conceivable and what isn't, and our judgments may depend on available empirical information. Knowing what we now know, we may not be able to conceive a world in which water is not H_2O, but people who didn't have the same information might have judged differently. In the case of qualitative characters of mental states, however, is there anything about them that, should we come to know it, would convince us that zombies and qualia inversions are not really possible? Don't we already know all we need to know, or can know, about these subjective phenomenal characters of our experience? Is there anything about them that we can learn from objective, empirical science? Research in neurophysiology will perhaps tell us more about the biological basis of phenomenal experiences, but it is difficult to see how that could be relevant as evidence for qualia supervenience. At best such discoveries will tell us more about lawful correlations between qualia and underlying neural states, but the question has to do with whether these correlations are *metaphysically necessary*—whether there are possible worlds in which the correlations fail. What's more, it isn't so obvious that neurophysiological research could even establish correlations between qualia and neural states. For, one might claim, the claimed correlations only correlate neural states with *verbal reports* of qualia, not qualia themselves, from which it follows that these correlations are consistent with qualia inversions. As we saw, we cannot easily eliminate the epistemic possibility of qualia inversions in our world, unless qualia supervenience is tacitly presupposed, and if this possibility is granted, we are accepting the possibility that either there are no lawful correlations between qualia and neural states or, even if there were, we could not know that they exist or ascertain what the specific correlations are.

The case against qualia supervenience, therefore, is not conclusive, though quite substantial. Are there, then, considerations in favor of qualia supervenience? It would seem that the only positive considerations are broad metaphysical ones that might very well be accused of begging the question. Say, you are already committed to physicalism: You then have two choices about qualia—either deny their existence or try to accommodate them somehow within a physicalist framework. Given this choice between accommodation and rejection, you opt for accommodation, since a flat denial of the existence of qualia, you may feel, makes your physicalism fly in the face of common sense. You may then find supervenience an appealing way for bringing qualia into the physical domain—close

enough to it, at any rate. For qualia supervenience at least guarantees that
once all the physical details of an organism, or a world, are fixed, that
fixes all the facts concerning that organism or world—and this of course
includes facts about qualia. If this doesn't make qualia full-fledged physical items, it at least makes them dependent on physical facts, and that
protects the primacy and priority of the physical. That, you may feel, is
good enough. Furthermore, qualia supervenience seems to open a way of
accounting for the causal relevance of qualia. If qualia are genuine existents, their existence must make a causal difference. But any reasonable
version of physicalism must consider the physical world to be causally
closed (see Chapter 6), and it would seem that if qualia are to be brought
into the causal structure of the world, they must at least be supervenient
on physical facts of the world. Supervenience by itself may not be enough
to confer *causal efficacy* to qualia, but it may suffice to make them *causally
relevant* in some broad sense. In any case, without qualia supervenience,
there may well be no hope of providing qualia with a place in the network of causal relations of this world.[25]

The Problem of Qualia

What is commonly referred to as "the problem of qualia" is
that of giving an account of qualia that is consistent with the basic tenets
of physicalism—that is, giving a physicalistically acceptable account of
qualia.[26] We have just discussed reasons for thinking that qualia are not
supervenient on the physical/biological processes going on in the brain.
But if qualia are not physically supervenient, they must be considered as
items that are in addition to the physical items of this world, and we must
consider facts about qualia to be extraphysical facts. The existence of non-
supervenient qualia thus poses a direct challenge to physicalism.

The physicalist, therefore, has two options at this point: (1) either argue
for a weaker form of the supervenience thesis or (2) argue that qualia, as
standardly conceived, do not exist—that there are no phenomenal, qualitative states or experiences with phenomenal characters. Let us consider
how each option plays out. We will discuss the first option in the balance
of this section and the next and take up the second option in a later section.

So our physicalist might concede that qualia do not supervene on phys-
ical/biological processes with metaphysical necessity, but they do so with
a weaker form of necessity, that is, nomological necessity. He concedes
that "zombie worlds" are metaphysically possible and that it is perfectly
conceivable that your physical duplicate has a visual spectrum that is inverted relative to yours. However, he claims that these things are not possible in worlds that are sufficiently like our world in that they are made
up of the same kinds of basic material particles that obey the same basic

physical laws. In speaking of qualia supervenience, we are not worried, he would say, about really weird worlds containing nonphysical spirits or in which very different physical laws prevail. Rather, we have in mind those worlds that are pretty much like this one, namely, the "nomologically possible worlds."[27]

This of course weakens physicalism. It now makes a claim only about the actual world and relevantly similar ones and says that in worlds like ours no two things can differ mentally—in particular, in phenomenal respects—without differing physically. Perhaps this is physicalism enough;[28] we might call it "nomological physicalism," distinguishing it from "metaphysical physicalism." And one may defend it along the following lines: Reduction of heat to molecular motion, that of the gene to the DNA molecule, and similar reductions in the sciences hold only in worlds sufficiently like ours, especially in regard to the nature of basic material stuff and fundamental physical laws. In worlds that are very remote from ours in which wholly different laws hold, it might not be the DNA molecule but some other type of molecule or mechanism that is causally responsible for the transmission of genetic information. Causal powers depend on prevailing laws, and given that the concept of the gene is defined in terms of causal roles (see below), it is apparent that the reduction of the gene to the DNA molecule holds only in worlds that are nomologically similar to ours. As long as DNA does the work in our world and worlds that are sufficiently close to it, that's good enough to count as reduction of the gene to the DNA molecule. What this shows is that questions of physicalism, supervenience, reduction, and such need to be considered only for nomologically possible worlds, worlds that are like ours in basic physical laws and material composition, and we may safely ignore far-out, exotic worlds.

Let us consider the claim of the nomological supervenience of qualia in the following form:

> For each phenomenal property P, whenever some organism x instantiates P there is a physical/biological property B such that x instantiates B at that time, and it is a law of nature (i.e., holds as a matter of nomological necessity) that whenever any organism y instantiates B, y instantiates P at that time.

So suppose you experience an itch at a given time: According to the supervenience thesis, then, you are in a certain physical/biological state (presumably some neural state of your brain)—call it "N"—such that the following generalization holds as matter of law:

> (S) Whenever N is instantiated in humans, they experience an itch ($N \rightarrow I$, for short)

We need not suppose that N is the only supervenience base for itch; it may be that in other species, different neural states may give rise to itchy sensations. What (S) says is that in humans, whenever N is realized, an itch will be experienced.

The question that now confronts the physicalist is this: Is nomological supervenience enough to accommodate qualia in a physical world—at least in physical worlds that are sufficiently like ours? There are reasons for thinking that there is more explaining to do. To see this, let us suppose ticklish sensations supervene on a certain neural state, M; that is, the following law holds:

(S*) $M \rightarrow T$

Regularities like (S) and (S*) hold in our world and other similar worlds. *But why?* Can this be explained in terms of the material constitution of these worlds (more specifically, the physical/biological constitution of humans) and basic physical laws? If correlations like (S) and (S*) hold only in worlds that are like ours in respect of basic laws and the material stuff they contain, we must expect an explanation of these correlations in terms of these laws and the properties of the material stuff the laws govern. But the prospects for such an explanation seem exceedingly remote. Terms like "itch" and "tickle" don't appear anywhere in the physical/biological sciences, not to mention basic physics; our basic physical sciences don't deal in properties like experiencing itches and tickles, sensing green, and such. It's difficult to see how from physical/biological premises we could infer, or somehow extract, facts about sensory qualia. If this is right, there would be facts about this world, facts concerning the occurrences of phenomenal experiences, that are not explainable in terms of physical facts and laws. The phenomena of the world would outrun the explanatory resources of physicalism.

If we had supervenience laws like (S) and (S*) as explanatory premises, we could of course explain why a particular instance of itchy sensation or ticklish sensation occurred in a person: She was itchy because she was in neural state N, and she was ticklish because she was in state M. *But precisely what is in need of explanation is why supervenience relations like (S) and (S*) hold in the first place.* Why do we experience itches just when we are in neural state N? Why don't we experience tickles instead? What is it about states N and M that account for the fact that itches emerge from N and tickles emerge from M, and not the other way around? Why does *any* phenomenal consciousness emerge at all? Why are there such things as qualia, in a world that is constituted entirely by material particles that behave according to physical laws? These are some of the questions that the physicalist needs to cope with.

Can Qualia Be Explained Physically?

Consider the case of temperature and mean kinetic energy. It would seem that we could explain perfectly well why the temperature of a gas supervenes on the mean kinetic energy of its molecules—in fact, why the temperature of a gas is nothing but its mean molecular energy of motion—somewhat along the following lines. To begin, the notion of temperature is a functional notion defined in terms of a cluster of laws that relate temperature with other properties. Temperature is the physical magnitude of an object that increases when the object is in contact with another object with a higher degree of that magnitude; that, when it is sufficiently high, will melt a ball of wax in proximity; that can, when very high, cause lumps of iron to glow and then become molten; that can, when sufficiently low, make steel brittle; and so on. The temperature of an object is that property of the object which occupies these causal roles, and it turns out that in this world and worlds physically like this one in respect of basic laws and material makeup, mean molecular energy is what fills these roles. Moreover, given the basic material constitution of the world and laws of physics, we can explain why mean molecular energy has these causal powers. And whatever property it is that meets these causal powers *is* temperature. This also explains why temperature supervenes on more basic microphysical facts. A similar story can be told about the gene and the DNA molecule: The gene is that biological factor or mechanism that does the causal work of transmitting phenotypic features from generation to generation in accordance with certain lawful patterns, and we find that the DNA molecule fills this causal role—it is exactly what performs this causal work in our world and worlds that are relevantly like ours. Moreover, we know, at least in rough but convincing outlines, just how DNA molecules accomplish this task. In any case these explanations of higher-level phenomena in terms of underlying physical mechanisms seem to exemplify the model of microreductive explanation in the sciences. Why can't we look to the sciences (presumably neurobiology) for a physical explanation of the qualia on the same model?

The kind of reductive explanation we have considered begins by construing the phenomena to be reduced in terms of their causal functions. Thus, as we saw, temperature is construed as that property of an object which stands in such and such causal/nomological relations to such and such phenomena. Similarly, the gene is understood as that biological mechanism, whatever it turns out to be, which is causally responsible for such and such phenomena involving the transmission of heritable characteristics. This means that the phenomena to be reduced are conceptualized *relationally* or *extrinsically*, in terms of their causal/nomological relationships to other phenomena, and not *intrinsically*, in terms of their internal qualitative character or compositional structure.

Thus, *properties that are up for reductive explanation must first be "primed" by being relationalized—that is, reconstrued, as extrinsic relational properties.* This makes sense for many macrophysical properties for which we seek, and have found in many instances, microphysical explanations. For something to be water soluble is for it to have a property that causes it to dissolve when immersed in water, for something to be transparent is for it to have the kind of structure that lets light beams through, and so on. But with phenomenal characters, we seem finally to have come face to face with paradigmatic instances of *intrinsic* properties. The hurtfulness of pain, the acrid smell of sulphur, the taste and flavor of pineapple—these things are intrinsic qualities if anything is. We often use, as we have just done, *extrinsic descriptions* to pick out these qualia (e.g., "the smell typically caused in humans by sulphur"), but what these descriptions pick out are not extrinsic properties but intrinsic ones. It may be precisely because the properties involved are intrinsic (and perhaps also subjective) that we need to resort to extrinsic, relational descriptions to make them communicable to other people. This procedure is not unique to qualia; it is used for fundamental physical magnitudes. For a stick to be 1 meter long is for it to coincide with the Standard Meter when the two are laid end to end (or it is so many times the wavelength of light emitted by cadmium or whatever). We do the same with mass: 1 kilogram is the mass of an object that accelerates at such and such rate when a net force of such and such magnitude is applied to it. But we standardly consider mass, length, electric charge, and the like to be basic intrinsic physical properties of material things.

If qualia are intrinsic properties, there seems little hope for their reductive explanation according to the standard model we have just described. If this is right, it seems that the N-itch, M-tickle, and other such correlations must be accepted as "brute" facts not subject to further explanation. We have no understanding of why itches emerge from N and tickles from M; all we know is that they do. As the emergentists have urged, we may have to accept these emergence or supervenience relations with "natural piety."

Those who hang their hope on neurobiological investigations for an account of consciousness urge us to look to some of the recent advances in neurobiology as a propitious omen of an eventual success in obtaining a physical explanation of phenomenal consciousness. For example, there is the recent speculation among the brain scientists that synchronized firings of certain neurons in the brain at a frequency in the range of 35–75 Hz (sometimes called "gamma oscillations" or "40-Hz oscillations") hold the key to a solution of the so-called binding problem, the problem of explaining how the separate pieces of information (color, shape, size, motion, smell, sound, texture, etc.) processed through different sensory-neural channels somehow get bound together to yield a coherent conscious awareness of, say, a moving bus as one unitary thing.[29] Some people appear to think that if this hypothesis turns out to be true, it would be a solution to "the problem of consciousness" or at least an important step toward a solution.[30]

Perhaps this hypothesis, if true, may be a partial solution to the *scientific* problem of consciousness. This is the problem of identifying neural mechanisms that subserve conscious states and processes.[31] Suppose that at some point in the future we have a detailed mapping of all sorts of qualia with distinct neural states (say, with the 40-Hz oscillations serving as the neural substrate of "unity of consciousness"). This would represent a very substantial scientific understanding of consciousness. But would it solve or make any advance toward solving the philosophical problem of consciousness?[32]

It is difficult to see how discovering neural mechanisms of consciousness, no matter how impressively detailed our knowledge of such mechanisms may be, can have anything to contribute toward dispelling the mystery of the phenomenal character of consciousness. As we noted, the deep mystery is why particular phenomenal characters correlate with, or arise out of, the neural substrates from which they in fact emerge. Neuroscientists may some day deliver to us an exhaustive list of qualia–brain-state correlations, and this would add to our knowledge of the brain and the particular ways in which our conscious life depends on what goes on in the brain. But these correlations are exactly what give rise to philosophical puzzles; what we need is an explanation of why this particular system of correlations, out of the myriad other possible ones, holds in our world.[33] And there is the deeper question: Why is there such a thing as phenomenal consciousness in a world that is fundamentally physical?

Who Needs Qualia?

We thus find ourselves in a dilemma: If qualia supervene on physical/biological processes, why they supervene—why they supervene on, or arise from, the specific neural substrates from which they in fact arise—remains a mystery, something that seems entirely inexplicable from the physical point of view. (This doesn't mean that this would be any easier to explain from a nonphysicalist perspective.) Yet if they do not supervene, they must be taken as phenomena entirely outside the physical domain. At this point some philosophers may feel that the basic physicalist approach to mentality is in deep trouble and that it is time to begin exploring nonphysicalist alternatives. But this strikes many philosophers as a dismal prospect, and some have taken the heroic (perhaps quixotic) route of denying the existence of qualia. This we may call "qualia nihilism" (or "qualia eliminativism").

Qualia nihilism comes in two varieties. The first is the claim that qualia, whether or not they really exist, have no place, no role to play, in the science of psychology, where psychology is understood as a science whose aim is law-based explanation and prediction of human behavior broadly construed. This form of qualia nihilism is to be distinguished from behaviorism; unlike the latter, it does not oppose the positing of inner states, whether these are physiological or psychological, in framing theories of behavior. And it need not shrink from mentioning consciousness: It can allow consciousness in the sense of awareness an active psychological role. It only says that the purely qualitative aspects of our consciousness have no role in explaining and predicting behavior. Let us call this "theoretical qualia nihilism."

You may be led to theoretical qualia nihilism by considerations along the following lines. Qualia are subjective and not intersubjectively accessible, and this makes their direct scientific study impossible. Moreover, unlike the unobservable theoretical posits of physical sciences, the intrinsic features of qualia do not seem to have any observably testable consequences; for as far as behavior goes, just what qualia a subject is experiencing seems to make no difference. What does make a difference is that the subject can distinguish, say red, from green—for example, she can tell reliably when the traffic lights say "Go!" or "Stop!"[34] On the basis of such discriminative behavior, we may even speculate that the subject is aware, in some direct and immediate way, of the qualitative difference between red and green, and this discriminative ability can play a role in explaining her behavior (e.g., her driving behavior). However, just what the intrinsic quality of her red experience is, how red looks to her or that her red quale is like *this* rather than *that*, seems of no importance whatever—it plays no role in explaining why she brakes her car when the red lights go on and starts up again when the lights turn green. What matters here is only that she can discriminate her red quale from her green quale. Therefore, what has behavioral consequences and hence is intersubjectively accessible is the subject's ability to discriminate between different qualia, not the intrinsic qualities of her experiences. Intrinsic qualities are there and serve a purpose, but the purpose served is relational, and it is the differences among qualia that carry information. To put it another way, if there were no intrinsic qualities, there would be nothing to discriminate! In this sense, therefore, there *must* be qualia, but the fact that a given quale is like *this* and another is like *that* does not matter; as far as the purpose of discrimination is concerned, it could have been the other way around and nothing would have changed as far as psychology is concerned. We should note, though, that these considerations do not support a total qualia nihilism; at best, they only show that the *intrinsic* properties of qualia play no causal-theoretical role, for they allow the relational and structural properties of qualia an indispensable role in our discriminative behavior.

Let us now briefly turn to what we may call "philosophical qualia nihilism." Proponents of this position argue that there "really" are no such things as qualia and that a close analysis of the concept of a quale will show qualia to be merely a piece of philosophical invention. Arguments for qualia nihilism of this sort typically begin with an enumeration of the properties usually associated with qualia, such as their infallible and incorrigible first-person accessibility, their ineffability and inaccessibility to the third person, and their intrinsicness. These arguments then attempt to show that either these concepts are incoherent or hopelessly obscure or that they are empty, applying to nothing recognizable in our mental life.[35] One problem with many of these arguments is that they tend to exaggerate the epistemic and other properties some philosophers have claimed in behalf of qualia, with the unsurprising result that nothing *could* qualify as qualia. To believe in qualia, it is not necessary, for example, to insist on absolute first-person infallibility or third-person inaccessibility. And then there are the all too facile analogies advanced by qualia-phobes[36] between belief in qualia and the discredited beliefs in witches, the phlogiston, and magnetic effluvia. The idea is that belief in qualia will be discredited when neuroscience reaches the stage where it can explain human behavior without recourse to an inner mental life, just as belief in phlogiston was abandoned when the oxidation theory of combustion took hold. But such arguments depend on the premise that qualia are only theoretical constructs posited to explain human behavior, an assumption that will be rejected by those who take qualia seriously.

Instead of reviewing these arguments, let us again remind ourselves of Wittgenstein's parable of "the beetle in the box" (first introduced in Chapter 2):

> Suppose everyone had a box with something in it; we call it a "beetle". No one can look into anyone else's box, and everyone says he knows what a beetle is only by looking at *his* beetle.—Here it would be quite possible for everyone to have something different in his box.[37]

As Wittgenstein says, the box might even be empty, and it isn't clear how the word "beetle" could have a role in public language, in communicating intersubjective information. The point is, of course, that our talk of private, directly accessible qualia, in our little private boxes (we call them "minds"), is just like this beetle talk.

It is difficult to know just how to respond to this and other arguments against qualia and the intelligibility of qualia talk—except to say that when I look inside my box, I find something there with just *these* characteristics. I can also add further explanations: I usually find something with similar characteristics when someone steps on my toes or a pin is stuck in my hand, but not when someone massages my back. If this doesn't help, perhaps nothing will. It is indeed a mystery how we could use words for qualia for intersubjective communication—at least what we normally assume to be intersubjective communication. There is the story that when Louis Armstrong was asked to explain what jazz was, he replied, "If you got to ask, you ain't never gonna get to know."[38] If there should be people who seriously and sincerely wanted to find out what qualia are, that would show not only that zombies are metaphysically possible but that some actually exist in this world!

Further Readings

The reader will find the sources mentioned in the endnotes useful. The following recent or forthcoming books discuss in detail many of the issues taken up in this chapter.

Daniel C. Dennett, *Consciousness Explained* (Boston: Little, Brown, 1992), offers an original account ("the multiple draft theory") of consciousness but defends a nihilist stance on qualia. Owen Flanagan, *Consciousness Reconsidered* (Cambridge: MIT Press, 1992), which includes a good survey of the current debate on consciousness, defends a middle-of-the road, reconciliationist position, arguing that a concerted effort by cognitive psychology, neural science, AI research, and philosophy can give a naturalistic account of consciousness.

In *Consciousness* (Cambridge: MIT Press, 1987), William G. Lycan offers a broadly functionalist account of consciousness, whereas Colin McGinn, *The Problem of Consciousness* (Oxford: Blackwell, 1991), argues that a solution to the problem of consciousness is beyond human intellectual powers.

William Seager, *Metaphysics of Consciousness* (London: Routledge, 1991), discusses many pertinent metaphysical issues relating to consciousness. John Searle, *The Rediscovery of the Mind* (Cambridge: MIT Press, 1992), mounts a sustained critique of the functionalist-computationalist approach to consciousness and intentionality. In his forthcoming book *The Conscious Mind* (New York: Oxford University Press), David Chalmers discusses many of the issues taken up in this chapter; I highly recommend the book.

Two useful anthologies of recent papers on consciousness by scientists and philosophers are *Consciousness in Contemporary Science*, ed. A. J.

Marcel and E Bisiach (Oxford: Oxford University Press, 1988); and *Consciousness*, ed. Martin Davies and Glyn W. Humphreys (Oxford: Blackwell, 1993). Also useful should be the forthcoming anthology *The Nature of Consciousness: Philosophical and Scientific Essays*, ed. Ned Block, Owen Flanagan, and Güven Güzeldere (Cambridge: MIT Press).

Notes

1. René Descartes, "Replies to the Fourth Set of Objections," in *The Nature of Mind*, ed. David M. Rosenthal (New York: Oxford University Press, 1991), p. 29.
2. Sometimes these terms are used to refer to states or events with these qualitative properties.
3. In Thomas Nagel, "What Is It Like to Be a Bat?" *Philosophical Review* 83 (1974):435–450; reprinted in Rosenthal, *The Nature of Mind*. The use of the expression "what it is like" in connection with consciousness is due to Nagel.
4. See, for example, John Searle, *The Rediscovery of the Mind* (Cambridge: MIT Press, 1992), especially ch. 4.
5. This has been discussed in some detail in Chapter 1.
6. "Cartesian" since it is often associated with Descartes. We leave open the question whether Descartes himself unambiguously advocated such a thesis.
7. This notion comes from Ned Block, who distinguishes between "phenomenal consciousness" (roughly, states with phenomenal properties) and "access consciousness." See his "On a Confusion About a Function of Consciousness," *Behavioral and Brain Sciences* 18 (1995):1–41.
8. For discussion of the relationship between access consciousness and phenomenal consciousness, ibid.
9. Nagel, "What Is It Like to Be a Bat?" p. 425. Emphasis added.
10. Thomas Nagel, "Subjective and Objective," in Nagel, *Mortal Questions* (Cambridge: Cambridge University Press, 1979), p. 201. Emphasis added.
11. See, for example, Roderick M. Chisholm, *The First Person* (Minneapolis: University of Minnesota Press, 1981), ch. 3.
12. David Armstrong, "The Nature of Mind," in Armstrong, *The Nature of Mind* (Brisbane: University of Queensland Press, 1981); reprinted in *Readings in Philosophy of Psychology*, vol. 1, ed. Ned Block (Cambridge: Harvard University Press, 1980). The quoted expression is from Block's volume, p. 199.
13. David Rosenthal, "The Independence of Consciousness and Sensory Quality," *Philosophical Issues* 1 (1991):15–36. (The quotation is from p. 31.)
14. David Chalmers makes this point in *The Conscious Mind* (New York: Oxford University Press, forthcoming).
15. The idea that a mind is really more like a committee than a single unified agent—or at any rate that there is no single center of mentality or consciousness—is found in many authors: for example, Marvin Minsky, *The Society of Minds* (New York: Simon and Schuster, 1985); Daniel C. Dennett, *Consciousness Explained* (Boston: Little, Brown, 1992)—see his arguments against the idea of a "Cartesian theater." For a functionalist approach to self-consciousness, see Robert Van Gulick, "A Functionalist Plea for Self-Consciousness," *Philosophical Review* 97 (1988):149–181.

16. For such an idea, see Daniel C. Dennett, *Content and Consciousness* (London: Routledge & Kegan Paul, 1969).

17. For an informal discussion of the concept of supervenience, see Chapter 1; the concept is discussed in greater detail in Chapter 9.

18. Saul Kripke, *Naming and Necessity* (Cambridge: Harvard University Press, 1980), pp. 153–154. The target of Kripke's argument is the identification of pain with C-fiber stimulation; however, his argument applies with equal force against the supervenience of pain on C-fiber stimulation.

19. This is based on Ned Block's "Inverted Earth," *Philosophical Perspectives* 4 (1990):51–79.

20. Arthur Rimbaud, "Voyelles."

21. For complexities and complications in the supposition of inverted spectra, see C. L. Hardin, *Color for Philosophers* (Indianapolis: Hackett, 1988). See also Sydney Shoemaker, "Absent Qualia Are Impossible—A Reply to Block" and "The Inverted Spectrum," in his *Identity, Cause, and Mind* (Cambridge: Cambridge University Press, 1984); Michael Tye, "Qualia, Content, and the Inverted Spectrum," *Noûs* 28 (1994):159–183.

22. This point is discussed in connection with functionalism; see Chapter 5.

23. It is consistent to hold the supervenience of qualia on physical properties but deny their supervenience on functional properties. One might, for example, hold that qualia arise out of biological processes and that an electromechanical system (e.g., a robot) that is functionally indistinguishable from us may lack consciousness. Searle, in *The Rediscovery of the Mind*, appears to hold a view of this kind.

24. For considerations against using imaginability as showing real possibility in connection with qualia supervenience, see Terence Horgan, "Supervenient Qualia," *Philosophical Review* 96 (1987):491–520.

25. For further discussion, see Chapter 6; also see Horgan, "Supervenient Qualia," for a causal argument for qualia supervenience.

26. Some writers speak of "naturalistic" rather than "physicalistic" accounts of qualia. However, what is to count as "naturalistic" is far less clear than what is to count as "physicalistic," and it isn't obvious why qualia should somehow be "naturalized" or what that means unless it means "physicalized." Why aren't qualia, unproblematically, part of the natural world? It is only when physicalistic considerations are brought in that qualia begin to pose problems.

27. For further discussion of this notion, see Terence Horgan, "Supervenience and Microphysics," *Pacific Philosophical Quarterly* 63 (1982):29–43.

28. For a contrary view, see Chalmers, *The Conscious Mind*.

29. For a popular account of this hypothesis, see Francis Crick, *The Astonishing Hypothesis: The Scientific Search for the Soul* (New York: Scribners, 1994), ch. 17 ("Oscillations and Processing Units").

30. Owen Flanagan seems to be suggesting something like this in his *Consciousness Reconsidered* (Cambridge: MIT Press, 1992), pp. 59–60.

31. Crick himself says: "Koch and I took this idea one stage further by suggesting that this synchronized firing on, or near, the beat of a gamma oscillation (in the 35- to 75-Hertz range) *might be the neural correlate of visual awareness*." *The Astonishing Hypothesis*, p. 245 (italics in the original).

32. The *New York Times* (27 October 1992, p. C10) quotes a scientist at California Institute of Technology as saying: "Progress in genetics came when we understood the molecular basis of the gene. . . . Similarly, to understand consciousness, you have to go to the level of nerve cells, electrical impulse codes and brain networks."

33. On these issues, see Joseph Levine, "Materialism and Qualia: The Explanatory Gap," *Pacific Philosophical Quarterly* 64 (1983):354–361; and "On Leaving Out What It's Like," in *Consciousness*, ed. Martin Davies and Glyn W. Humphreys (Oxford: Blackwell, 1993).

34. Even when the positions of green, yellow, and red lights are randomized (I understand that color-blind people use the relative positions of these lights as cues).

35. For arguments along these lines, see Daniel C. Dennett, "Quining Qualia," in *Consciousness in Contemporary Science*, ed. A. J. Marcel and E. Bisiach (Oxford: Oxford University Press, 1988). See also Gilbert Harman, "The Intrinsic Quality of Experience," *Philosophical Perspectives* 4 (1990):31–52.

36. Who call the believers in qualia "qualia-freaks."

37. Ludwig Wittgenstein, *Philosophical Investigations*, trans. G.E.M. Anscombe (Oxford: Blackwell, 1953), sec. 293.

38. This anecdote is taken from Ned Block who uses it to make the same point in his "Troubles with Functionalism," in *Minnesota Studies in the Philosophy of Science*, vol. 9, ed. C. Wade Savage (Minneapolis: University of Minnesota Press, 1978), p. 281; reprinted in Block, *Readings in Philosophy of Psychology*.

8

Mental Content

You hope that it will be a clear day tomorrow, and I believe that it will. But Mary doubts it and in fact hopes that she is right. Here we have various intentional states: your *hoping* that it will be a clear day tomorrow, my *believing*, and Mary's *doubting* that it will be so. All of these states, though they are states of different persons and represent different attitudes (believing, hoping, and doubting), have the same *content*, expressed by the sentence "It will be a clear day tomorrow." And this content *represents* (or *is*) a certain state of affairs, namely, its being a clear day tomorrow. Different subjects can adopt the same intentional attitudes toward it, and the same subject can bear different attitudes toward it (e.g., you believe it and are pleased about it; later you come to disbelieve it). But in virtue of what do these intentional states have this content and represent the state of affairs they represent? It can't be a brute fact about these states that they have this particular content and not some other; it must have an explanation. This is the basic question about mental content.

The question can be raised another way. It is not just persons who have mental states with content. All sorts of animals perceive their surroundings through their various senses, process this information, store and use it to guide their behavior. We humans do this in our own distinctive ways but probably not in ways that are fundamentally different from the higher species of animals. It is clear, then, that certain physical/biological states of organisms, presumably states of their brains or nervous systems, can carry information about their surroundings, representing them as being this way or that way (e.g., that here is a red apple, that yonder is a moving brown object shaped like a cow, and the like), process and store these representations, make inferences from them, and use them to guide their actions and behavior in coping with their environment. That is to say, these physical/biological states have representational content—they are *about* things, inside or outside an organism, and *represent them to be such and such*. In a word, these states have *meaning*. But how does such a state, presumably a complex neural state, come to have meaning? Just what makes it the case that a configuration of nerve fibers or a pattern of their activation represents the state of affairs of there being a red apple on the table rather than, say, there being cows in Canada or even nothing at all?

This question about the nature of mental content has a companion question, a question about how contents are *attributed* to the mental states of persons and other intentional systems. We routinely ascribe states with content to persons, animals, and even some nonbiological systems. If we had no such practice—if we were to stop attributing to our fellow human beings beliefs, desires, emotions, and the like—our communal life would surely suffer a massive collapse. There would be little understanding or anticipating of what other people will do, and this would severely undermine interpersonal transactions. Moreover, it is by attributing these states to ourselves that we come to understand ourselves as cognizers and agents. Self-attribution of beliefs, desires, and the rest is arguably a precondition of personhood. Moreover, we often attribute such states to nonhuman animals and purely mechanical or electronic systems. On what basis, then, do we attribute contentful states to persons and other organisms and systems? What procedures and principles do we follow when we do this? As we will see, the two questions, one about the nature of mental content and the other about its attribution, are intimately related.

Interpretation Theory

Suppose you are a field anthropologist-linguist visiting a tribe of people never before visited by an outsider. Your job is to find out what these people believe, remember, desire, hope, fear, and so on—that is, to determine their "mental world"—and to develop a dictionary and grammar for their language—that is, to be able to understand their speech. So your project is twofold: to interpret their minds and to interpret their speech. This is the project of "radical interpretation": You are to construct an interpretation of the natives' speech and mental states from scratch, on the basis of your observation of their behavior (including their speech behavior), without the aid of a native translator or a dictionary.[1]

But the twin projects of determining the natives' beliefs, desires, and the rest of their mental world and of understanding their speech are interconnected and interdependent. In particular, belief, among all mental states, can be seen to hold the key to radical interpretation: It is the crucial link between a speaker's utterances and their meanings. If a native speaker sincerely asserts sentence S, and S means that there goes a rabbit, then the speaker believes that there goes a rabbit. Conversely, if the speaker believes that there goes a rabbit and uses sentence *S* to express this belief, *S* means that there goes a rabbit. If you knew how to interpret the native's speech, it would be relatively easy to find out what she believes by observing her speech behavior (you can ask her whether she believes that *p*, and then see what she says). If you had complete knowledge of what she believes on a given occasion, interpreting her utterances on that occasion—what she means by her words—would be relatively simple. But you have knowledge of neither, and by observing how she behaves in the context of her environment, you have to secure both. There are, then, three variables involved: behavior, belief, and meaning. One of the three, behavior, is known, since you can observe it, and you must solve for the two unknowns, belief and meaning. Where do you start?

Suppose you find that Karl, one of the natives, affirmatively utters[2] the sentence "Es regnet" when, and only when, it is raining in his vicinity. (This is highly idealized, but the main point should apply, with suitable provisos, to real-life situations.) You observe a similar behavior pattern in many others in Karl's speech community, and you project the following general hypothesis:

(R) Speakers of language *L* (as we will call it) affirm "Es regnet" at time *t* if and only if it is raining at *t* in their vicinity.

From this it would be natural to entertain the following two hypotheses:

(S) In language *L* "Es regnet" means that it is raining (in the utterer's vicinity).

(M) When speakers of *L* affirm (or are disposed to affirm) "Es regnet," this indicates that they believe that it is raining (in their vicinity) and use "Es regnet" to express this belief.

In this way you get your first toehold in the language and minds of the natives, and something like this seems like the only way.

But what sanctions the move from (R) to (S) and (M)? When you observe Karl utter the words "Es regnet," you see yourself that it is raining out there. You have assumed that Karl is expressing a belief about the current condition of the weather. This assumption is reinforced when you observe him, and others, doing this time after time. But what belief? What is the content of the belief that Karl expresses when he affirms "Es regnet"? It seems clear that the answer is that this belief has the content "it is raining." But why? Why not the belief with the content "it is a sunny day" or "it is snowing"? What are the tacit principles that help to rule out these possibilities?

You attribute the content "it is raining" to Karl's belief *because you assume that his belief is true.* You know, or have assumed, that his belief is about the weather outside, and you see that it is raining. What you need, and all you need, to get to the conclusion that his belief has the content "it is raining" is the further premise that his belief is true. In general, then, the following principle gives you what you need:

[The principle of charity] The speakers' beliefs are by and large true. (Moreover, they are largely correct in making inferences and rational in forming expectations and making decisions.[3])

With this principle on hand, we can make sense of the transition from (R) to (S) and (M) in the following way:

In uttering "Es regnet," Karl is expressing a belief about the current weather condition in his vicinity, and we may assume, by the charity principle, that this belief is true. The current weather condition is that it is raining. So Karl's belief has the content that it is raining, and he is using the sentence "Es regnet" to express this belief (M), whence it further follows that "Es regnet" means that it is raining (S).

You do not attribute the content "it is not raining" or "it is snowing" because that would make Karl's and his friends' beliefs about whether or not it is raining around them invariably false. That is a bare logical possibility; there is no logical contradiction in the idea that a group of otherwise normal people are almost always wrong about rain in their vicinity, but it is not something that can be taken seriously; it is a possibility we have to exclude if we are to have any chance at constructing a workable interpretive scheme.

Clearly, the same points apply to interpreting utterances about colors, shapes, and so on. When Karl and his friends invariably respond with "rot" when we show them red apples, ripe tomatoes, and red sunsets and withhold it when they are shown lemons, eggplants, and snowballs, it would make no sense to speculate that "rot" might mean *green* and that Karl and his friends systematically misperceive colors and in consequence have massively erroneous beliefs about colors of objects around them. The only plausible thing to say is that "rot" means *red* in Karl's language and that Karl is expressing the (true) belief that the apple held in front of him is red. All this isn't to say that our natives never have false beliefs; they may have them in huge numbers. But unless we assume that their beliefs, especially those about the manifestly observable properties of things and events around them, are largely correct, we have no hope of gaining an entry into their cognitive world.

So what happens is that we interpret the natives in such a way that they are credited with beliefs that are largely true and coherent—in particular, their beliefs about the observable features of their environment. But since *we* are doing the interpreting, this in effect means *largely true and coherent by our light*. Under our interpretation, therefore, our subjects come out with beliefs that largely agree with our own. The attribution of a system of beliefs and other intentional states is essential to the understanding of other people, of what they say and do. It follows, then, that we can understand only those whose belief systems are largely like our own.

The charity principle requires our interpretive project to attribute to our subjects a system of beliefs that by and large are true. It rules out, a priori, interpretations that attribute to them beliefs that are mostly false or incoherent; any interpretive scheme according to which our subjects' beliefs are massively false or manifestly inconsistent (e.g., they come out believing that there are round squares) cannot, for that very reason, be a correct interpretation. Further, we can think of a generalized charity principle that enjoins us to interpret all of our subjects' intentional states, including desires, aversions, intentions, and the rest, in a way that renders them maximally coherent among themselves and enables us to make the best sense of their observed behavior. In any case, we should note the following important point: There is no reason to think that in any interpretive project there will be a single unique interpretation that best meets this requirement. This is evident when we reflect on the fact that the charity principle only requires that the entire *system* of beliefs attributed to the subject be by and large true but doesn't tell us which ones of her beliefs must come out true. In practice as well as in theory, there are likely to be ties, or indeterminate and unstable near-ties, among possible interpretations: That is, we are likely to end up with more than one maximally true, coherent, and rational scheme of interpretation that can explain all the observational data. We can see that this will almost certainly be the case when we note that our criteria of coherence and rationality are bound to be vague and imprecise and that their applications to specific situations will likely be fraught with ambiguities. At any rate, it is easy to see how interpretational indeterminacy can arise by considering a simple example.

We see Karl eating raw spinach leaves. Why is he doing that? We can easily see that there are indefinitely many belief-desire pairs that we could attribute to Karl that would explain why he is doing what he is doing. For example:

- Karl believes that eating raw spinach will improve his stamina, and he is eager to improve his stamina.
- Karl believes that eating raw spinach will help him get rid of his bad breath, and he has been unhappy about his bad breath.
- Karl believes that eating raw spinach will please his mother, and he will do anything to please her.
- Karl believes that eating raw spinach will annoy his mother, and he will go to any length to annoy her.

And so on without end. We can expect many of these potential explanations to be excluded by further observation of Karl's behavior and by consideration of coherence with other beliefs and desires we want to attribute to him. But it is difficult to imagine that this will eliminate all but one of the indefinitely many possible belief-desire pairs that can explain Karl's spinach eating. Moreover, it is likely that any one of these pairs could be protected no matter what if we are willing to make drastic enough adjustments elsewhere in Karl's total system of beliefs, desires, and other mental states.

Suppose, then, there are two schemes of interpretation of Karl's mental states that, as far as we can determine, satisfy the charity principle to the same degree and work equally well in explaining his behavior, and that one of these systems attributes to Karl the belief that eating raw spinach is good for one's stamina and the other instead attributes to him the belief that eating spinach will please his mother. As far as interpretation theory goes, the schemes are tied, and neither could be pronounced to be better than the other. But what is the fact of the matter concerning Karl's belief system? Does he or doesn't he believe that eating raw spinach improves stamina?

There are two possible approaches one could take in response to these questions. The first is to take interpretation as the rock-bottom foundation of contentful mental states and declare that for Karl to have the belief that p is for this belief to be part of the best (that is, maximally true, coherent, and explanatory) total scheme of beliefs, desires, and other mental states to be attributed to Karl, and there is no further fact of the matter that determines whether or not Karl has this belief.[4] When several interpretive schemes are tied for first and the belief that p is not an element of each of these schemes, then there is no fact of the matter about whether or not this belief actually exists. Whether Karl believes that p, therefore, is a question without a determinate answer. To be sure, the question about this particular bit of belief may be settled by further observation of Karl; however, indeterminacies are almost certain to remain even when all the observations are in (surely, at some point after Karl is dead, there is nothing further to observe that will be relevant!). Some will see in this kind of position a version of *content irrealism*: If beliefs are among the objectively existing entities of the world, either Karl believes that raw spinach is good for his stamina or he doesn't. There must be a fact about the existence of this belief, independent of any holistic interpretive scheme that someone might construct to explain Karl's total behavior. So if the existence of beliefs is genuinely indeterminate, we would have to conclude, it seems, that beliefs are not part of objective reality. Evidently, the same conclusion would apply to all content-bearing mental states.

An alternative line of consideration can lead to *content relativism* rather than content irrealism: Instead of accepting the indeterminacy of belief existence, one might hold that whether or not a given belief exists is *relative to a scheme of interpretation*. It is not a question that can be answered absolutely, independently of a choice of an interpretative scheme. Whether or not Karl has that particular belief depends on the interpretive scheme relative to which we view Karl's belief system. But a relativism of this kind gives rise to a host of difficult and puzzling metaphysical questions. What is it for a belief to "exist relative to a scheme" to begin with? Is it anything more than "the scheme says that it exists"? If so, shouldn't we ask the further question whether what the scheme says is *true*? But this takes us right back to the nonrelativized notion of belief existence. Moreover, is all existence relative to some scheme or other, or is it just the existence of belief that is relative in this way? Either way, many further questions and puzzles await us.

We have been led to these considerations by the assumption that interpretation is fundamental to the very existence of belief and other intentional states. But we may question whether this assumption is covertly question-begging. Interpretation involves an interpreter, and the interpreter herself is an intentional system, a person with beliefs, desires, and so on. How do we account for *her* beliefs and desires—*how do her intentional states get their contents*? And when she tries to maximize agreement between her beliefs and her subject's beliefs, how does she know what she believes? That is, *how is self-interpretation possible*? Don't we need an account of how we can know the contents of our own beliefs and desires? Do we just look inward—are they just there for us to see? It is clear that the interpretation approach to mental content must, on pain of circularity, confront the issue of self-interpretation.

Alternatively, one could try to stand for a robustly realist position about intentional states, insisting that there must be a fact of the matter about the existence of Karl's belief about spinach that is independent of any interpretive schemes. If Karl is a real and genuine intentional system, there must be a determinate answer to the question whether or not he has this belief; whether or not someone is trying to interpret Karl, or what any interpretive scheme says about Karl's belief system, should be entirely irrelevant to that question. This is *content realism*, a position that views interpretation only as a way of *finding out* what Karl's belief system is, not as constitutive of it. Interpretation, therefore, is given only an epistemological function, that of ascertaining what intentional states a given subject has; it does not have the ontological role of grounding their existence. You may find content realism appealing. If so, there is more work to do; you must provide an alternative realist account of what constitutes the content of intentional states—what it is about an intentional state that makes it the case that it has the content it has.

The Causal/Correlational Approach

A fly flits across a frog's visual field, and the frog's tongue darts out, snaring the fly. The content of the frog's visual perception is a moving fly. Or so we would say. Suppose now that in a world very much like our own (or some unknown region of this world) frogs that are just like our frogs exist but there are no flies. Instead there are "schmies," very small reptiles roughly the size, shape, and color of earthly flies, and they fly around just the way our flies do and are found in the kind of habitat that our flies inhabit. In that world frogs feed on schmies, not flies. Now, in this other world a schmy flits across a frog's visual field, and the frog flicks out its tongue and catches it. What is the content of this frog's visual perception? What does the frog's visual percept represent? The obvious answer is: a moving schmy.

From the frogs' internal perspectives, there is no difference between our frog's perceptual state and the other-earthly frog's perceptual state: Both register a black speckle moving rapidly across the visual field. However, we attribute different contents to them, and the difference here lies outside the frogs' perceptual systems; it is a difference in the kind of object that stands in a certain relationship to the perceptual states of the frogs. It isn't only that in these particular instances a fly caused the perceptual state of our frog and a schmy caused a corresponding state in the other-earthly frog; there is also a more general fact, namely, that the habitat of earthly frogs includes flies, not schmies, and it is with flies, not schmies, with which they are in daily perceptual and other causal contact. The converse is the case with other-earthly frogs and schmies.

Suppose that under normal conditions a certain state of an organism *covaries* regularly and reliably with the presence of a horse. That is, this state occurs in you when, and only when, a horse is present in your vicinity (and you are awake and alert, sufficient illumination is present, you are appropriately oriented in relation to the horse, etc.). The occurrence of this state, then, can serve as an *indicator*[5] of the presence of a horse; it carries the information "horse" (or "a horse is present nearby"). And it seems appropriate to say that this state, which covaries with the presence of horses, *represents* the presence of a horse and has it as its content. The suggestion is that something like this account will work for intentional content in general, and this is the causal/correlational approach. This approach seems to work well with contents of perceptual states, as we just saw in the fly-schmy case. I perceive *red*, and my perceptual state has "red" as its content, because I am having the kind of perceptual experience typically correlated with—in fact, caused by—the presence of a red object. Whether I perceive red or green has little to do with the intrinsic properties of my internal states (however these are conceived); rather, it depends essentially on the properties of the objects with which I am in causal-perceptual relations. Those internal states that are typically caused by red objects, or correlate with the presence of red objects nearby, have the content "red," for that very reason, not because of any of their intrinsic properties.

How well does this approach work with intentional states in general? We may consider a simple version of this approach, perhaps something like this:[6]

(C) Subject S has the belief with content p (that is, S believes that p) just in case, under optimal conditions, S has this belief if and only if p obtains.

To make (C) at all viable, we should restrict it to cases of "observational beliefs," beliefs about matters that are perceptually observable to S. For (C) is obviously implausible when applied to beliefs like the belief that God exists or that light travels at a finite velocity and beliefs about abstract matters (say, the belief that the continuum hypothesis is true); it is much more plausible for observational beliefs like the belief that there are red flowers on my desk or that there are horses in the field. The proviso "under optimal conditions" is included since for the state of affairs p (e.g., the presence of horses in the field) to correlate with, or cause, subject S's belief that p, favorable perceptual conditions must obtain, such as that S's visual organs are functioning properly, that the condition of illumination is adequate, that S's attention is not seriously distracted, and so on.

But there are some serious difficulties with (C), which we will enumerate below. However, (C) is only a rough-and-ready version of the approach, and none of the objections need be taken as delivering a disabling blow to the general approach itself.

(1) Suppose the belief that there are horses in the field correlates reliably with the presence of horses in the field. But it also correlates reliably with the presence of horse genes in the field (since the latter correlates reliably with the presence of horses). According to (C), someone observing horses in the field should have the belief that there are horse genes in the field. But this surely is wrong. Moreover, the belief that there are horses in the field also correlates with the special array of light rays, reflected by the horses, traveling from the field to the observer, but, again, the observer does not have the belief that these light rays are traveling toward him. The general problem, then, is that an account like (C) cannot differentiate between belief with p as its content and belief with q as its content if p and q reliably correlate with each other. For any two correlated states of affairs p and q, (C) entails that one believes that p if and only if one believes that q, which seems prima facie false.

(2) Someone is looking at the horses in the field. Does she have the be-

lief that there are horses in the field? Not necessarily, for it may be that her ontology does not include whole objects like horses and cows but only things like horse parts, time-slices of horses, and the like. If so, the content of her belief is not that there are horses in the field but that there are (un-detached) horse parts in the field.

(3) Belief is *holistic* in the sense that what you believe is influenced, often crucially, by what else you believe. When you observe horselike fig-ures in the field, you may not believe that there are horses in the field if you have been told by someone you trust that many cardboard horses have been put up there for a children's fair or if you believe you are hallu-cinating, and so on. Correlational accounts make beliefs basically atom-istic, at least for observational beliefs, but even our observational beliefs are constrained by other beliefs we hold, and it isn't clear how the correla-tional approach could do justice to this systemic aspect of belief.

(4) Belief that there are horses in the field is caused not only by horses in the field but also by cows and moose at dusk, cardboard horses at a distance, robot horses, and so on. In fact, the belief correlates more reli-ably with the disjunction "horses or cows and moose at dusk or card-board horses or. . . ." If so, why should we not say that when you are look-ing at the horses in the field, your belief has the content "there are horses *or* cows *or* moose at dusk *or* cardboard horses *or* robot horses"? This so-called disjunction problem has turned out to be a highly recalcitrant prob-lem for the causal/correlational approach; it is being actively discussed, but no solution that is likely to command a consensus is in sight.[7]

These are some of the initial difficulties that face the correlational ap-proach; whether, or to what extent, these difficulties can be overcome without compromising the naturalistic/reductive spirit of the correla-tional approach remains an open question. Quite possibly, most of the dif-ficulties are not really serious and can be resolved by further elaborations and supplementations. It may well be that this approach is the most promising one—in fact, the only viable one that promises to give a non-question-begging, "naturalistic" account of mental content.

Narrow Content and Wide Content

One thing that the correlational account of mental content high-lights is this: Content has a lot to do with what is going on in the world, outside the physical boundaries of the subject. As far as what goes on in-side is concerned, the earthly frog and the other-earthly frog are indistin-guishable—they are in the same relevant neural/sensory state: Both regis-ter a moving black dot. But in describing the representational content of their states, what the frogs "see," we advert to the factors in the environment of the frogs. Or consider a simpler case: Peter is looking at a tomato, and Mary is also looking at one (a different tomato, but let's suppose that it looks pretty much the same as the one Peter is looking at). Mary thinks to herself, "This tomato has gone bad," and Peter, too, thinks, "This tomato has gone bad." From the internal point of view, Mary's perceptual experience is indistinguishable from Peter's (we may suppose their neural states, too, are relevantly similar), and they would express their thoughts using the same words. But it is clear that the contents of their beliefs are different. For they involve different objects: Mary's belief is about the thing she is gazing at, and Peter's belief is about a different thing altogether. Moreover, and this is a related point, Mary's belief may be true and Peter's false. On the standard understanding of the notion of "content," beliefs with the same content must be true together or false together (that is, contents are "truth conditions"). Obviously, the fact that Peter's and Mary's beliefs have different content is due to facts external to them; the difference in content cannot be explained in terms of what is going on inside the perceivers. It seems, then, that at least in this and other similar cases belief contents are differentiated, or "individuated," by reference to conditions external to the believer.

Beliefs whose content is individuated in this way are said to have "wide" or "broad" content. In contrast, beliefs whose content is individuated solely on the basis of what goes on inside the persons holding them are said to have "narrow" content. Alternatively, we may say that the content of an intentional state is narrow just in case it supervenes on the internal/intrinsic properties of the subject who is in that state and that it is wide otherwise. This means that two individuals who are exactly alike in all intrinsic/internal respects must have the same narrow-content beliefs but may well diverge in their wide-content beliefs. Thus, our two frogs are exactly alike in internal/intrinsic respects but unlike in what their perceptual states represent. So the contents of these states do not supervene internally and are therefore wide.

Several well-known thought experiments have been instrumental in persuading many philosophers that most of our ordinary beliefs (and other intentional states) have wide content, that what beliefs and desires we hold is not simply a matter of what's going on inside our minds or heads. Among these thought experiments, the following two, the first due to Hilary Putnam and the second to Tyler Burge,[8] have been particularly influential.

Thought Experiment 1: Earth and Twin Earth

Imagine a planet, "twin earth," somewhere in the remote region of space, which is just like the earth we inhabit except in one respect: On twin earth a certain chemical substance with the molecular structure XYZ, which has all the observable characteristics of water (it is transparent, dissolves salt and sugar, quenches thirst, puts out fire, freezes at 0°C, etc.), replaces water everywhere. So lakes and oceans on twin earth are filled with XYZ, not H_2O (that is, water), and twin earthians drink XYZ when they are thirsty, do their laundry in XYZ, and so on. Some twin earthians speak English, which is indistinguishable from earthian English, and they use their expression "water" in the way we use our word "water."

But there is a difference between our English and the English spoken on twin earth: The twin-earthian "water" and our "water" refer to different things (they have different "extensions," as logicians will say). The first refers to XYZ, not water, and the second refers to water, not XYZ. If you are the first visitor to twin earth and find out the truth about their "water," you may report back to your friends on earth as follows: "At first I thought that the transparent stuff that fills the oceans and lakes around here was water, and it really looks and tastes like our water. But I just found out that it isn't water at all, although people around here call it 'water.' It's really XYZ, not H_2O." You will not translate the twin-earthian word "water" into the English word "water"; you will need to invent a new word, perhaps "twater." There is a sense of meaning, then, in which the twin-earthian "water" and our "water" have different meanings, although what goes on inside the minds, or heads, of twin earthians may be exactly the same as what goes in ours, and our speech behavior involving the two words is also indistinguishable. This semantic difference between our "water" and twin-earthian "water" is reflected in the way we describe and individuate mental states of earthians and twin earthians. When a twin earthian says to the waiter, "Please bring me a glass of water!" she is expressing her desire for twater, and we will report, in *oratio obliqua*, that she wants some twater, not that she wants some water. When an earthian says the same thing, she is expressing a desire for water, and we will say that she wants water. You believe that water is wet, and your twin-earthian doppelganger believes that twater is wet. And so on. To summarize, then, earthians have water-thoughts and water-desires, whereas twin earthians have twater-thoughts and twater-desires, and this difference is due to environmental factors external to the subjects who have the beliefs and desires.

Suppose an earthian astronaut, Jones, lands on twin earth. She of course doesn't realize at first that the liquid she sees in the lakes and coming out of the tap isn't water. She is offered a glass of this transparent liquid by her twin-earthian host and thinks to herself, "That's a nice, cold glass of water—just what I needed." Consider Jones's belief that the glass contains cold water. This belief is false, since the glass contains not water but XYZ, or twater. Although she is now on twin earth, in an environment full of twater and devoid of water, she is still subject to earthian standards: Her words mean, and her thoughts are individuated, in accordance with the criteria that prevail on earth. What this shows is that a person's *past associations* with her environment play a role in determining her meanings and thought contents. If Jones stays on twin earth long enough, we will eventually interpret her word "water" to mean twater, not water, and attribute to her twater-thoughts rather than water-thoughts, although of course it is difficult to say exactly when this change will come about.

If these considerations are by and large correct, they show that two supervenience theses fail: First, the meanings of our expressions do not in general supervene on our *internal* physical/psychological states. Twin earthians are indistinguishable from us in all relevant respects as far as our internal lives, both physical and mental, are concerned, and yet our words have different meanings. We can imagine that there is a twin-earth doppelganger of you who is molecule-for-molecule identical with you;[9] you and she are in the same neural state when you and she use the word "water," but your word "water" means water and hers mean twater. Second, and this is what is of immediate relevance to us, the contents of beliefs and other intentional states also fail to supervene on our internal physical/psychological states. You have water-thoughts and your twin-earthian doppelganger has twater-thoughts. And there is strong reason for thinking that beliefs are individuated by content; that is, beliefs with the same content are regarded as being of the same belief type, and beliefs with different content count as falling under different belief types. What particular beliefs you hold depends on your relationship, past as well as present, to the things and events in your surroundings, as well as what goes on inside you. The same goes for other content-bearing intentional states. If this is in general right, the thought experiment establishes the existence of wide content.

Thought Experiment 2: Arthritis and "Tharthritis"

Consider a person, call him "Fred," in two situations.

1. *The actual situation.* Fred thinks "arthritis" means inflammation of the bones (it actually means inflammation of the joints). Feeling pain and swelling in his thigh, Fred complains to his doctor, "I have arthritis in my thigh." His doctor tells him that people can have arthritis only in their joints. Two points to keep in mind: First, Fred believed, before he talked to his doctor, that he had arthritis in his thigh, and, second, this belief was false.

2. *A counterfactual situation.* Nothing has changed with our Fred—he is experiencing swelling and pain in his thigh and complains to his doctor, ex-

claiming, "I have arthritis in my thigh." What is different about the counterfactual situation concerns the use of the word "arthritis" in Fred's
speech community: In the situation we are imagining, the word is used to
refer to inflammation of bones, not just bone joints. That is, in the counterfactual situation Fred has a correct understanding of the word "arthritis,"
unlike in the actual situation. In the counterfactual situation, then, Fred is
expressing a true belief when he utters, "I have arthritis in my thigh." But
how would we report Fred's belief concerning the condition of his thigh—
that is, report in *our* language (in this world)? We can't say that Fred believes that he has arthritis in his thigh, because in our language "arthritis"
means inflammation of joints, and he clearly doesn't have that, which
would render his belief false. We might coin a new expression (to be part
of our language), "tharthritis," to mean inflammation of bones as well as
of joints, and say that Fred, in the counterfactual situation, believes that he
has tharthritis in his thigh. Again, note two points: First, Fred, in the counterfactual situation, believes not that he has arthritis in his thigh but that
he has tharthritis in his thigh, and, second, this belief is true.

What this thought experiment shows is that the content of belief depends, at least in part but crucially, on the speech practices of the linguistic community in which we situate the subject. Fred in the actual situation
and Fred in the counterfactual situation are exactly alike when taken as
an individual person (that is, when we consider his internal/intrinsic
properties alone), including his speech habits (he speaks the same idiolect
in both situations) and inner mental life. Yet he has different beliefs in the
two situations: Fred in the actual world has the belief that he has arthritis
in his thigh, which is false, but in the counterfactual situation he has the
belief that he has tharthritis in his thigh, which is true. If this is right, beliefs and other intentional states do not supervene on the internal physi-
cal/psychological states of persons; if supervenience is wanted, we must
also include in the supervenience base the linguistic practices of the community to which persons belong.

Burge argues plausibly that the example can be generalized to show
that almost all contents are wide—that is, externally individuated. Take
the word "brisket" (another of his examples): Some of us mistakenly
think that brisket comes only from beef, and it is easy to see how a case
analogous to the arthritis example can be set up. In fact, the same situation will arise for any word whose meaning is incompletely understood—in fact, any word whose meaning *could* be incompletely understood, which includes pretty much every word. When we profess our
beliefs using such words, our beliefs will be identified and individuated
by the socially determined meanings of these words (recall Fred and his
"arthritis" in the actual situation), and it is easy to see how a Burge-style

counterfactual situation can be set up for each such word. Moreover, we seem standardly to identify our own beliefs by reflecting on what words we would use to express them, even if we know that our understanding of these words is incomplete or even possibly defective (how many of us know the correct meaning of, say, "mortgage," "justice of the peace," or "galaxy"?). This shows, one might argue, that almost all of our ordinary belief attributions involve wide contents.

If this is right, the question naturally arises: Are there beliefs whose content isn't determined by external factors? That is, are there beliefs with narrow content? There certainly are beliefs, and other intentional states, that do not imply the existence of anything, or refer to anything, outside the subject who has them. For example, Fred's belief that he is in pain or that he exists or that there are no unicorns does not require that anything other than Fred exist, and it would seem that the content of these beliefs is independent of conditions external to Fred. If this is right, the narrowness of these beliefs is not threatened by considerations of the sort that emerged from Thought Experiment 1. But what of Thought Experiment 2? Consider Fred's belief that he is in pain. Could we run on the word "pain" Burge's argument involving "arthritis"? Surely it is possible for someone to misunderstand the word "pain" or any other sensation term, as well as "arthritis" and such. Suppose Fred thinks that "pain" applies to both pains and severe itches and that on experiencing bad itches on his shoulder, he complains to his wife about his annoying "pains" in the shoulder. If the Burge-style considerations apply here, we would have to say that Fred is expressing his belief that he is experiencing pain in his shoulder, and that this is a false belief.

The question is whether that is what we should, or want to, say. It would not seem implausible to say that knowing what we know about Fred's misunderstanding of the word "pain" and the sensation he is actually experiencing, the correct thing to say is that he believes, and in fact knows, that he is experiencing severe itches in his shoulder. It's only that in saying "I am having pains in my shoulder" he is misdescribing his sensation and hence misreporting his belief. Now consider the following counterfactual situation: In the linguistic community to which Fred belongs, "pain" is in fact used to refer to pains and severe itches. How would we report, in our own words, the content of Fred's belief in the counterfactual situation? There are these possibilities: (1) We say, "He believes that he is experiencing pains in his shoulder"; (2) We say, "He believes that he is experiencing severe itches in his shoulder"; and (3) we don't have a word in English that can be used for expressing the content of his belief (we could introduce a neologism, "painitch," and say, "Fred believes that he is experiencing painitches in his shoulder"). Obviously, (1) has to be ruled out; if (3) is what we should say, the arthritis argument applies to the present case as well, since this would show that a change in the social environment of the subject can change the belief content attributed to him. But it isn't obvious that this, rather than (2), is the correct option. It seems to be an open question, then, whether the arthritis argument applies to cases involving beliefs about one's own sensations, and there seems to be a reason for the inclination to say of Fred in the actual world that he believes that he is having severe itches rather than that he believes that he is having pains. The reason is that if we were to opt for the latter, it would make his belief false, and this is a belief about his own current sensations. But we assume that under normal circumstances people don't make mistakes in identifying their current sensory experiences. This assumption need not be taken as a contentious philosophical doctrine; arguably, recognition of first-person authority on such matters, too, reflects our common social/linguistic practices, and this may very well override the kinds of consideration so plausibly advanced by Burge in the case of arthritis.

Another point to consider is beliefs of nonlinguistic animals. Do cats and dogs have beliefs and other intentional states whose contents can be reported in the form: "Fido believes that *p*," where *p* stands for a declarative sentence? Clearly, the arthritis-style arguments cannot be applied to such beliefs since these animals don't belong to any linguistic community and the only language that is involved is our own, namely, the language of the person who makes such belief attributions. In what sense, then, could animal beliefs be externally individuated? There may or may not be an obvious answer to this question, but anyhow this example can cut both ways, as far as Burge's argument is concerned; for one might argue, as some philosophers have,[10] that nonlinguistic animals are not capable of having intentional states (in particular, beliefs) and that this is connected with the inapplicability of the arthritis argument. The details here are complicated, and we must set them aside. We will return to the question of narrow content in a subsequent section.

The Metaphysics of Wide-Content States

The considerations involved in the two thought experiments show that many, if not all, of our ordinary beliefs and other intentional states have wide content. Their contents are "external": That is, they are determined, at least in part, by factors outside the subject, in her physical and social environment. Before these externalist considerations were brought to our attention, philosophers used to think that beliefs, desires, and the like are in the mind, or at least in the head. Putnam, the inventor of twin earth with its XYZ, said: "Cut the pie any way you like, 'meanings' just ain't in the head."[11] Should we believe that beliefs and desires aren't in the head, or in the mind, either? If so, where are they? Outside the head? Let us consider three possibilities.

1. One might say that the belief that water and oil don't mix is constituted in part by water and oil, that the belief itself, in some sense, involves the actual stuff, water and oil, in addition to the person having the belief (or her "head"). A similar response in the case of arthritis would be that Fred's belief that he has arthritis is in part constituted by his linguistic community. The general idea is that all the factors that play a role in the determination of the content of a belief *ontologically constitute* that belief, that the belief is a state that comprises these items within itself. Thus, we have a simple explanation for just how your belief that water is wet differs from your twin-earthian twin's belief that twater is wet: Yours includes water as a constituent and hers includes twater as a constituent. On this approach, then, beliefs extrude from the subject's head into the world, and there are no bounds to how far they can reach. The whole universe would, on this approach, be a constituent of your beliefs about the universe! Moreover, all beliefs about the universe would appear to have exactly the same constituent, namely, the universe. This sounds absurd, and it is absurd. We can also see that this general approach would make causation of beliefs difficult to explain.

2. One might consider the belief that water and oil don't mix as a certain relation holding between the subject on the one hand and water and oil on the other. Or, alternatively, one takes the belief as a *relational property* of the subject involving water and oil. (That Socrates is married to Xanthippe is a relational fact; Socrates also has the relational property of being married to Xanthippe, and, conversely, Xanthippe has the relational property of being married to Socrates.) This approach makes causation of beliefs more tractable: We can ask, and will sometimes be able to answer, how a subject came to bear this belief relation to water and oil, just as we can ask how Xanthippe came to have the relational property of being married to Socrates. But what of other determinants of content? As we saw, belief content is determined in part by the history of one's interaction with one's environment. And what of the social-linguistic determinants, as in Burge's examples? It seems at least highly awkward to consider beliefs as relations with respect to these factors.

3. The third possibility is to consider beliefs to be wholly internal to the subjects who have them but consider their contents as giving *relational specifications* of the beliefs. On this view, beliefs may be neural states or other types of physical states of organisms and systems to which they are attributed. Contents, then, are viewed as ways of specifying these inner states; wide contents, then, are specifications in terms of, or under the constraints of, factors and conditions external to the subject, both physical and

social, both current and historical. We can refer to, or pick out, Socrates by relational descriptions or by specifying his relational properties, for example, "the husband of Xanthippe" (or the property of being married to Xanthippe), "the teacher of Plato" (or the property of being a teacher of Plato), and so on. But this doesn't mean that Xanthippe or Plato is a constituent part of Socrates, nor does it mean that Socrates is some kind of relational entity. Similarly, when we specify Jones's belief as the belief that water and oil don't mix, we are specifying this belief relationally, in terms of water and oil, but this doesn't mean that water and oil are constituents of the belief or that the belief itself is a relation to water and oil.

Let us look into this last approach in a bit more detail. Consider physical magnitudes such as mass and length, which are standardly considered to be paradigm examples of intrinsic properties of material objects. But how do we *specify, represent,* or *measure* the mass or length of an object? The answer: relationally. To say that this rod has a mass of 5 kilograms is to say that it bears a certain relationship to the International Prototype Kilogram (it would balance, on an equal-arm balance, five objects each of which balances the Standard Kilogram). Likewise, to say that the rod has a length of 2 meters is to say that it is twice the length of the Standard Meter (or twice the distance traveled by light in a vacuum in a certain specified fraction of a second). These properties are intrinsic, but their specifications or representations are extrinsic and relational, involving relationships to other things and properties in the world. It may well be that the availability of such extrinsic representations are essential to the utility of these properties in the formulation of scientific laws and explanations.

In physical measurements we use numbers to represent properties of objects, and these numbers involve relationships to other objects. Similarly, in attributing to persons beliefs with wide content, we use propositions, or content sentences, to represent them, and these propositions (often) involve relations to things outside the persons. When we say that Jones believes that water is wet, we are using the content sentence "Water is wet" to specify this belief, and the appropriateness of this sentence as a specification of the belief depends on Jones's relationship, past and present, to her environment. What Burge's examples show is that the choice of a content sentence depends also on the social/linguistic facts about the person holding the belief. In a sense, we are "measuring" people's mental states using sentences, just as we measure physical magnitudes using numbers.[12] Moreover, just as the assignment of numbers in measurement depends on relationships to things other than the things whose magnitudes are being measured, the use of content sentences in the specification of intentional states makes use of, and depends on, factors outside the subject. In both cases the informativeness and utility of the specifications, assigned numbers or sentences, depend crucially on the involvement of external factors and conditions.[13]

The approach we have just sketched has much to recommend itself over the other two. It locates beliefs and other intentional states squarely within the subjects; they are internal states of the persons holding them, not something that somehow extrudes from them. This is a more elegant metaphysical picture than its alternatives. What is "wide" about these states is their specifications or descriptions, not the states themselves. And there are good reasons for the wideness of content specifications. For one, we want them to specify the representational contents of beliefs— what states of affairs in the world are represented by beliefs—and it is no surprise that this involves reference to conditions external to the believer. For another, the sorts of social/linguistic constraints involved in Burge's examples seem crucial to the uniformity, stability, and intersubjectivity of content attributions. But it is important not to conflate the ontological status of internal states with the modes of their specification.

Narrow Content?

You believe that water extinguishes fires, and your twin on twin earth believes that twater extinguishes fires. The two beliefs have different contents: What you believe is not the same as what your twin believes. But leaving the matter here is unsatisfying; it seems to ignore something important—something psychologically important—that you and your twin share in holding these beliefs. "Narrow content" is supposed to capture this something shared you and your twin share.

First, we seem to have a strong sense that both you and your twin conceptualize the same state of affairs in holding the beliefs about water and twater respectively; the way things seem to you when you think that water extinguishes fires must be the same, we feel, as the way things seem to your twin when she thinks that twater extinguishes fires. From an internal psychological perspective, your thought and her thought seem to have the same significance. In thinking of water, you perhaps have the idea of a substance that is transparent, flows a certain way, tastes a certain way, and so on; and in thinking of twater, your twin has the same associations. Or take the frog case: Isn't it plausible to suppose that the earthly frog that detects a fly and the other-earthly frog that detects a schmy are in the same perceptual state—a state whose content consists in a black dot flitting across the visual field? There is a strong intuitive pull toward the view that there is something important that is common to your psychological life and your twin's, the earthly frog's perceptual state and the other-earthly frog's, that could reasonably be called "content."

Second, consider your and your twin's behaviors: They show a lot in common. For example, when you find your couch on fire, you pour water on it; when your twin finds her couch on fire, she pours twater on it. If you were visiting twin earth and found a couch on fire there, you would pour twater on it, too (and conversely if your twin is visiting the earth). Your behavior involving water is the same as her behavior involving twater; moreover, your behavior would remain the same if twater were substituted for water everywhere, and her behavior would remain the same if water were substituted for twater. It's almost as though the water-twater difference seems psychologically irrelevant—irrelevant for behavior causation or explanation. That is, the difference between water-thoughts and twater-thoughts cancels itself out, so to speak, in the context of psychological explanation and causation. What is important for psychological explanation seems to be what you and your twin share, namely, thoughts with narrow content. So the question arises: Does psychological theory need wide content? Can it get by with narrow content alone (assuming there is such a thing)?

We have seen some examples of beliefs that plausibly do not depend on the existence of anything outside the subject holding them: Your belief that you exist, that you are in pain, that unicorns don't exist, and the like. Although we left open the question whether the arthritis argument applies to them, they are at least "internal" or "intrinsic" to the subject in the sense that for these beliefs to exist, nothing outside the subject needs to exist. There seems no reason not to think that the occurrence of these beliefs logically entails anything external to the believer and therefore that these beliefs supervene solely on the factors internal to him (again barring the Burge-style considerations).

However, a closer look at the situation reveals that some of these beliefs are not supervenient only on internal states of the believer. For we need to consider the involvement of the subject herself in the belief. Consider Mary's belief that she is in pain. The content of this belief is that she, that is, Mary, is in pain. This is the state of affairs represented by the belief, and this belief is true just in case that state of affairs obtains—that is, just in case Mary is in pain. (That is to say, we take contents to be *truth conditions*, as standardly done.) Now, put Mary's twin on twin earth (or a perfect physical replica of Mary on this earth) in the same internal physical state that Mary is in when she has this belief. If mind-body supervenience, *as usually conceived*, holds, it would seem that Mary's twin, too, will have the belief that she is in pain. However, her belief has the content *she* (twin-earth Mary) is in pain, not the content that *Mary* is in pain. The belief is true if and only if Mary's twin is in pain. This means that the content of the belief that one is in pain, where content is understood as truth conditions, does not supervene on the internal physical state of the believer.

Thus, the following two ideas that are normally taken to lie at the core of the notion of "narrow content" fail to coincide: (1) Narrow content is internal and intrinsic to the believer and doesn't involve anything outside her current state; (2) narrow content supervenes on the current internal physical states of the believer. Mary's belief that she is in pain and other beliefs whose content sentence includes a reference back to the subject (e.g., her belief that she exists, that she is taller than her sister), satisfy (1) but not (2). Nor do beliefs whose contents involve reference to particular objects: Mary believes that Clinton is left-handed, but if you put Mary's twin in the same neural state, she will believe not that Clinton is left-handed but that twin-Clinton (Clinton's doppelganger on twin earth) is left-handed.

One may think that this shows not that these beliefs don't supervene on the internal physical states of the believer but rather that we should revise the notion of "same belief" involved here—that is, revise the criteria of belief individuation. In our discussion thus far, individual beliefs (or "belief tokens") have been considered to be "the same belief" (or "belief type") just in case they have the same content, that is, the same truth condition. As we saw, Mary's belief that she, Mary, is in pain and her twin's belief that she, the twin Mary, is in pain don't have the same content and hence must count as belonging to different belief types. That is why supervenience fails for these beliefs. However, there is an obvious and natural sense in which Mary and her twin have "the same belief"—even beliefs with "the same content"—when each believes that she is in pain. The same is true of Mary's belief that Clinton is left-handed and twin-Mary's belief that twin-Clinton is left-handed. More work, however, needs to be done to capture this notion of "content" or sameness of belief,[14] and that is part of the project of explicating the notion of narrow content.

It is widely accepted that most of our ordinary belief attributions, and attributions of other intentional states, involve wide content. Some hold not only that all contents are wide but that the very notion of narrow content makes no sense. One point that is often made against narrow content is its alleged ineffability: How do we capture the shared content of Jones's belief that water is wet and her twin's belief that twater is wet? And if there is something shared, why is it a kind of "content"?

One way the friends of narrow content have tried to deal with such questions is to treat narrow content as an abstract technical notion, roughly in the following sense. The thing that Mary and her twin share has this role: If anyone has it and has acquired her language on earth (or in an environment containing water), then her word "water" refers to water and she has water-thoughts, and if anyone has it and has acquired her language on twin earth (or in an environment containing twater), then her word "water" refers to twater and she has twater-thoughts. The same idea applies to the frog case. What the two frogs, one on this earth and the other on a planet with schmies but no flies, have in common is this: If a frog has it and inhabits an environment with flies, it has the capacity to have flies as part of its perceptual content and similarly for frogs in a schmy-inclusive environment. Technically, narrow content is taken as a *function* from environmental contexts (including contexts of language acquisition) to wide contents (or truth conditions).[15] Whether or not such an approach is ultimately viable is a complex question that we must set aside.

Two Problems with Wide Content

We will survey here two outstanding issues confronting the thesis that all, or most, of our psychological states have wide content.

The Causal Relevance of Wide Content

Even if we acknowledge that commonsense psychology individuates intentional states widely and formulates causal explanations of behavior in terms of wide-content states, we might well ask whether this is an ineliminable feature of such explanations. Several considerations can be advanced to cast doubt on the causal/explanatory efficacy of wide-content states. First, we have already noted the similarity between the behaviors of earthians and those of twin earthians in relation to water and twater respectively. We saw that in formulating causal explanations of these behaviors, the difference between water-thoughts and twater-thoughts somehow drops out. Second, to put the point another way, if you are a psychologist who has already developed a working psychological theory of earthians, formulated in terms of content-bearing intentional states, you obviously would not start all over again from scratch when you want to develop a psychological theory for twin earthians. In fact, you are likely to say that earthians and twin earthians have "the same psychology"—that is, the same psychological theory is valid for both. In view of this, isn't it more appropriate to take the difference between water-thoughts and twater-thoughts merely as a difference in the values of a contextual parameter to be fixed to suit the situations to which the theory is applied, rather than as an integral element of the theory itself? If this is correct, doesn't wide content drop out as part of the theoretical apparatus of psychological theory?

Moreover, there is a metaphysical point to consider: The proximate cause of my physical behavior (e.g., bodily motions) must be "local"—it must be a certain series of neural events originating in my central nervous system that causes the contraction of appropriate muscles and such. This means that what these neural events represent in the outside world is irrelevant to behavior causation: If the same neural events occur in a different environment so that they have different representational (wide) content, they would still cause the same physical behavior. That is, we have reason to think that proximate causes of behavior are locally supervenient on the internal physical states of an organism, but wide-content states are not so supervenient. Hence, the wideness of wide-content states is not relevant to causal explanations of physical behavior.

One way in which the friends of wide content have tried to counter these considerations goes as follows. What we typically attempt to explain in commonsense psychology is not physical behavior but action—not why your right hand moved thus and so, but why you turned on the stove, why you boiled the water, why you made the tea. To explain why your hand moved in a certain way, it may suffice to advert to causes "in the head," but to explain why you turned on the stove or why you boiled the water, we must invoke wide-content states: because you wanted to heat the kettle of water, because you wanted to make a cup of tea for your friend, and so on. Behaviors explained in typical commonsense explanation are given under "wide descriptions," and we need wide-content states to explain them. So the point of the reply is that we need wide content to explain "wide behavior." Whether or not this response is sufficient is another question. In particular, one might raise questions whether the wideness of thoughts and the wideness of behavior are playing any real role in the causal/explanatory relation involved or merely ride piggyback, so to speak, on an underlying causal/explanatory relationship between the neural states, or narrow-content states, and physical behavior.

Wide Content and Self Knowledge

How do we know that Mary believes that water is wet and that Mary's twin on twin earth believes that twater is wet? Because we know that Mary's environment contains water and that Mary's twin's environment contains twater. But consider the matter from Mary's point of view: How does she know that she believes that water is wet? How does she know the content of her own thoughts?

We believe that a subject has special, direct access to her own mental states. Perhaps the access is not infallible and doesn't extend to all mental states, but it is uncontroversial that there is special first-person authority in regard to one's own occurrent thoughts. When you consciously think something, you know immediately, without inference or further evidence, what you think. If you think that the shuttle bus is late and you might miss your flight, you know, almost in the very act of thinking, that you think that. You don't make observations, or make inferences, to come to know that. First-person knowledge of the contents of one's own thoughts is direct and immediate and carries a special sort of authority (Chapters 1, 7).

Let us now return to Mary and her knowledge of the content of her belief. It would seem that in order for her to know that her thought is about water, not about twater, she is in the same epistemic situation that we are in with respect to the content of her thought. For her to know that she believes that water is wet, not that twater is wet, she must know, it would seem, that she is in a water-inclusive environment, not a twater-inclusive one. To make this more vivid, suppose that twin earth exists in a nearby planetary system and we can travel freely between earth and twin earth. It seems plausible to suppose that if one spends a sufficient amount of time on earth (or twin earth), one's word "water" becomes locally acclimatized, as it were, and begins to refer to the local stuff, water or twater, as the case may be. Now, Mary, an inveterate space traveler, forgets which planet she has been living on for the past several years—whether it's earth or twin earth. Can she know, directly and without further investigation, whether her thoughts are about water or twater? It would seem that just as she cannot know, without external evidence, whether her present use of the word "water" refers to water or twater, she cannot know, without investigating her environment, whether her thought about the steaming liquid in her kettle has the content that this water is boiling or that this twater is boiling. If something like this is right, then content externalism, the thesis that almost all, if not all, of our ordinary intentional state attributions involve wide content, would have the consequence that most of our knowledge of our own intentional states is indirect and must be based on external evidence. That is to say, content externalism appears to be prima facie incompatible with first-person epistemic access to one's own mind.

These issues concerning wide and narrow content are likely to be with us for some time. Their importance could hardly be exaggerated: Content-bearing states, that is, propositional attitudes like belief, desire, and the rest, constitute the central core of our commonsense psychological practices, providing us with a framework for formulating explanations and predictions of what we and our fellow humans do. Without this essential tool for understanding and anticipating human action and behavior, a communal life would be unthinkable. The issues, however, go beyond commonsense psychology. There is, for example, this important question about scientific psychology: Should systematic psychology make use of these content-bearing intentional states in formulating its laws and explanations? Or should it—or could it—transcend them by formulating its theories and explanations in purely nonintentional (perhaps ultimately neurobiological) terms? These questions concern the centrality of contentful intentional states to the explanation of human action and behavior—both in everyday psychological practices and in theory construction in scientific psychology. Many of these issues remain wide open and are being vigorously discussed in the field.

Further Readings

On interpretation theory, see W. V. Quine, *Word and Object* (Cambridge and New York: Technology Press of MIT and John Wiley & Sons, 1960); Donald Davidson, *Essays on Truth and Interpretation* (Oxford: Oxford Univsity Press, 1984); David Lewis, "Radical Interpretation," in *Philosophical Papers*, vol. 1 (New York: Oxford University Press, 1983); Daniel C. Dennett, "True Believers," in *The Nature of Mind*, ed. David M. Rosenthal (New York: Oxford University Press, 1991); Daniel C. Dennett, "Intentional Systems," in his *Brainstorms* (Montgomery, Vt.: Bradford Books, 1978).

On causal/correlational theories of content, see Fred Dretske, *Knowledge and the Flow of Information* (Cambridge: MIT Press, 1981); Robert Stalnaker, *Inquiry* (Cambridge: MIT Press, 1984); J. A. Fodor, *Psychosemantics* (Cambridge: MIT Press, 1987) and his *Theory of Content and Other Essays* (Cambridge: MIT Press, 1990); Dennis Stampe, "Toward a Causal Theory of Linguistic Representation," *Midwest Studies in Philosophy* 2 (1977):42–63; Brian McLaughlin, "What Is Wrong with Correlational Psychosemantics?" *Synthese* 70 (1987):271–286; and essays by Louise Antony and Joseph Levine, Lynne Rudder Baker, and Paul Boghossian in *Meaning in Mind*, ed. Barry Loewer and Georges Rey (London: Routledge, 1991); and Robert Cummins, *Meaning and Mental Representation* (Cambridge: MIT Press, 1989), especially ch. 4–6. Another useful recent book on issues of mental content, including some not discussed in this chapter, is Lynne Rudder Baker, *Explaining Attitudes* (Cambridge: Cambridge University Press, 1995).

On narrow and wide content, the two principal texts that introduced the issues are Hilary Putnam, "The Meaning of 'Meaning,'" in his *Mind, Language, and Reality: Philosophical Papers*, vol. 2 (Cambridge: Cambridge University Press, 1975); and Tyler Burge, "Individualism and the Mental," *Midwest Studies in Philosophy* 4 (1979):73–121. See also Burge's "Individualism and Psychology," *Philosophical Review* 95 (1986):3–45; Fodor's *Psychosemantics* and "A Modal Argument for Narrow Content," *Journal of Philosophy* 88 (1991):5–26; the papers by Ned Block and Robert Stalnaker in Loewer and Rey, *Meaning in Mind*. The more ambitious reader may wish also to tackle Block's "Advertisement for a Semantics for Psychology," *Midwest Studies in Philosophy* 10 (1986):615–678.

On wide content and self-knowledge, see Donald Davidson, "Knowing One's Own Mind," *Proceedings and Addresses of the American Philosophical Association* 60 (1986):441–458; Tyler Burge, "Individualism and Self-Knowledge," *Journal of Philosophy* 85 (1988):654–655; Paul Boghossian, "Content and Self-Knowledge," *Philosophical Topics* 17 (1989):5–26; John Heil, *The Nature of True Minds* (Cambridge: Cambridge University Press, 1992), ch. 5.

Notes

1. The discussion in this section is based on the works of W. V. Quine and Donald Davidson. See Quine on "radical translation" in his *Word and Object* (Cambridge and New York: Technology Press of MIT and John Wiley & Sons, 1960), ch. 2. Davidson's principal essays on interpretation are included in his *Essays on Truth and Interpretation* (Oxford: Oxford University Press, 1984); in particular, see "Radical Interpretation" and "Belief as the Basis of Meaning." See also David Lewis, "Radical Interpretation," reprinted in his *Philosophical Papers*, vol. 1 (New York: Oxford University Press, 1983).

2. We are assuming here that affirmative utterances of sentences (roughly cases of what Davidson calls "holding a sentence true") are observable or at least ascertainable on the basis of observable behavior, independently of ascription of contentful mental states or attitudes to the speaker. (The account would be circular otherwise.)

3. The parenthetical part is often assumed without being explicitly stated. Some writers state it as a separate principle, sometimes called the "requirement of rationality." There are many inequivalent versions of the charity principle in the literature.

4. Such a position seems implicit in, for example, Daniel Dennett's "True Believers," in his *Intentional Stance* (Cambridge: MIT Press, 1987); reprinted in *The Nature of Mind*, ed. David M. Rosenthal (New York: Oxford University Press, 1991).

5. To use Robert Stalnaker's term in his *Inquiry* (Cambridge: MIT Press, 1984), p. 18.

6. This captures the gist of the correlational approach, which has many diverse versions. For accounts in this spirit, see Fred Dretske, *Knowledge and the Flow of Information* (Cambridge: MIT Press, 1981); Stalnaker, *Inquiry*; and J. A. Fodor, *Psychosemantics* (Cambridge: MIT Press, 1987) and *A Theory of Content and Other Essays* (Cambridge: MIT Press, 1990). The correlational approach was initiated by Dennis Stampe in his "Toward a Causal Theory of Linguistic Representation," *Midwest Studies in Philosophy* 2 (1977):42–63. For a critique of this approach see, for example, Brian McLaughlin, "What Is Wrong with Correlational Psychosemantics?" *Synthese* 70 (1987):271–286; and papers by Louise Antony and Joseph Levine, Lynne Rudder Baker, and Paul Boghossian in *Meaning in Mind*, ed. Barry Loewer and Georges Rey (London: Routledge, 1991). In this section I am indebted to McLaughlin's paper.

7. For discussion of this issue, see the items listed in note 6.

8. Hilary Putnam, "The Meaning of 'Meaning,'" in Putnam, *Mind, Language, and Reality: Philosophical Papers*, vol. 2 (Cambridge: Cambridge University Press, 1975); Tyler Burge, "Individualism and the Mental," *Midwest Studies in Philosophy* 4 (1979):73–121. The use of the terms "narrow" and "wide" in this context is due to Putnam.

9. We will ignore here the inconvenient but inessential detail that since your body contains lots of H_2O molecules and your twin on twin earth has XYZ where you have H_2O, you two couldn't be "molecule-for-molecule" identical.

10. Most notably Descartes and Davidson. See Davidson's "Thought and Talk" in his *Essays on Truth and Interpretation*.

11. Putnam, "The Meaning of 'Meaning,'" p. 227.

12. This idea is explicitly stated by Paul M. Churchland in his "Eliminative Materialism and the Propositional Attitudes," *Journal of Philosophy* 78 (1981):67–90. It has been systematically elaborated by Robert Matthews in "The Measure of Mind," *Mind* 103 (1994):131–146. However, these authors do not relate this approach to the issues of content externalism. For another perspective on the issues see Ernest Sosa, "Between Internalism and Externalism," *Philosophical Issues* 1 (1991):179–195.

13. This point concerning content sentences is made by Burge in "Individualism and the Mental."

14. In this connection see Roderick Chisholm's theory, which takes beliefs not as relations to propositions but construes them as attributions of properties, in his *First Person* (Minneapolis: University of Minnesota Press, 1981). David Lewis has independently proposed a similar approach in his "Attitudes *De Dicto* and *De Se*," reprinted in his *Philosophical Papers*, vol. 1.

15. See Stephen White, "Partial Character and the Language of Thought," *Pacific Philosophical Quarterly* 63 (1982):347–365; Fodor, *Psychosemantics*.

9

Reductive and
Nonreductive Physicalism

As we have seen, the classic dualism of Descartes is *substance dualism*, a position that posits two distinct domains of entities, one consisting of immaterial minds ("mental substances") and the other consisting of physical things ("material substances"). Associated with these two domains of entities are two families of properties, one consisting of mental properties and kinds and the other of physical properties and kinds, which characterize the entities of the two domains, minds and bodies, respectively. Thus, Descartes's dualism combines substance dualism and *property dualism*: two disparate domains of substances and two mutually exclusive families of properties. Arguably, substance dualism entails property dualism: It would be prima facie incoherent to accept two fundamentally different types of substance and yet maintain that a single set of properties suffices to characterize all substances.

In contemporary philosophy of mind, substance dualism has largely been abandoned, for various reasons. The idea that there are nonphysical substances outside the framework of spacetime and in causal interaction with physical processes, as Descartes believed, has seemed to many thinkers as deeply puzzling, mysterious, and ultimately incoherent.[1] Thus, *ontological physicalism*,[2] the view that there are no concrete existents, or substances, in the spacetime world other than material particles and their aggregates, has been a dominant position on the mind-body problem. In most contemporary debates, ontological physicalism forms the starting point of discussion rather than a conclusion that needs to be established. In consequence, the most intensely debated issue—in fact, the only substantive remaining issue—concerning the mind-body relation has centered on *properties*—that is, the question *how mental and physical properties are related to each other.* Here, the main focus of the debate has been, and continues to be, the controversy between reductionism and nonreductionism. The reductionist, or the reductive physicalist, takes the position that mental properties are reducible to, and hence ultimately turn out to be, physical properties. On this view, then, there are no nonphysical properties in this world; all properties are ultimately reducible to the properties countenanced in fundamental physics. For over two decades, however, reductionism has been in deep decline, and the most influential version of physicalism has been *nonreductive physicalism*, the view that mental properties, along with other "higher-level" properties, constitute an autonomous domain that resists reduction to the physical domain. A nonreductionist view of this kind has also served as an influential philosophical foundation of "cognitive science," providing support for the claim that cognitive science, including psychology, linguistics, artificial intelligence, and so on, forms an autonomous and irreducible science with its own distinctive vocabulary and methodology and not answerable to the methodological or explanatory constraints of the more fundamental sciences, such as physics and biology. Thus, the most widely accepted form of physicalism today combines ontological physicalism with property dualism: All concrete particulars in this world are physical, but certain complex structures and configurations of physical particles can, and sometimes do, exhibit properties that are not reducible to "lower-level" physical properties.

What Is Reduction?

The account of reduction that has been assumed, explicitly or implicitly, in the contemporary debate on reductionism was originally formulated by Ernest Nagel in the 1950s.[3] This account, which we may call the Nagel model, takes reduction primarily as a relation between two *scientific theories*, the target theory that is up for reduction and the theory that serves as its reduction base ("the reducer" or "base theory"). A theory in this context is taken to be a set of statements, which represent its "laws." It's convenient to think of a theory as constituted by its "basic laws" (or "axioms") plus all statements logically (and mathematically) derivable from them. Each theory T will have its characteristic vocabulary, V, of nonlogical, descriptive expressions (e.g., "mass," "magnetic," "temperature," "ductility," "gene," etc.) in terms of which its laws are formulated.

What, then, is the relation between target theory T_2 and base theory T_1 that makes it the case that T_2 is reduced to T_1? As Nagel conceived it, the relation of reducibility is, at bottom, that of *logical derivability* or *provability*: For T_2 to be reducible to T_1, the laws of T_2 must be derivable from laws of T_1—that is, T_2-laws are theorems of T_1, provable from the basic T_1-laws. This would in effect show T_2 to be implicitly contained in T_1 as a subtheory and not an independent theory concerning its domain. But how can T_2-laws, formulated in their distinctive theoretical vocabulary (say, that of chemistry), be logically derived from T_1-laws, which are formulated in a different, perhaps totally disjoint, vocabulary (say, that of theoretical physics)? Take a T_2-law with the following simple form:

(1) For anything x, if x has property F, x has property G ($F \rightarrow G$, for short)

where "F" and "G" are expressions of T_2 that are not part of the T_1-vocabulary. To derive (1) from T_2, then, we need special auxiliary premises connecting T_2-expressions with T_1-expressions—that is, "bridge principles" correlating the two vocabularies. Suppose, then, that we have the following bridge principles:

(2a) For anything x, x has property F iff x has property F^* ($F \leftrightarrow F^*$)

(2b) For anything x, x has property G iff x has property G^* ($G \leftrightarrow G^*$)

where F^* and G^* are predicates of the base theory T_1. These are likely to be complex expressions built up from the basic terms in the vocabulary of T_1. It is easy to see that given these two bridge principles, our T_2-law, (1), can be easily derived from the following T_1-statement:

(3) For anything x, if x has property F^*, x has property G^* ($F^* \rightarrow G^*$).

This means that if (3) is a law of T_1, our T_2-law, (1), can be reduced to T_1. Nagel reduction, therefore, may be stated as follows:

T_2 is *Nagel-reduced* to T_1 just in case all laws of T_2 are logically (and mathematically) derivable from laws of T_1 augmented with appropriate "bridge principles" connecting the expressions of T_2 with expressions of T_1.

What is the status of these bridge principles, like (2a) and (2b), which connect expressions of two different theories? The two possibilities are these: (i) they are *definitions* that define the T_2-expressions "F" and "G" in terms of the T_1-expressions "F^*" and "G^*," respectively; (ii) they are empirically certified *correlation laws* that affirm that as a matter of empirical law properties F and G are correlated, respectively, with properties F^* and G^*. These possibilities need not be taken as mutually exclusive options: They would be so only if we assumed that definitions could be based only on analytic relations between the meanings of expressions, not on empirically motivated and warranted correlations between the properties signified by them. We should also keep in mind that in any given case of theory reduction, some of the bridge principles involved may be definitions that are largely grounded in meanings, and others may be empirical correlation laws. In some cases of reduction, the main warrant for certain bridge principles may well be that they enable the desired reduction, and when a reduction becomes well entrenched, the bridge principles, whatever their provenance may have been, may come to be viewed as definitions (consider the stock case of "temperature" and "mean kinetic energy"). In any case, for terminological uniformity we will henceforth use the term "bridge law" rather than "bridge principle"; this is also in conformity with the general usage in this area.

Must bridge laws be *biconditionals* in form—that is, "iff" ($\leftrightarrow$) statements—rather than one-way "if-then" ($\rightarrow$) conditionals? Nagel does not require them to be biconditionals: The derivability of the higher laws from the laws of the reducer is his main focus, and the only requirement on bridge laws is that they must be available in sufficient numbers and strength to make the derivation possible. This means that just what sorts of bridge laws are needed will vary from case to case, depending on the strength of the laws to be derived and that of the laws available as premises. On Nagel's approach, then, nothing general can be said about the form, or strength, of bridge laws. Current discussions of reductionism, however, standardly assume that these laws, like (2a) and (2b), must be biconditionals in form, giving for each property to be reduced a nomologically coextensive property in the base theory.

There are at least two good reasons for making this assumption. First, it states a general requirement, simple and perspicuous, that guarantees the derivability of the laws of the target theory from the laws of the reduction base (assuming the target theory to be true). This is easy to see:.By using these biconditionals in effect as definitions, we can rewrite every T_2-law in the vocabulary of T_1 (by replacing F by F^*, G by G^*, and so on; in the above example, (3) is a T_1-rewrite of (1)). Now, the T_1-rewrite of a T_2-law is either derivable from the laws of T_1, in which case all is well, or it isn't. In the latter case, we may simply add it to T_1 as an additional law, since it is a true T_1-statement with the form of a law. In either case the T_2-law is easily derived from its T_1-rewrite, using the biconditional bridge laws as auxiliary premises. To be sure, T_1 may have to be augmented by the addition of new laws, as described; however, the new laws are formulated entirely in the original vocabulary of T_1, and we have not expanded its domain of entities or properties. Thus, this will not diminish in any way the philosophical and methodological interest of the reduction. In this way, the biconditional bridge laws, if available for every predicate of the target theory, guarantee Nagel reduction.

A second reason for wanting biconditionals as bridge laws is ontological: When reduction has been successfully carried out, we may very well want to *identify* the properties of the reduced theory with properties of the base theory. That is, we may want to upgrade (2a) and (2b) to the identities:

(2a*) Property F = property F^*

(2b*) Property G = property G^*

Such identities, one could argue, are essential to the ontological simplification that we seek in theory reduction, for they enable us to dispense with facts involving F and G as something in addition to facts involving F^* and G^*. They also allow us to give simple answers to potentially embarrassing questions of the form, "But why does property F correlate this way with property F^*?" Our answer: "Because F just is F^*." In short, these property identities give us *reduction of higher-level properties*, and hence *reduction of higher-level facts*, and this is something that mere correlations cannot deliver. But these identities presuppose biconditional correlation laws: the identity "$F = F^*$" requires the correlation "$F \leftrightarrow F^*$" and cannot be grounded merely on "$F \rightarrow F^*$" or "$F^* \rightarrow F$."

Nagel reduction, therefore, is in essence the deductive absorption of the target theory by a wider base theory supplemented with appropriate bridge laws. Later writers have argued, plausibly, that reduction so conceived is a highly idealized model that is at best only approximated by actual cases of theory reduction in science, and that the requirement of derivability of the laws of the reduced theory must be weakened, especially in view of the fact that these laws are often only approximately true. One natural and popular way of relaxing the derivability requirement is to say that *appropriately corrected versions* of these laws, rather than the laws as given, be derivable from the laws of the base theory; a similar idea is that the reduced laws must have "images," or "counterparts," among the laws of the base theory that can serve essentially the same explanatory and predictive purposes. These possible modifications will require corresponding changes in the conception of "bridge laws," but these issues will not significantly affect the discussion to follow concerning mind-body reduction.

What exactly is the payoff, philosophical or scientific, of theory reduction? What does the talk of "unification" and "systematization" supposedly achieved by reduction really amount to? Our initial answer to this question must be this: By reducing one theory to another, we reduce the number of independent assumptions about the world. Reduction, on the Nagelian model, shows that the laws of the reduced theory are derivable from, and hence are not independent of, the laws of the reducer. It shows that fewer basic laws, and fewer basic expressions, fully suffice for the description and explanation of the phenomena of a given domain. That in itself is a sufficient justification for the reductive procedure, but we can be more explicit about the significance of the unification and simplification effected by reduction. First, theory reduction when appropriately carried out provides us with *explanations* of the laws of the reduced theory in terms of the laws of the base theory. When we reduce the gas laws by deriving them from mechanical laws about the behavior of molecules constituting gases, we explain why these gas laws hold (to the extent that they do)—why, for example, the temperature and volume of a gas under constant pressure are inversely correlated with each other. The explanation describes a micromechanism, involving gas molecules, that explains the observed macroregularities. "Microreduction" of this kind is seen all over science: We explain why objects and systems of objects have the properties they have (e.g., solubility in water, ductility, transparency) by analyzing their microstructure—that is, by deriving statements describing their macroproperties and regularities from laws governing the behaviors and properties of their microconstituents. The reduction of genetic laws to laws of molecular biology about DNA and so on is another example of microreduction; this gives us a reductive explanation of why the observed patterns of transmission of phenotypic features occur from generation to generation. Microreductions provide us with explanatory insight into how and why the observed regularities hold at the macrolevel.

Second, there is the metaphysical payoff of *ontological simplicity*. When light is reduced to electromagnetic radiation or the gene is reduced to DNA molecules, a measure of simplicity is achieved: Phenomena involving light are just events and processes involving electromagnetic radiation, and similarly for the gene and the DNA molecules. As we have seen, bridge laws may be upgraded to identities yielding reductive identifications of properties of a higher-level theory with those of its reducer.[4] Thus, in the kinetic theory of gases, temperature is identified with average kinetic energy (of the molecules constituting a gas). Given this identification, there are no facts about temperatures of gases over and above facts about average kinetic energies of molecules; that this gas has this temperature is not a fact over and above the fact that its molecules have a certain average translational energy, and there is no need to give an explanation of why this gas has this temperature just when it has the corresponding micromolecular property.

Arguments Against Mind-Body Reduction

Most antireductionist arguments focus on the unavailability of bridge laws to effect a Nagelian reduction of psychological theory to physical theory ("physical" here, as elsewhere, is construed broadly to include biology as well as physics and chemistry). In particular, the emphasis has been on the unavailability of bridge laws of the biconditional form specifying for each mental term, or property, a nomologically necessary and sufficient condition in physical terms. Demand for bridge laws of this form, not just any connection between mental and physical properties, seems both appropriate and justified. First, we are not even close to having a finished psychological theory to reduce nor a completed neurobiology to serve as a reduction base, and this means that we can have no clear idea just what psychophysical bridge laws might be minimally sufficient for the Nagelian derivation of psychological laws from neurophysiological laws. Biconditional psychophysical laws are attractive because they would guarantee, as we saw, the required derivation and thereby free the discussion of psychophysical reduction from the details of just what our finished psychology and neurophysiology will look like, something that we may never know.

To be sure, we don't have a clear idea either about exactly what concepts will be used or what properties will be invoked in a finished psychological theory. However, here we seem better off: At least we can focus on the concepts used in commonsense psychology or the systematic scientific psychology of today and discuss the prospects of finding biconditional bridge laws for them, making sure that our considerations don't depend on what may turn out to be the idiosyncratic local features of the chosen examples. A second reason for going for biconditional laws is that, as we saw, bridge laws of this form could underwrite property identities, thereby simplifying our ontology. Note in this connection the following important fact: Biconditional bridge laws make it possible for us to discuss mind-body reduction independently of any particular model of theory reduction, Nagel's or anyone else's. This is so because these bridge principles by themselves may be sufficient to underwrite, or at least support, property identities, which after all is the ultimate goal of reduction. Thus, if we have reason to believe that for every psychological property or kind M a necessary and sufficient physical/biological property P exists—that is, we have a bridge principle of the form "$M \leftrightarrow P$"—these laws alone could motivate property identities of the form "$M = P$."[5] Conversely, and more importantly, reasons for thinking that such biconditional bridge laws cannot be had would yield a powerful argument against the possibility of reductive identification of mental properties with physical properties and hence against mind-body reductionism. In sum, then, bridge laws are what provide the crucial reductive linkages, and their form and availability are critical factors in the discussion of mind-body reduction.

Behaviorism can be considered an attempt to reduce the mental to the physical by connecting mental properties with behavioral properties via *definitional* bridge principles. If every mental expression M can be given a behavioral definition B that would give us a bridge principle, "$M \leftrightarrow B$," and a complete system of such biconditionals encompassing all mental properties would suffice to reduce mentality to behavior. Objections to the possibility of such behavioristic definitions of mental terms (Chapter 2), therefore, are reasons for thinking that mind-body reduction cannot be achieved by definitional or semantic reduction. The collapse of logical behaviorism encourages us to look for empirically grounded bridge laws; that is, if we are to have mind-body reduction, we will need *psychophysical laws*, laws correlating mental and physical properties, as our bridge principles. The reduction of psychology to physical theory, then, must be nomological reduction, not definitional reduction.

So the question of mind-body reduction comes to this: Are there psychophysical laws, in sufficient numbers and of an appropriate form, to serve as bridge laws? We now see the significance of Davidson's psychophysical anomalism for mind-body reduction and his reasons for advocating "anomalous monism," a version of nonreductive physicalism (Chapter 6). For if psychophysical anomalism is true, there are no laws to serve as mind-body bridge laws—not only no laws of the biconditional form but no laws of any form. Obviously, then, any argument for psychophysical anomalism is ipso facto an argument against the possibility of mind-body reductionism.[6]

Davidson's psychophysical anomalism, though it is an arresting doctrine, has not been embraced by everyone; what has had a far greater impact in persuading physicalists to abandon reductionism, and hence type physicalism, is an argument based on the phenomenon of multiple realizability of mental properties. As we saw (Chapters 2 and 3), this is the widely accepted thesis that any mental property can have diverse physical realizations in a wide variety of biological organisms—and perhaps in complex nonbiological systems as well. Consider a mental property M with its diverse physical realizers $P_1, P_2, \ldots$ (this, as many nonreductivists will claim, is likely to be an open-ended list). For P_i to be a realizer of M, the following conditional must hold, as a matter of law:

(PR1) $P_i \to M$

That is to say, each physical realizer must be a lawfully sufficient condition for the mental property it realizes. Thus, if C-fiber activation realizes pain in humans, it must be the case that the occurrence of C-fiber activation guarantees the occurrence of pain. Now, since each of $P_1, P_2, \ldots,$ which are all distinct from one another, is sufficient for M, none of them can be necessary for it. That is, P_1 cannot be necessary for M, since M can occur in the absence of P_1 as long as another one of its many realizers, P_2 or P_3 or $\ldots$, is present. So for no i can we have a biconditional law:

(PR2) $P_i \leftrightarrow M$

That is, none of these Ps is a "nomic coextension" of M, a property that something instantiates, as a matter of law, if and only if it instantiates M. And for this reason, we cannot hope to arrive at our reductive goal, namely, the identity:

(I) $P_i = M$

since (I) entails (PR2), and therefore if (PR2) doesn't hold, (I) cannot hold.

An immediate and natural reaction to this antireductionist argument is the "disjunction strategy": Given that $P_1, P_2, \ldots$ are all the realizers of M, M is instantiated on a given occasion only if one or another of these Ps is instantiated. So why not take the disjunction of the Ps, namely, the property of having *either P_1 or P_2 or* . . . (which we can abbreviate as $\cup P_i$) as a physical property that is both necessary and sufficient for M? The idea, then, is that since

(PR3) $\cup P_i \leftrightarrow M$

holds, we can take it as the required biconditional bridge law for M and consider M to be reduced to $\cup P_i$ via the identity:

(Id) $\cup P_i = M$

The standard reply of the antireductionist to this disjunction strategy is to question the propriety of $\cup P_i$ as a legitimate property. She will first make a general point about disjunctive properties, to the effect that from the fact that R and S are properties it does not follow that their disjunction, R or S, is also a property. Take an example: *being round or green*. Round things resemble each other in virtue of being round, and similarly for green things; but two things each of which has the (supposed) property of being round or green may show no resemblance whatever, for one can be round and orange and the other square and green. It will be pointed out further that resemblance or similarity is the very core of our concept of a property and that things that share a property must resemble one another in some significant respect. Resemblance would seem to be exactly what fails to be preserved when we form disjunctions of properties. Given the extreme heterogeneity of the actual and possible physical realizers of M (see Chapters 3 and 4), we cannot expect $\cup P_i$ to be a well-behaved property that captures a point of significant resemblance among the items that have it.

Moreover, apart from the point about resemblance and similarity, which basically appeals to our intuitive ideas of propertyhood, the antireductionist can go on as follows: When we note the possibility that some of M's realizers are neurological properties of organisms and others may well be electromechanical properties of robots (remember $\cup P_i$ has as its disjuncts not only actual but *all nomologically possible* realizers of M), we see that there isn't likely to be a *single scientific theory* that can deal with hopelessly heterogeneous disjunctions like $\cup P_i$. That is, the expression "$\cup P_i$" isn't going to be a predicate of any scientific theory.[7] If so, there will be no scientific theory to which psychology can be reduced via bridge laws like (PR3).

To this the reductionist can try the following reply: Insisting on some unanalyzed, primitive notion of resemblance as a criterion for respectable properties is both dogmatic and myopic. When we debate the reducibility of ethical properties by defining them in terms of descriptive or naturalistic properties (as "ethical naturalists" would attempt), it would be highly artificial and unmotivated to disallow the use of such basic logical/grammatical constructions as disjunction ("or") and negation ("not"). If we could define terms like "good," "right," "just," and so on, using only certifiably descriptive expressions and their logical compounds, everyone would agree that would be reduction enough. So why disallow disjunction in the case of psychophysical reduction?

Another antireductionist reasoning may proceed as follows: No scientific theory can make use of an open-ended expression (whether it's a disjunction or conjunction or whatnot) like "$\cup P_i$" (remember this is short for "P_1 or P_2 or . . ."), unless it is *finitely characterizable*. But in our case the only way of doing so seems to be to make use of M itself, replacing the ellipsis with something like "any other physical property that realizes M." There is no other way we can define membership in the open-ended disjunction "P_1 or P_2 or. . . ." If this is correct, the expression "$\cup P_i$" is at least partly but ineliminably mentalistic, since the mentalistic expression "M" covertly occurs in it, and this means that it cannot be a term in some underlying physical/biological theory. To put it another way, if (PR3) is to be acceptable as a bridge law, its left-hand side must be an expression made up of purely physical terms, but on the current understanding, "$\cup P_i$" fails this requirement. It follows, then, that (PR3) cannot be considered an acceptable bridge law. Moreover, there seems to be no hope of purging "$\cup P_i$" of its mentalistic involvement by identifying all actual and possible realizers of M exclusively in physical terms. We must conclude, then, that the disjunction strategy cannot ever yield a physical/biological expression suitable for a bridge law.

This argument is persuasive as a point about theory reduction. The reductionist, however, can perhaps formulate a rejoinder along the following lines: The antireductionist argument concedes one important point of principle, namely, that the disjunctiveness of the expression "$\cup P_i$" itself does not impugn its legitimacy as an expression that may occur in a bridge law. The only question is whether or not it could be given a finite physical characterization. But this is a contingent question whose answer depends on factors like the expressive resources of the physical language and our ingenuity and persistence in doing science. Thus, the multiple realizability of mental properties does not by itself entail an antireductionist conclusion, namely, that a finite and purely physical characterization, no matter how logically complex, does not or cannot exist for the property referred to by "$\cup P_i$." From an ontological point of view, the reductionist continues, (PR3) and its companion identity, (I), do justify a reductionist conclusion, since the expression "$\cup P_i$," as presently understood, does refer to *a purely physical property*, although in doing so it makes use of the mentalistic expression "*M*."

So goes the debate. We will return to the issue of multiply realizable mental properties later in this chapter.

Supervenience Physicalism

The antireductionist claim is a negative thesis; it does not provide us with a positive statement about how mental properties are related to physical properties, telling us only that this relation is not that of reducibility. This claim is something that will be welcomed by Cartesians, neovitalists, emergentists, and other antiphysicalists as good news. It is only proper and natural, then, that most physicalists want to give a positive characterization of the mental-physical relation that recognizes the primacy and priority of the physical over the mental. If you want to call yourself a "physicalist," you will probably want to go beyond mere ontological physicalism and clarify a sense in which physical theory and its properties give a description of the world at its most fundamental level.

Cartesian dualism presents a *bifurcated* picture of reality: The world consists of two nonoverlapping spheres of equal ontological standing, one consisting of material bodies and the other of minds, existing side by side. The basic ontological picture implicit in contemporary discussions of the mind-body problem is strikingly different: It presents the world as a *multilayered* hierarchy consisting of "levels" or "tiers" of entities and their characteristic properties. It is usually supposed that there is a bottom level consisting of what according to microphysics are the most basic particles out of which all matter is composed. Above this bottom level there are levels consisting of atoms, of molecules, of cells, of organisms, and so on. Entities belonging to a given level are supposed to be characterized by properties distinctive to that level (although lower-level properties may apply to them also); thus, basic physical magnitudes like mass, energy, and spin are some of the properties of the basic particles, and properties like electrical conductivity and temperature are properties of aggregates of molecules. Mental properties, at least in our world, emerge only at the level of organisms. Notice that entities at a given level are composed entirely of entities belonging to lower levels; no new entities appear at a higher level that are not aggregates of entities at the lower levels. What, then, of the properties of the higher-level entities? How are they related to properties of the entities at lower levels?

The assumption that is widely shared by physicalists is that higher-level properties are in some sense *dependent* on, or *determined* by, their lower-level properties. More specifically, what higher-level properties a given entity has are totally fixed by the lower-level properties and relations characterizing its parts. Generally, then, a dependency relation characterizes both the entities and properties at adjacent levels. Higher-level entities are determined by the lower-level ones in that they are "mereological" structures wholly decomposable into parts that belong to the lower level. It is this asymmetric and transitive part-whole relation that generates a hierarchy of levels or tiers of entities. But in what sense are higher-level properties determined by lower-level properties? Are the properties, too, ordered hierarchically by some significant relationship?

This is where the idea of "supervenience" comes in. Some physicalists will state their position like this: Higher-level properties of a thing are *supervenient* on its lower-level properties. But what does this mean? Suppose you are working on an art project, say, a piece of marble sculpture. Your aim is to create a work with certain aesthetic qualities (e.g., beauty, drama, expressiveness), but the work you do on a slab of marble is laborious physical work, cutting, drilling, chipping, and chiseling at a piece of hard material substance. You are giving it a physical shape and texture; that is, you are endowing the piece of marble with a set of physical properties. When the physical work has been finished, there is no *further* aesthetic work to do, no further step of attaching beauty and other desired aesthetic properties to the material object you have created. Once the physical work is done, the whole project is done. This is so because the physical properties of the object wholly determine its aesthetic properties. And we may justify the attribution of an aesthetic property to it on the basis of the physical properties on which it supervenes (e.g., it is beautiful and expressive because its physical shape, texture, etc. are thus and so). In this sense, aesthetic properties of an object or situation *supervene* on its physical properties. This can be seen another way: Suppose that you and your friend each had a project of sculpting a marble bust of Aristotle and that by sheer coincidence the bust you have created is entirely indistinguishable from your friend's bust in all physical details—the same size and shape, same material, same color and texture, and so on. If this happened, the two busts could not differ in some aesthetic respect—say, one of them is dramatically expressive and the other isn't. Any two works of art that are physically indiscernible must of necessity be aesthetically indiscernible.

Supervenience in this sense, therefore, opens up an interesting possibility: It may seem to provide us with a relationship that gives us *determination, or dependence, without reduction,* just what those who reject mind-body reductionism but wish to retain the dependence of the mental on the physical have been looking for. For supervenience seems, at least at first blush, consistent with irreducibility. Although aesthetic properties supervene on physical properties in the sense explained, we do not believe that beauty, say, can be given a physical definition or reduction; the aesthetic character of a work of art is distinct from, and irreducible to, its physical properties—or so we are inclined to think. The situation seems quite similar in the case of moral properties: If Socrates is a good person, then anyone who is exactly like him in respect of all descriptive, nonethical properties (e.g., the same character and personality traits, behavioral dispositions, etc.) must also be a good person. If a murder is morally reprehensible, then another murder that is indistinguishable from it in all descriptive respects must also be morally reprehensible, exactly to the same degree. In this way moral properties supervene on nonmoral (descriptive, naturalistic) properties; yet most philosophers doubt that moral properties are definable in nonmoral terms or are otherwise reducible to them. Certainly, many moral theorists who have rejected ethical naturalism, the view that ethical properties are naturalistically definable, have subscribed to the supervenience of the moral on the nonmoral.[8]

Supervenience, therefore, looks like just what the nonreductive physicalist has ordered: It promises to be a nonreductive dependency relation that can do justice to both her physicalism and antireductionism. The thesis that the mentality of an organism supervenes on its physical nature seems to capture both the physicalist requirement that mentality depends on and is determined by physical properties and the antireductionist thesis that this dependency falls short of reducibility. Note the following important point: Although supervenience perhaps doesn't imply reducibility, it need not be taken to imply irreducibility either—that is, supervenience suffices for the purposes of the nonreductive physicalist if it is consistent with both reducibility and irreducibility.

Let us consider the following formulation of supervenience physicalism:

(SP1) Mental properties supervene on physical properties in that for every mental property M, if something has M, it has a physical property P such that necessarily if anything has P it has M.

As an example, suppose a person experiences pain. If mind-body supervenience holds in the sense of (SP1), then that person instantiates some physical property, perhaps the property of being in some neural state, that is a "supervenience base" for pain in the sense that whenever any person or organism is in that neural state, he/she/it experiences pain. (SP1) says that every mental property has a supervenience base in physical properties that constitutes a sufficient condition for it.[9] If the modal qualifier "necessarily" is understood as metaphysical necessity, the base property is metaphysically sufficient for—it "necessitates" or "entails"—the supervenient mental property; if it is understood to mean nomological necessity, the base property will be sufficient, as a matter of empirical law, for the mental property.

Under certain plausible assumptions about property composition, (SP1) can be shown to be equivalent to the following version of supervenience physicalism:[10]

> (SP2) Mental properties supervene on physical properties in that if any x (in any possible world) and y (in any possible world) have the same physical properties (in their respective worlds), then x and y have the same mental properties (in those worlds).

This formulation recapitulates the informal explanation of supervenience with which we began, but having (SP1) is convenient for many purposes. For example, it brings out the close similarity between supervenience physicalism and the physical realization principle (discussed in Chapter 4), which goes as follows:

> (PR) If anything has a mental property M, it is a material thing with a certain physical property P such that P realizes M.

If, as we suggested earlier, any realizer of M must be a lawfully sufficient condition for M, (PR) clearly entails (SP1). Note in particular that just as (PR) permits multiple physical realizers of M, (SP1) allows multiple physical bases on which M may supervene. This means that functionalists, who by and large accept (PR), must believe in mind-body supervenience; they are also supervenience physicalists. It is also easy to see how functionalists are committed to (SP2): If two organisms or systems are physically indistinguishable, they must be functionally equivalent and realize the same psychology.

You will recall our discussion in the preceding section whether the multiple physical realizability of mental properties entails their physical irreducibility—in particular, the question whether the "disjunction strategy" shows (PR) to entail the reducibility, rather than irreducibility, of the mental. The close similarity between supervenience and physical realization should alert us to the possibility that the same issues, and the ensuing dialectic, may arise in regard to supervenience. That is exactly the case. For there is a simple parallel argument that starts with (SP1) as premise that will run as follows. Consider any mental property M: According to (SP1), it supervenes on physical properties, so let $P_1, P_2, \ldots$ be all of its subvenient physical bases. It is easily seen that the disjunction

P_1 or P_2 or . . . (which we can again abbreviate as $\cup P_i$) is necessarily coextensive with M. So why not use "$\cup P_i \leftrightarrow M$" as a bridge law and reductively identify M with $\cup P_i$? As you would expect, the dialectic of argument from this point on will simply recapitulate what we have seen before with multiple realizability. It remains, therefore, an unsettled issue whether supervenience physicalism in the form of (SP1) is a viable form of nonreductive physicalism. That is why some philosophers have looked to "global supervenience" to formulate their favored version of nonreductive physicalism.

Consider, then, the following claim:

> (GS) Mental properties globally supervene on physical properties in that worlds that are physically indiscernible are also psychologically indiscernible; in fact, physically indiscernible worlds are one and the same world.

This form of supervenience is called "global supervenience" because indiscernibility considerations are applied to whole worlds, not to the individuals within them. Suppose you are creating a world: (GS) says that once you have fixed the total physical character of a world, its psychological character is fixed thereby; there is no further work you need to do or indeed can do. But what does it mean to say that two worlds are physically indiscernible? To avoid technical complications, let us assume that the worlds being compared share the same individuals—that is, the same individuals exist in all of them. We can then say that two worlds are physically indiscernible just in case the way physical properties are distributed over the individuals of one world (that is, which individuals have which physical properties) is exactly identical with the way they are distributed in the other.[11]

It can be seen that (GS), the global supervenience of the mental on the physical, is entailed by (SP1). The thought that (GS) does not in turn entail (SP1), and hence may be free of the likely reductionist commitments of (SP1), is based on the fact that in speaking globally of the mental and physical character of whole worlds, it does not seem to require direct correlations of specific mental properties with specific physical properties, type-type correlations of the sort (e.g., bridge laws) thought to be required for reduction. As a proof of this, proponents of global mind-body supervenience might point to the following sort of possibility, which is apparently ruled out by (SP1) but not by (GS), showing that the latter is essentially weaker than the former:

> There are two worlds, w_1 and w_2, and one mental property, M, and one physical property, P. There are two individuals a and b in both

worlds. In w_1, a has P and M, and b, too, has P and M; in w_2, a has P but not M, and b does not have P.

Consider now the following two claims:

(S) M supervenes on P (in the sense of [SP1]).

(G) M globally supervenes on P (in the sense of [GS]).

If the situation as described is possible, (S) is falsified, since "Necessarily if anything has P, it has M" is made false by w_2 (because a has P but not M in w_2). But apparently it is compatible with (G), since w_1 and w_2 are not physically indiscernible (for b has P in w_1 but not in w_2); to defeat (G) we need a pair of worlds that are physically indiscernible but psychologically discernible.[12]

But things are not as simple as they may seem. For if w_1 and w_2, as described, are possible, and if a and b are distinct individuals and hence each could exist even if the other didn't,[13] the following two worlds, w_3 and w_4, would also seem possible:

a is the lone individual in w_3 and in w_4. In w_3 a has P and M; in w_4 a has P but not M.

Notice that w_3 and w_4 are "contractions" of w_1 and w_2 respectively, in that the former pair result from the latter by simply removing individual b. (Think of it this way: w_1 is a world with two persons, Tom and Dick, where Tom is tall and happy and Dick, too, is tall and happy. If that is a possible world, the following, w_3, must also be a possible world, one in which Tom alone exists and is tall and happy. Similarly for w_2 and w_4.) But if w_3 and w_4 are possible worlds, (G) as well as (S) are defeated; for w_3 and w_4 are physically indiscernible and yet psychologically discernible. Thus, if this reasoning is correct, the original pair, w_1 and w_2, is incompatible after all, not only with (S) but with (G) as well, because it entails the existence of another pair of worlds, w_3 and w_4, which contradicts (G).

Thus, whether or not supervenience in one of its various forms can provide a way of formulating nonreductive physicalism remains an open question.[14]

Emergentism

Emergentism, which flourished during the first half of the twentieth century, was the first systematic formulation of nonreductive physicalism as well as of the multilayered model of the world. Its main proponents included not only academic philosophers such as Samuel Alexander, C. D. Broad, and A. O. Lovejoy[15] but also those, like C. Lloyd Morgan,[16] who were scientists by training. It seems to hold a continuing fascination for practicing scientists who have an interest in the philosophical issues arising within their disciplines, as witness Roger Sperry,[17] the noted neurophysiologist.

We can think of emergentism as consisting of the following three doctrines:

1. [Ontological physicalism] All that exists in the spacetime world are the basic particles recognized in physics and their aggregates.

Thus, the emergentist agrees with contemporary physicalists in the claim that material particles exhaust all of concrete reality (although some emergentists, unlike modern physicalists, believed in an empty spacetime frame). There are to be no spirits, vital forces, or entelechies that make their appearance at higher levels; everything that exists must be made up of physical particles, atoms, molecules, and so on.

2. [Property emergence] When aggregates of material particles attain an appropriate level of structural complexity ("relatedness"), genuinely novel properties emerge to characterize these structured systems.

The emergentist distinguishes between two types of properties that a whole may have: those that are merely "resultant" and those that are "emergent." Resultant properties are "additive" or "subtractive"; for example, the weight of this table is merely the arithmetic sum of the weight of its top and the weight of its base, and hence it is predictable from the properties of its parts. For this reason, it is a resultant property. This would be so even if nothing had existed that had exactly the weight of this table before the table came into being. Thus, the property of weighing, say, exactly 174.34556899999 lbs. might be a "new" property, a property that has never been exemplified till now, but it still would not be a "genuinely novel" one in the sense the emergentist has in mind. An example emergentists sometimes used as a genuinely novel property is the transparency of water: This property is totally alien to hydrogen and oxygen atoms and not predictable from the properties of these atoms. You can know all about the physical properties of hydrogen and oxygen atoms and not know that when they are combined in a certain way, they result in a substance with this property of transparency. Or so some emergentists argued. However, this probably was not a good example; perhaps it is possible to predict, on the basis of what we now know from solid-state physics, that lumps of H_2O molecules will have the property of letting light beams through intact. But the example gives us a serviceable idea of what the emergentists have in mind.

This leads to the following doctrine, which is the definitive doctrine of emergentism:

3. [The irreducibility of the emergents] Emergent properties are irreducible to, and unpredictable from, the lower-level phenomena from which they emerge.

The multilayered model of contemporary physicalism is all but explicit in these three doctrines, and the first and third doctrines together make emergentism a form of nonreductive physicalism, combining as they do a physicalist ontological monism with property dualism. For the emergentist, emergent properties are not only irreducibly distinct from lower-level properties but they represent richer and fuller levels of reality, toward which the universe is supposed to approach in its "emergent evolution."

But why does the emergentist think that higher-level properties, in particular mental properties, are irreducible to lower-level properties? Why are mental properties "emergent" and not merely "resultant" from physicochemical or biological properties? Notice, first of all, that the emergentist would have had no problem with laws connecting emergent properties and their underlying lower-level bases. Indeed, they are committed to there being such laws: *When appropriate "basal conditions" are present, emergent properties must of necessity emerge.* When the same basal conditions recur, we have every reason to expect the appearance of the same emergent property. The emergentist would happily grant that on the basis of such observed correlations between emergent properties and their basal conditions, we can predict *further* occurrences of emergent properties; all we need to do is to make sure that appropriate basal conditions are, or will be, present. Moreover, there is no reason to think that the emergentist would have had any problems with biconditional bridge laws connecting emergent properties with lower-level properties. For the emergentist, the issue of mind-body reduction has nothing to do with the availability of psychophysical laws. So why does the emergentist object to mind-body reduction?

The answer is that the emergentist has a different conception of what reduction ought to accomplish. She would reject the purely inferential model of Nagelian reduction as sufficient for the reduction of psychology to physical theory, for she conceives of reduction primarily as an *explanation*, something that renders the reduced phenomena intelligible by explaining why they occur under just those conditions in which they do in fact occur. Suppose that pain emerges from C-fiber excitation. What the emergentist would have us answer before she would acknowledge the reduction of pain to C-fiber excitation are the following two questions:

Why does pain emerge just when C-fibers are excited, not when, say, A-delta-fibers are excited?

Why does pain rather than itch or tickle emerge when C-fibers are excited? Indeed, why does any conscious experience emerge at all when C-fibers are excited?

This means that from the emergentist's point of view, *the bridge laws are precisely what need to be explained: Why do these mental-physical correlations hold*? To derive psychological laws from neurobiological laws with these correlation laws as additional premises is, the emergentist will argue, just not relevant to the explanatory project. Such derivations may serve certain scientific purposes, but they fail to fulfill the central goal of reduction, namely, that of enhancing our understanding of why emergent phenomena occur as they do (see the discussion of qualia in Chapter 7).

The emergentist will make a similar point about the unpredictability of emergent phenomena: She will grant that on the basis of the unexplained, "brute" correlation between pain and C-fiber excitation, we can predict occurrences of pain. I have information to the effect that your C-fibers are going to be stimulated, so I predict that you will experience pain. But this ability to predict comes only *after* I have ascertained the brute correlation. Before I have observed occurrences of pain, there is no way I could have found out that just this type of sensation would occur when one's C-fibers are stimulated; complete neurophysiological information concerning the workings of C-fibers would not, the emergentist argues, suffice for such knowledge. This contrasts with the case of resultant properties: Even if no lump of pure gold weighing 1 million tons has ever been observed, we can predict that if we were to put together so many lumps of gold each weighing such and such, there would be a lump of pure gold weighing 1 million tons. According to the emergentist, why pain emerges when C-fibers are excited will forever remain a mystery; we have no choice but to accept it as an unexplainable brute fact.

The Problem of "Downward Causation"

The appearance of emergent properties depends, as we saw, on the presence of appropriate basal conditions, and this means that mental properties emerge only when the right neurobiological and other types of conditions obtain. In this sense, mental properties are dependent on neurobiological properties. But the emergentist holds that once they have emerged, these higher-level properties begin to lead a life of their own, so to speak, and manifest their powers by causally affecting lower-level phenomena. This is the so-called "downward causation," the causal influence exerted by higher-level phenomena on the processes going on at a lower level. Downward causation is a fundamental commitment of emergentism, and we will see how the basic doctrines of emergentism lead to that commitment. More generally, we can also see how the basic tenets of nonreductive physicalism lead to a commitment to mental-to-physical causation, a form of downward causation. Let us see how this happens with nonreductive physicalism.

The nonreductive physicalist is a mental realist; she takes mental properties as real, genuine features of the world. But what does it mean to say that mental properties are "real"? As we saw (Chapter 6), to be real, arguably, is to have causal powers. Anything real must be part of the causal structure of the world. So if mental properties are real features of the world, they must have causal powers; that is, having a mental property must endow the thing that has it with powers to affect courses of events in its neighborhood. But nonreductive physicalism holds that mental properties are irreducible to, and distinct from, their underlying physical and biological properties. If being real means having causal powers, being real and irreducible must mean having causal powers that are irreducible. That is, if mental properties are irreducible to those of physical/biological properties, as the nonreductivist claims, this must mean that they have causal powers that are different from those of physical/biological properties. If their causal powers are simply those of some lower-level properties, there would be little point in advertising them as real and irreducible properties in their own right. For, arguably, properties must be individuated in terms of their causal powers. (The corresponding reasoning involving emergentism will go like this: If mental properties are "genuinely novel properties," they must bring with them *genuinely novel causal powers*, powers not had by their basal conditions. If they are really novel phenomena, they must make novel causal contributions.)

So let M be a mental property. How does M manifest its causal powers? We can distinguish between two cases: (1) M has the power to cause another mental property, M^*, to be instantiated; (2) M has the power to cause a physical property P to be instantiated. (1) is "same-level causation," as we might call it; (2) of course is downward causation. We will show that (1) presupposes (2)—that is, mental-to-mental causation (same-level causation) is possible only if mental-to-physical causation (downward causation) is possible. Suppose, then, that M causes M^* to be instantiated. But M^*, as a mental property, must be physically realized (or supervenient on a physical base or emerge from certain physical basal conditions—the argument to follow could be formulated in any of these idioms); let us assume that on this occasion M^* occurs by being realized by a physical property, say P^*. So the picture we have is like this:

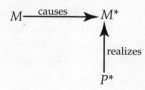

We can see that this picture depicts an unstable set of relationships. For ask: Why is M^* instantiated on this occasion? We get two different answers: (1) because M caused it to be instantiated (*ex hypothesi*) and (2) because P^* realized it on this occasion. If P^* is a realizer of M^*, then when P^* is present, M^* must be there, too, *no matter what happened before* (in particular, whether or not M was there); P^* alone is sufficient to bring about M^*'s instantiation on this occasion. Moreover, unless P^*, or some other realizer of M^*, were present on this occasion, M^* could not have been instantiated. All this puts into doubt the role of M in the causation of M^*; P^* seems to preempt the causal role of M. It is plausible to think that the only way for validating M's causal role is for the following to be the case: M *causes M^* by causing its realizer, P^*, to be instantiated*. In general, the following principle about causation of physically realized properties is both natural and plausible:

[The causal realization principle] If $P_1, P_2, \ldots$ are the realizers of Q, then to cause Q to be instantiated, you must cause one of the P's to be instantiated.

To bring about an occurrence of pain in a human, you must bring about an instance of C-fiber excitation. There is no way you can somehow "directly" cause pain; to control pain—that is, to cause it or eliminate it—you must "work through" its physical realizer, that is, some neural process, and that is precisely what we do when we take Demerol to relieve severe pains. So the picture we now have of the situation is as follows:

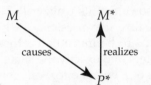

But the causation of P^* by M is of course downward causation, an instance of mental-to-physical causation. This establishes our claim that same-level causation is possible only if downward causation is possible; the former presupposes the latter.

Now it is tempting to extend these considerations further and modify this picture in the following way: Since M, too, must have a physical realization base, why not say that M's causation of P^* consists in the fact that M's physical realizer, say, P, causes P^* to be instantiated. Surely a mental event could not telekinetically cause a physical event P^*; if the sharp pain in your elbow causes you to cry, "Ouch!" it could not be that your pain, as a nonphysical mental event, could somehow directly cause your vocal cords to vibrate! We must expect the causal path from the pain to "Ouch!"

to coincide with the chain of neural events that culminates in the appropriate vibrations of your vocal cords, and it seems inescapable that we must locate the origin of this physical causal chain at the physical realizer of the pain, if we indeed want to give the pain a causal role. This leads to the following picture:

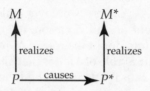

You may recall the model of supervenient causation discussed earlier (Chapter 6); the above model of mental causation is exactly the same except that "physical realization" replaces "supervenience." Given the close similarity between supervenience and the realization relation, we may regard the two models as essentially identical in philosophical import. Both construe higher-level causal relations as grounded in, or derivative from, the causal processes at a more basic level. If physical facts determine all the facts, as physicalists are fond of saying, then physical facts, including causal facts about physical processes, must determine all the causal facts, including facts about mental causation.

But is this view of mental causation something that the nonreductive physicalist and the emergentist could accept? The answer, arguably, is in the negative. For on this approach the causal powers of M are wholly derived from the causal powers of its realizer P: This instance of M causes whatever its physical realizer P causes. Since whatever causes P to be instantiated also causes M to be instantiated thereby, it follows that the given instance of M enters into exactly the same causal relations that the corresponding instance of P enters into: Something is a cause or effect of the M-instance if and only if it is a cause or effect of the P-instance. There are no new causal powers that magically accrue to M over and beyond the causal powers of P. The approach to mental causation last pictured, therefore, is essentially reductionist: No new causal powers emerge at higher levels, and this goes against the claim of the emergentist and the nonreductive physicalist that higher-level properties are novel causal powers irreducible to lower-level properties.

It follows, then, that the nonreductive physicalist, like the emergentist, is committed to irreducible downward causation, causation of physical processes by nonphysical properties, and this of course means that the causal closure of the physical is breached. The emergentist perhaps will not be troubled by it, but the nonreductive physicalist, insofar as he is a physicalist, should be. As we saw earlier (Chapter 6), to abandon the physical causal closure is to retrogress to the Cartesian picture that does not allow, even in principle, a complete and comprehensive physical theory of the physical world. On the Cartesian dualist model, any theory that gives full coverage of the physical would have to invoke nonphysical causal agents. This is something that no serious physicalist will find palatable.

Local Reductions and the Status of Mental Properties

Let us return to multiple realization. Earlier we observed that if P is a realizer of M, the conditional "$P \to M$" must hold as a matter of law. Actually, this isn't quite right, in two respects. First, the property P may realize M in organisms or systems of one kind but not another; it may be that although C-fiber activation is a realizer of pain in humans, it need not be in an organism with a very different neural structure. In such an organism C-fibers may subserve a totally different mental function or none at all. So the conditional "$P \to M$" must be explicitly relativized to organism or structure types. Second, relative to such types, the realizer P must be both necessary and sufficient for M; that is, the occurrence of M must be "controllable" by controlling the occurrence of P. This is most evident if we think in terms of building a physical realizer (that is, a computer) of an abstract computing machine (e.g., a Turing machine). Roughly speaking, we must design a machine that has a series of physical states realizing its computational states, and we should be able to guarantee the *nonoccurrence* as well as occurrence of a computational state by manipulating its physical realizer. This of course means that a physical realizer of a computational state must be both necessary and sufficient for it. The same is true when we think of designing a physical device that realizes a psychology: We must design into such a device a set of physical states corresponding to the given set of psychological states such that each member of the former is both necessary and sufficient for its corresponding psychological state.

All this can be summarized as follows: If P is a realizer of M in organisms or structures of type S, the following relationship holds as a matter of law:

$$S \to (M \leftrightarrow P)$$

This says that if anything is a structure of type S, it instantiates mental property M (at a time) if and only if it instantiates physical property P (at that time). Laws of this form are biconditional bridge laws *restricted to specific species and structures*; we may call them "structure-restricted bridge laws."

What multiple realizability tells us is that unrestricted bridge laws are in general unavailable and that these structure-restricted bridge laws are all we can get. In fact, in conjunction with the physical realization principle, it guarantees that there are restricted bridge laws of this form for all organisms and systems that have a psychology. It is the task of human neurophysiology to discover and identify those neural states that realize psychological properties in humans; similarly for other species. Moreover, although these restricted bridge laws will not give us a global or uniform Nagel reduction of psychology, they will generate "local reductions"; thus, a complete set of these laws for humans will reduce human psychology to human neurophysiology. Such a reduction, on the Nagelian model, will consist in the derivation of psychological laws restricted to humans (if L is a psychological law, "$H \rightarrow L$" is L restricted to humans) from laws of human neurophysiology in conjunction with these restricted biconditional laws. Such a reduction would be extremely valuable: It would tell us exactly how psychology is biologically implemented in human organisms. Given the assumption that the same psychology can be realized in a diverse variety of species and structures, "local reductions" of this kind are what we ought to expect and aim at. Even if a global reduction were possible, it would likely be too abstract to yield the kind of concrete information we want out of reduction.

The multiple realizability of mental properties, as we saw, has been used by many nonreductivists as the main weapon against the possibility of psychophysical reduction. What we have just seen is this: Although it may well rule out uniform, global mind-body reduction, *it in fact entails the possibility of locally reducing psychological theories and states to physical/biological bases.* Perhaps this is all the reduction we need or could want—indeed, the only kind of reduction that we can get anywhere in science if, as the friends of multiple realization often claim, multiple realizability is a pervasive feature of the relationship between higher-level properties and lower-level properties.

The local physical reducibility of mental properties has interesting implications for the metaphysical status of mental properties. Suppose mental property M is multiply realized by, and hence locally reduced to, three physical realizers P_1, P_2, and P_3. The claim that these are distinct and diverse ("wildly heterogeneous," as it is sometimes said) must mean that they are *diverse as causal powers.* Unless they are causally diverse in virtue of entering into diverse sets of causal laws, there would be little reason to stress their diversity as physical properties and speak of multiple realization to begin with. As we argued in the preceding section, it is highly plausible to regard the causal powers of an instance of M as deriving from the causal powers of its realizer. When we put these pieces together, the following picture emerges: All instances of M fall into three nonoverlapping groups, each with its distinctive causal powers, namely, those M-instances that are realized by P_1, those realized by P_2, and those realized by

P_3. These three groups of M-instances are exactly as causally heterogeneous as are their realizers, P_1, P_2, and P_3, and this puts into doubt the unity and systematicity of M itself as a scientific kind—that is, a kind in terms of which we can hope to formulate causal laws and explanations. For M cannot be a "single," unified property any more than the widely despised disjunctive property, P_1 or P_2 or P_3, can be.

Thus, what we see is the potential undermining of psychological properties as scientific kinds. Our two assumptions, the multiple realizability of psychological properties and the principle that scientific kinds must group causally homogeneous instances, seem to lead inexorably to that conclusion. This does not mean that psychology is unscientific or that its accomplishments cannot be theoretically illuminating and practically useful. It only means that psychology may lose its status as a single, unitary science that generates laws and explanations uniformly valid for all species and structures—that is, universal laws that hold for psychological properties as such. Of course human psychology could be formally identical with, or isomorphic to, the psychology of some exotic extraterrestrial species whose biology is wholly inorganic. But that would be a pure coincidence. If we believe in the multiple realizability of psychological states, we must also believe in the multiple realizability of psychology itself.

A possible reply to the foregoing line of consideration might go like this: Multiple realizability goes wider and deeper than species, and even within a single species we cannot expect to find uniform physical realizers for mental properties. We often hear about how the mental function of a damaged part of the brain can be taken over by another part, and it is quite possible that in the process of maturation and development, the brain substrates of our cognitive capacities change over time. Neural differences among individual humans are probably as common and significant as any other kinds of individual differences, such as height, weight, eye color, and so on. How reasonable is it, for example, to expect that the belief that Bill Clinton will win in 1996 is realized by exactly the same neural state in every human who has that belief?

These points are sound and plausible. But what they show is only that the possibility of human psychology as a science depends on the contingent and fortuitous fact that humans as a species show sufficient similarities in their neural anatomy and functions to make them exhibit sufficiently similar mental characteristics. It is because humans, as conspecifics, share a sufficiently similar biology—in particular neurobiology—that it is possible and fruitful to study their psychology as a unified scientific subject. This is one reason why we do not, and cannot, expect precise and exceptionless laws in psychology; for "sufficiently similar" doesn't mean "exactly identical." (Humans probably differ more among themselves than, say, the tokens of the 1991 Chevrolet Camaro do; we don't look for exact "laws" applicable to all 1991 Chevrolet Camaros, although we would expect to find useful statistical regularities for them.) If this supposition were false and psychological states are realized by "wildly heterogeneous" neural states even among humans, then human psychology would be impossible to pursue as a unitary scientific project. So the possibility of human psychology, or any other species-specific psychology, depends on the fact that conspecifics share a largely identical biology and hence have sufficiently similar neural realizers for their psychological states.

Qualia and Reductionism: A Dilemma

If we accept a broadly objectivist perspective on mentality, the local reducibility of mental properties to a physical/biological basis is a plausible doctrine as a metaphysical underpinning of psychology as a science. The doctrine is perhaps also unavoidable if we are to give a metaphysical account of how mental causation is possible. But does this mean that we are home free with this limited form of reductionism? As you would expect about any serious philosophical problem, the answer is no; in philosophy there never seems to be an occasion where you can tidy up the mess and go home.

The main obstacle to mind-body reductionism, whether global or local, is qualia—the phenomenal, qualitative characters of our experiences. We discussed various issues about qualia earlier (Chapter 7), and they do not need to be rehearsed here. But it is easy to see how qualia may resist any attempt at reduction. For qualia seem to be *intrinsic* properties of our experiences; the painful, hurting character of a sharp pain in the elbow is intrinsically different as a felt quality from, say, the itchiness of an itch you experience on your shoulder. There are of course cases in which we are not sure whether we are feeling pain (is that a pain I am feeling in my stomach or just a sore and uncomfortable sensation?). But that isn't the issue: There are cases in which we know a pain to be painful and an itch to be itchy without knowing how they are caused or what they in turn cause—in general, without knowing how they are related to anything else. Qualia, or phenomenal properties of experiences, seem to be intrinsic, not extrinsic, in that sense.

If qualia are intrinsic properties, it is difficult to see how they could be reductively identified with anything else. How could the hurtfulness of this pain be the very same property as some physical property of some neural state? The emergentists may have been right after all in despairing of giving an intelligible account of how consciousness could, or should, emerge from the molecular processes of the nervous system. It would seem that any correlation we might find between a phenomenal quality of experience and a neural property must be taken as brute and fundamental, not amenable to further explanation. There have been various attempts, some of them impressively subtle and ingenious, to dissipate the problem of qualia in one way or another—from attempts to turn them into functional (thus, extrinsic) properties to an outright denial that they exist. In the end the issue of reductionism comes down to this: Are we prepared to abandon qualia as intrinsic properties in their own right? If we are, then at least we can have the local mind-body reductionism discussed in the preceding section; if we are not, reductionism has to go. But before you rejoice at the thought that reductionism has been defeated, remember this: If our considerations on emergentism and downward causation are generally correct, then if reductionism goes, so goes the intelligibility of mental causation.

So we find ourselves in a profound dilemma: If we are prepared to embrace reductionism, we can explain mental causation. However, in the process of reducing mentality to physical/biological properties, we may well lose the intrinsic, subjective character of our mentality—arguably, the very thing that makes the mental mental. In what sense, then, have we saved "mental" causation? But if we reject reductionism, we are not able to see how mental causation should be possible. But saving mentality while losing causality doesn't seem to amount to saving anything worth saving. For what good is the mind if it has no causal powers? Either way, we are in danger of losing mentality. That is the dilemma.

The problem of qualia—or consciousness—and the problem of mental causation are the two most profound and difficult issues in the philosophy of mind. These two intractable problems come together in this dilemma. It is not happy to end a book with a dilemma, but we should all take it as a challenge, a challenge to find an account of mentality that respects consciousness as a genuine phenomenon that gives us and other sentient beings a special place in the world and that also makes consciousness a causally efficacious factor in the workings of the natural world. The challenge, then, is to find out what kind of beings we are and what our place is in the world of nature.

Further Readings

The classic source on reduction is Ernest Nagel, *The Structure of Science* (New York: Harcourt, Brace & World, 1961). Also useful are Robert Causey, *Unity of Science* (Dordrecht: Reidel, 1977) and Patricia S. Churchland, *Neurophilosophy* (Cambridge: MIT Press, 1986), ch. 7. Paul Oppenheim and Hilary Putnam, "Unity of Science as a Working Hypothesis," in *Minnesota Studies in the Philosophy of Science*, vol. 2, ed. Herbert Feigl, Michael Scriven, and Grover Maxwell (Minneapolis: University of Minnesota Press, 1958), contains a useful presentation of the "multilayered model" and the thesis of unified science through microreduction.

On nonreductive physicalism, see Donald Davidson, "Mental Events," reprinted in his *Essays on Actions and Events* (New York: Oxford University Press, 1980); J. A. Fodor, "Special Sciences, or the Disunity of Science as a Working Hypothesis," in *Readings in Philosophy of Psychology*, vol. 1, ed. Ned Block (Cambridge: Harvard University Press, 1980); and Geoffrey Hellman and Frank Thompson, "Physicalism: Ontology, Determination, and Reduction," *Journal of Philosophy* 72 (1975):551–564. The latter also includes one of the first formulations of supervenience physicalism. For a critique, see Jaegwon Kim, "The Myth of Nonreductive Physicalism" and "Multiple Realization and the Metaphysics of Reduction," both in Kim, *Supervenience and Mind* (Cambridge: Cambridge University Press, 1993). For nonreductivist replies, see Derk Pereboom and Hilary Kornblith, "The Metaphysics of Irreducibility," *Philosophical Studies* 63 (1991):125–145; Robert Van Gulick, "Nonreductive Materialism and the Nature of Intertheoretical Constraint," in *Emergence or Reduction?* ed. Ansgar Beckermann, Hans Flohr, and Jaegwon Kim (Berlin: De Gruyter, 1992); Ausonio Marras, "Nonreductive Physicalism and Mental Causation," *Canadian Journal of Philosophy* 24 (1994):465–493.

For discussion of supervenience, see John Heil, *The Nature of True Minds* (Cambridge: Cambridge University Press, 1992), ch. 3; and Jaegwon Kim, "Supervenience as a Philosophical Concept" in Kim, *Supervenience and Mind*.

A highly useful survey of emergentism is contained in Brian McLaughlin's "The Rise and Fall of British Emergentism," in Beckermann, Flohr, and Kim, *Emergence or Reduction?*

For an argument against physicalism based on qualia ("the knowledge argument") that is different from the one presented in the text, see Frank Jackson, "What Mary Didn't Know," in *The Nature of Mind*, ed. David M. Rosenthal (New York: Oxford University Press, 1991).

For a general defense of nonreductivist metaphysics and philosophy of science, see John Post, *The Faces of Existence* (Ithaca: Cornell University Press, 1987); John Dupre, *The Disorder of Things* (Cambridge: Harvard University Press, 1993).

Jeffrey Poland's *Physicalism* (Oxford: Clarendon Press, 1994) is a comprehensive discussion of contemporary physicalism. The following anthologies contain useful articles relevant to the topics of this chapter: *Reduction, Explanation, and Realism*, ed. David Charles and Kathleen Lennon (Oxford: Clarendon Press, 1992); *Objections to Physicalism*, ed. Howard Robinson (Oxford: Clarendon Press, 1993); *Contemporary Materialism*, ed. Paul K. Moser and J. D. Trout (London: Routledge, 1995). *The Philosophy of Science*, ed. Richard Boyd, Philip Gasper, and J. D. Trout

(Cambridge: MIT Press, 1991) includes articles on the general issue of reduction and reductionism.

Notes

1. For recent dissenting views, see Richard Swinburne, *The Evolution of the Soul* (Oxford: Clarendon, 1986); W. D. Hart, *The Engines of the Soul* (Cambridge: Cambridge University Press, 1988); John Foster, *The Immaterial Self* (London: Routledge, 1991).

2. "Substance physicalism" would be a more appropriate term; however, I follow the common usage here.

3. See Ernest Nagel, *The Structure of Science* (New York: Harcourt, Brace & World, 1961), ch. 11. For a different account of reduction or reductive explanation, see the discussion of qualia and physical explanation of qualia in Chapter 7.

4. Some have argued, plausibly, that if real reductions are to be accomplished, bridge laws must be identities, not merely "iff" correlations; see, for example, Lawrence Sklar, "Types of Inter-theoretic Reduction," *British Journal for the Philosophy of Science* 18 (1967):109–124.

5. Whether or not they actually do will depend on many other considerations that we cannot go into here. An ordinary biconditional "*F* iff *G*" clearly does not suffice for the identity "property *F* = property *G*"; compare the property of having kidneys to the property of having a heart.

6. On a popular interpretation of Davidson—apparently confirmed by Davidson himself in his recent "Thinking Causes," in *Mental Causation*, ed. John Heil and Alfred Mele (Oxford: Clarendon Press, 1993)—although anomalous monism denies the possibility of "strict laws" between the mental and the physical, it acknowledges "nonstrict" psychophysical laws hedged with ceteris paribus clauses, endowing them with important explanatory and causal roles. If this is accepted, it is not obvious just why nonstrict laws cannot also serve as bridge laws enabling the physical reduction of the mental. See for further discussion Kim, "Can Supervenience and 'Nonstrict' Laws Save Anomalous Monism?" in *Mental Causation*, ed. Heil and Mele.

7. The reader should consider here the possibility of taking, as the base theory, the conjunction of all the scientific theories that concern the disjuncts of ∪*Pi*.

8. Two important examples are G. E. Moore and R. M. Hare. See especially R. M. Hare, *The Language of Morals* (Oxford: Clarendon Press, 1952).

9. When supervenience claims like this are considered in regard to mental states with "wide content," that is, intentional states whose contents are individuated at least in part by conditions extrinsic to the subject, care has to be exercised. In particular, one should be clear about what one means by "physical property"— for example, whether relational physical properties are to be included in the supervenience base. The same issues arise when one uses terms like "emergence," "determination," "realization," and the like rather than "supervenience" in discussing the interlevel relationship of properties.

10. For details, see Kim, "'Strong' and 'Global' Supervenience Revisited," in Kim, *Supervenience and Mind* (Cambridge: Cambridge University Press, 1993).

11. This characterization is not entirely unproblematic, but this will not affect

our discussion. For more details, see Kim, "Supervenience for Multiple Domains," in Kim, *Supervenience and Mind*.

12. This example comes from Bradford Petrie, "Global Supervenience and Reduction," *Philosophy and Phenomenological Research* 48 (1987):119–130.

13. This is the case if *a* and *b* are "substances" in the traditional sense. Substances, as traditionally conceived, are "independent existents," things that could exist even if nothing else did.

14. For further details, see Kim, "'Strong' and 'Global' Supervenience Revisited" and "Postscripts on Supervenience," both in Kim, *Supervenience and Mind*; Cranston Paull and Theodore Sider, "In Defense of Global Supervenience," *Philosophy and Phenomenological Research* 52 (1992):833–854.

15. See Samuel Alexander, *Space, Time, and Deity*, 2 vols. (London: Macmillan, 1920); C. D. Broad, *The Mind and Its Place in Nature* (London: Routledge & Kegan Paul, 1962).

16. See C. Lloyd Morgan, *Emergent Evolution* (London: Williams & Norgate, 1923).

17. See Roger W. Sperry, "A Modified Concept of Consciousness," *Psychological Review* 76 (1969):532–536.

Bibliography

This is a list of works cited in the text. Although it is not intended as a comprehensive bibliography of philosophy of mind, it is representative of the current literature on the topics discussed in the book.

Alexander, Samuel. Space, Time, and Deity, 2 vols. (London: Macmillan, 1920).

Antony, Louise. "Anomalous Monism and the Problem of Explanatory Force," *Philosophical Review* 98 (1989):153–158.

Armstrong, David M. *A Materialist Theory of Mind* (New York: Humanities Press, 1968).

_____. "The Nature of Mind." In *Readings in Philosophy of Psychology*, vol. 1, ed. Ned Block (Cambridge: Harvard University Press, 1980).

Armstrong, David M., and Norman Malcolm. *Consciousness and Causality* (Oxford: Blackwell, 1984).

Atkinson, J. W., and D. Birch. *The Dynamics of Action* (New York: Wiley, 1970).

Baker, Lynne Rudder. *Explaining Attitudes* (Cambridge: Cambridge University Press, 1995).

Bechtel, William. *Philosophy of Mind: An Overview for Cognitive Science* (Hillsdale, NJ: Lawrence Erlbaum, 1988).

Beckermann, Ansgar, Hans Flohr, and Jaegwon Kim, eds. *Emergence or Reduction?* (Berlin: De Gruyter, 1992).

Block, Ned. "Are Absent Qualia Impossible?" *Philosophical Review* 89 (1980):257–274.

_____. "Psychologism and Behaviorism," *Philosophical Review* 90 (1981):5–43.

_____. "Advertisement for a Semantics for Psychology," *Midwest Studies in Philosophy* 10 (1986):615–678.

_____. "Can the Mind Change the World?" in *Meaning and Method*, ed. George Boolos (Cambridge: Cambridge University Press, 1990).

_____. "Inverted Earth," *Philosophical Perspectives* 4 (1990):51–79.

_____. "On a Confusion About a Function of Consciousness," *Behavioral and Brain Sciences* 18 (1995):1–41.

Block, Ned, ed. *Readings in Philosophy of Psychology*, vol. 1 (Cambridge: Harvard University Press, 1980).

Block, Ned, Owen Flanagan, and Güven Güzeldere, eds. *The Nature of Consciousness: Philosophical and Scientific Essays* (Cambridge: MIT Press, forthcoming).

Block, Ned, and Jerry A. Fodor. "What Psychological States Are Not." In *Readings in Philosophy of Psychology*, vol. 1, ed. Ned Block.

Boghossian, Paul. "Content and Self-Knowledge," *Philosophical Topics* 17 (1989):5–26.

Boyd, Richard, Philip Gasper, and J. D. Trout, eds. *The Philosophy of Science* (Cambridge: MIT Press, 1991).

Brentano, Franz. *Psychology from an Empirical Standpoint*, trans. Antos C. Rancurello, D. B. Terrell, and Linda L. McAlister (New York: Humanities Press, 1973).

Broad, C. D. *The Mind and Its Place in Nature* (London: Routledge & Kegan Paul, 1962).

Burge, Tyler. "Individualism and the Mental," *Midwest Studies in Philosophy* 4 (1979):73–121.

_____. "Individualism and Self-Knowledge," *Journal of Philosophy* 85 (1988):654–655.

_____. "Individualism and Causation in Psychology," *Pacific Philosophical Quarterly* 70 (1989):303–322.

Causey, Robert. *Unity of Science* (Dordrecht: Reidel, 1977).

Chalmers, David. *The Conscious Mind* (New York: Oxford University Press, forthcoming).

Charles, David, and Kathleen Lennon, eds. *Reduction, Explanation and Realism* (Oxford: Clarendon Press, 1992).

Chisholm, Roderick M. *Perceiving* (Ithaca: Cornell University Press, 1957).

_____. *The First Person* (Minneapolis: University of Minnesota Press, 1981).

Chomsky, Noam. Review of *Verbal Behavior* by B. F. Skinner. *Language* 35 (1959):26–58.

Churchland, Patricia S. *Neurophilosophy* (Cambridge: MIT Press, 1986).

Churchland, Paul M. "Eliminative Materialism and the Propositional Attitudes," *Journal of Philosophy* 78 (1981):67–90.

_____. *Matter and Consciousness* (Cambridge: MIT Press, 1988).

Crick, Francis. *The Astonishing Hypothesis: The Scientific Search for the Soul* (New York: Scribners, 1994).

Cummins, Robert. *Meaning and Mental Representation* (Cambridge: MIT Press, 1989).

Davidson, Donald. *Essays on Actions and Events* (New York: Oxford University Press, 1980).

_____. *Essays on Truth and Interpretation* (Oxford: Oxford University Press, 1984).

_____. "Knowing One's Own Mind," *Proceedings and Addresses of the American Philosophical Association* 60 (1986):441–458.

_____. "Thinking Causes." In *Mental Causation*, ed. John Heil and Alfred Mele (Oxford: Clarendon Press, 1993).

Davies, Martin, and Glyn W. Humphreys, eds. *Consciousness* (Oxford: Blackwell, 1993).

Davis, Martin. *Computability and Unsolvability* (New York: McGraw-Hill, 1958).

Dennett, Daniel C. *Content and Consciousness* (London: Routledge & Kegan Paul, 1969).

_____. *Brainstorms* (Montgomery, Vt.: Bradford Books, 1978).

_____. "True Believers." In Daniel C. Dennett, *Intentional Stance* (Cambridge: MIT Press, 1987).

_____. "Quining Qualia." In *Consciousness in Contemporary Science*, ed. A. J. Marcel and E. Bisiach (Oxford: Oxford University Press, 1988).

_____. *Consciousness Explained* (Boston: Little, Brown, 1991).

Descartes, René. *Meditations*. In *The Philosophical Writings of Descartes*, ed. John Cottingham, Robert Stoothoff, and Dugald Murdoch, 3 vols. (Cambridge: Cambridge University Press, 1985).

_____. *The Passions of the Soul*, book 1. In *The Philosophical Writings of Descartes*, ed. John Cottingham, Robert Stoothoff, and Dugald Murdoch, 3 vols. (Cambridge: Cambridge University Press, 1985).

_____. "Replies to the Fourth Set of Objections." In *The Nature of Mind*, ed. David Rosenthal (New York: Oxford University Press, 1991).

Dretske, Fred. *Knowledge and the Flow of Information* (Cambridge: MIT Press, 1981).

_____. *Explaining Behavior* (Cambridge: MIT Press, 1988).

Dupre, John. *The Disorder of Things* (Cambridge: Harvard University Press, 1993).

Enc, Berent. "Redundancy, Degeneracy, and Deviance in Action," *Philosophical Studies* 48 (1985):353–374.

Feigl, Herbert. "The 'Mental' and the 'Physical.'" In *Minnesota Studies in the Philosophy of Science*, vol. 2, ed. Herbert Feigl, Michael Scriven, and Grover Maxwell (Minneapolis: University of Minnesota Press, 1958).

Flanagan, Owen. *Consciousness Reconsidered* (Cambridge: MIT Press, 1992).

Fodor, Jerry A. "Special Sciences, or the Disunity of Science as a Working Hypothesis," *Synthese* 28 (1974):97–115.

_____. *Psychosemantics* (Cambridge: MIT Press, 1987).

_____. *A Theory of Content and Other Essays* (Cambridge: MIT Press, 1990).

_____. "A Modal Argument for Narrow Content," *Journal of Philosophy* 88 (1991):5–26.

Foster, John. *The Immaterial Self* (London: Routledge, 1991).

Ginet, Carl. *On Action* (Cambridge: Cambridge University Press, 1990).

Goldman, Alvin I. "Interpretation Psychologized." In Alvin I. Goldman, *Liaisons* (Cambridge: MIT Press, 1992).

Gordon, Robert M. "Folk Psychology as Simulation," *Mind and Language* 1 (1986):159–171.

Graham, George. *Philosophy of Mind: An Introduction* (Oxford: Blackwell, 1993).

Guttenplan, Samuel, ed. *A Companion to Philosophy of Mind* (Oxford: Blackwell, 1994).

Hannan, Barbara. *Subjectivity and Reduction* (Boulder: Westview Press, 1994).

Hardin, C. L. *Color for Philosophers* (Indianapolis: Hackett, 1988).

Hare, R. M. *The Language of Morals* (Oxford: Clarendon Press, 1952).

Harman, Gilbert. "The Intrinsic Quality of Experience," *Philosophical Perspectives* 4 (1990):31–52.

Hart, W. D. *The Engines of the Soul* (Cambridge: Cambridge University Press, 1988).

Heil, John. *The Nature of True Minds* (Cambridge: Cambridge University Press, 1992).

Heil, John, and Alfred Mele, eds. *Mental Causation* (Oxford: Clarendon Press, 1993).

Hellman, Geoffrey, and Frank Thompson, "Physicalism: Ontology, Determination, and Reduction," *Journal of Philosophy* 72 (1975):551–564.

Hempel, Carl G. "The Logical Analysis of Psychology." In *Readings in Philosophy of Psychology*, vol. 1, ed. Ned Block (Cambridge: Harvard University Press, 1980).

Hill, Christopher S. *Sensations: A Defense of Type Materialism* (Cambridge: Cambridge University Press, 1991).

Horgan, Terence. "Supervenience and Microphysics," *Pacific Philosophical Quarterly* 63 (1982):29–43.

_____. "Supervenient Qualia," *Philosophical Review* 96 (1987):491–520.

_____. "Mental Quausation," *Philosophical Perspectives* 3 (1989):47–76.

Huxley, Thomas H. *Methods and Results: Essays* (New York: D. Appleton, 1901).

Jackson, Frank. "What Mary Didn't Know." In *The Nature of Mind*, ed. David M. Rosenthal (New York: Oxford University Press, 1991).

James, William. *The Principles of Psychology* (1890; reprint, Cambridge: Harvard University Press, 1981).

Kim, Jaegwon. "Can Supervenience and 'Nonstrict' Laws Save Anomalous Monism?" In *Mental Causation*, ed. John Heil and Alfred Mele (Oxford: Clarendon Press, 1993).

_____. *Supervenience and Mind* (Cambridge: Cambridge University Press, 1993).

Kim, Jaegwon, and Ernest Sosa, eds. *A Companion to Metaphysics* (Oxford: Blackwell, 1995).

Kripke, Saul. *Naming and Necessity* (Cambridge: Harvard University Press, 1980).

Lashley, Karl. *Brain Mechanisms and Intelligence* (New York: Hafner, 1963).

LePore, Ernest, and Barry Loewer. "Mind Matters," *Journal of Philosophy* 84 (1987):630–642.

Levine, Joseph. "Materialism and Qualia: The Explanatory Gap," *Pacific Philosophical Quarterly* 64 (1983):354–361.

_____. "On Leaving Out What It's Like." In *Consciousness*, ed. Martin Davies and Glyn W. Humphreys (Oxford: Blackwell, 1993).

Lewis, David. *Counterfactuals* (Cambridge: Harvard University Press, 1973).

_____. "Psychophysical and Theoretical Identifications." In *Readings in Philosophy of Psychology*, vol. 1, ed. Ned Block (Cambridge: Harvard University Press, 1980).

_____. *Philosophical Papers*, vol. 1 (New York: Oxford University Press, 1983).

Loewer, Barry, and Georges Rey, eds. *Meaning in Mind* (London: Routledge, 1991).

Lycan, William G. *Consciousness* (Cambridge: MIT Press, 1987).

Lycan, William G., ed. *Mind and Cognition* (Oxford: Blackwell, 1990).

Macdonald, Cynthia. *Mind-Body Identity Theories* (London: Routledge, 1989).

Macdonald, Cynthia, and Graham Macdonald, eds. *Philosophy of Psychology: Debates on Psychological Explanation* (Oxford: Blackwell, 1995).

Mackie, J. L. "Counterfactuals and Causal Laws." In *Analytic Philosophy*, ed. R. J. Butler (Oxford: Blackwell, 1962).

Marcel, A. J. and E. Bisiach, eds. *Consciousness in Contemporary Science* (Oxford: Oxford University Press, 1988).

Marras, Ausonio. "Nonreductive Physicalism and Mental Causation," *Canadian Journal of Philosophy* 24 (1994):465–493.

Matthews, Robert. "The Measure of Mind," *Mind* 103 (1994):131–146.

McGinn, Colin. *The Problem of Consciousness* (Oxford: Blackwell, 1991).

McLaughlin, Brian. "Event Supervenience and Supervenient Causation," *Southern Journal of Philosophy* 22 (1984), the Spindel Conference Supplement: 71–92.

_____. "What Is Wrong with Correlational Psychosemantics?" *Synthese* 70 (1987):271–286.

_____. "Type Epiphenomenalism, Type Dualism, and the Causal Priority of the Physical," *Philosophical Perspectives* 3 (1989):109–136.

_____. "The Rise and Fall of British Emergentism." In *Emergence or Reduction?* ed. Ansgar Beckermann, Hans Flohr, and Jaegwon Kim (Berlin: De Gruyter, 1992).

Melzack, Ronald. *The Puzzle of Pain* (New York: Basic Books, 1973).

Menzies, Peter. "Against Causal Reductionism," *Mind* 97 (1988):551–574.

Millikan, Ruth G. *Language, Thought, and Other Biological Categories* (Cambridge: MIT Press, 1984).

Minsky, Marvin. *The Society of Minds* (New York: Simon and Schuster, 1985).

Morgan, C. Lloyd. *Emergent Evolution* (London: Williams & Norgate, 1923).

Moser, Paul K., and J. D. Trout, eds. *Contemporary Materialism* (London: Routledge, 1995).

Nagel, Ernest. *The Structure of Science* (New York: Harcourt, Brace & World, 1961).

Nagel, Thomas. "What Is It Like to Be a Bat?" *Philosophical Review* 83 (1974):435–450.

_____. "Subjective and Objective." In Thomas Nagel, *Mortal Questions* (Cambridge: Cambridge University Press, 1979).

Oppenheim, Paul, and Hilary Putnam. "Unity of Science as a Working Hypothesis." In *Minnesota Studies in the Philosophy of Science*, vol. 2, ed. Herbert Feigl, Michael Scriven, and Grover Maxwell (Minneapolis: University of Minnesota Press, 1958).

Paull, Cranston, and Theodore Sider. "In Defense of Global Supervenience," *Philosophy and Phenomenological Research* 52 (1992):833–854.

Pereboom, Derk, and Hilary Kornblith. "The Metaphysics of Irreducibility," *Philosophical Studies* 63 (1991):125–145.

Petrie, Bradford. "Global Supervenience and Reduction," *Philosophy and Phenomenological Research* 48 (1987):119–130.

Place, U. T. "Is Consciousness a Brain Process?" *British Journal of Psychology* 47, pt. 1 (1956):44–50.

Poland, Jeffrey. *Physicalism* (Oxford: Clarendon Press, 1994).

Post, John. *The Faces of Existence* (Ithaca: Cornell University Press, 1987).

Putnam, Hilary. *Mind, Language, and Reality: Philosophical Papers*, vol. 2 (Cambridge: Cambridge University Press, 1975).

_____. "Brains and Behavior." In *Readings in Philosophy of Psychology*, vol. 1, ed. Ned Block (Cambridge: Harvard University Press, 1980).

_____. *Representation and Reality* (Cambridge: MIT Press, 1988).

Quine, W. V. *Word and Object* (Cambridge and New York: Technology Press of MIT and John Wiley & Sons, 1960).

Robinson, Howard, ed. *Objections to Physicalism* (Oxford: Clarendon Press, 1993).

Rosenthal, David M. "The Independence of Consciousness and Sensory Quality," *Philosophical Issues* 1 (1991):15–36.

Rosenthal, David M., ed. *The Nature of Mind* (New York: Oxford University Press, 1991).

Ryle, Gilbert. *The Concept of Mind* (New York: Barnes and Noble, 1949).

Seager, William. *Metaphysics of Consciousness* (London: Routledge, 1991).

Searle, John. *Intentionality* (Cambridge: Cambridge University Press, 1983).

_____. "Minds, Brains, and Programs." In *The Nature of Mind*, ed. David M. Rosenthal (New York: Oxford University Press, 1991).

_____. *The Rediscovery of the Mind* (Cambridge: MIT Press, 1992).

Segal, Gabriel, and Elliott Sober. "The Causal Efficacy of Content," *Philosophical Studies* 63 (1991):1–30.

Shaffer, Jerome. "Mental Events and the Brain." In *The Nature of Mind*, ed. David M. Rosenthal (New York: Oxford University Press, 1991).

Shoemaker, Sydney. *Identity, Cause, and Mind* (Cambridge: Cambridge University Press, 1984).

Skinner, B. F. *Science and Human Behavior* (New York: Macmillan, 1953).

Sklar, Lawrence. "Types of Inter-theoretic Reduction," *British Journal for the Philosophy of Science* 18 (1967):109–124.

Smart, J.J.C. "Sensations and Brain Processes." In *The Nature of Mind*, ed. David M. Rosenthal (New York: Oxford University Press, 1991).

Sosa, Ernest. "Mind-Body Interaction and Supervenient Causation," *Midwest Studies in Philosophy* 9 (1984):271–281.

_____. "Between Internalism and Externalism," *Philosophical Issues* 1 (1991):179–195.

Sperry, Roger W. "A Modified Concept of Consciousness," *Psychological Review* 76 (1969):532–536.

Stalnaker, Robert. *Inquiry* (Cambridge: MIT Press, 1984).

_____. "A Theory of Conditionals." In *Conditionals*, ed. Frank Jackson (Oxford: Oxford University Press, 1991).

Stampe, Dennis. "Toward a Causal Theory of Linguistic Representation," *Midwest Studies in Philosophy* 2 (1977):42–63.

Swinburne, Richard. *The Evolution of the Soul* (Oxford: Clarendon, 1986).

Turing, Alan M. "Computing Machinery and Intelligence," *Mind* 59 (1950):433–460.

Tye, Michael. "Qualia, Content, and the Inverted Spectrum," *Noûs* 28 (1994):159–183.

Van Fraassen, Bas. *The Scientific Image* (Oxford: Clarendon, 1980).

Van Gulick, Robert. "A Functionalist Plea for Self-Consciousness," *Philosophical Review* 97 (1988):149–181.

_____. "Nonreductive Materialism and the Nature of Intertheoretical Constraint." In *Emergence or Reduction?* ed. Ansgar Beckermann, Hans Flohr, and Jaegwon Kim (Berlin: De Gruyter, 1992).

von Eckardt, Barbara. *What Is Cognitive Science?* (Cambridge: MIT Press, 1993).

von Wright, G. H. *Explanation and Understanding* (Ithaca: Cornell University Press, 1971).

Watson, J. B. "Psychology as the Behaviorist Views It," *Psychological Review* 20 (1913):158–177.

White, Stephen. "Partial Character and the Language of Thought," *Pacific Philosophical Quarterly* 63 (1982):347–365.

Wilson, George M. *The Intentionality of Human Action* (Stanford: Stanford University Press, 1989).

Wittgenstein, Ludwig. *Philosophical Investigations*, trans. G.E.M. Anscombe (Oxford: Blackwell, 1953).

Yablo, Stephen. "Mental Causation," *Philosophical Review* 101 (1992):245–280.

About the Book and Author

The philosophy of mind has always been a staple of the philosophy curriculum. But it has never held a more important place than it does today, with both traditional problems and new topics often sparked by the implications of modern psychology, cognitive science, and computer science.

In this concise but comprehensive survey, Jaegwon Kim explores, maps, and interprets this difficult terrain. Designed as a textbook for upper-level undergraduates and graduate students, *Philosophy of Mind* succeeds brilliantly on these terms. It manages to offer riches to experienced philosophers while remaining accessible to readers new to philosophy.

Focusing on the traditional mind-body problem, Kim canvasses the traditional attempts to explain the mind as soul, as certain forms of behavior, as brain, or as a type of computer as well as more recent complex attempts to meet objections raised by these accounts. The author also includes extensive coverage of the issues surrounding content and consciousness.

Throughout, Kim allows readers to come to their own terms with these views. At the same time, the author's own emerging views are on display and serve to advance the discussion. Readers of Kim's previous work will especially welcome this aspect of the text.

Comprehensive, clear, and fair, *Philosophy of Mind* is a model of philosophical exposition. It is a major contribution to the study and teaching of the philosophy of mind.

Jaegwon Kim is William Perry Faunce Professor of Philosophy at Brown University. He is the author of *Supervenience and Mind* (1993) and of many important papers in the philosophy of mind, metaphysics, epistemology, and the philosophy of science.

Index